D1570554

SURVIVING THE
FORGOTTEN GENOCIDE

SURVIVING THE FORGOTTEN GENOCIDE

An Armenian Memoir

John Minassian

Introduction by Wendy Lower and Anoush Baghdassarian

Foreword by Roderic Ai Camp

Edited by Richard Hovannisian, Wendy Lower, and Kirsti Zitar
with the assistance of Jeremy Anderson, Anoush Baghdassarian,
Larissa Peltola, and Rebecca Shane

ROWMAN & LITTLEFIELD
Lanham • Boulder • New York • London

Published by Rowman & Littlefield
An imprint of The Rowman & Littlefield Publishing Group, Inc.
4501 Forbes Boulevard, Suite 200, Lanham, Maryland 20706
www.rowman.com

6 Tinworth Street, London SE11 5AL, United Kingdom

British Library Cataloguing in Publication Information Available

Library of Congress Cataloging-in-Publication Data

Names: Minassian, John, author. | Hovannisian, Richard G., editor. | Lower, Wendy,
  editor. | Zitar, Kirsti, editor.
Title: Surviving the forgotten genocide : an Armenian memoir / John Minassian ;
  introduction by Wendy Lower and Anoush Baghdassarian ; foreword by Roderic Ai
  Camp ; edited by Richard Hovannisian, Wendy Lower, and Kirsti Zitar.
Other titles: Many hills yet to climb | Armenian memoir
Description: Lanham : Rowman & Littlefield, [2020] | Includes bibliographical references
  and index.
Identifiers: LCCN 2019050137 (print) | LCCN 2019050138 (ebook) | ISBN
  9781538133705 (cloth) | ISBN 9781538133712 (epub)
Subjects: LCSH: Minassian, John, 1895-1991. | Armenian massacres, 1915-1923—
  Personal narratives. | Armenian massacres survivors—United States—Biography. |
  World War, 1914-1918—Atrocities—Turkey. | Sivas (Turkey)—Biography.
Classification: LCC DS195.5 .M534 2020 (print) | LCC DS195.5 (ebook) | DDC
  956.6/20154092 [B]—dc23
LC record available at https://lccn.loc.gov/2019050137
LC ebook record available at https://lccn.loc.gov/2019050138

∞™ The paper used in this publication meets the minimum requirements of
American National Standard for Information Sciences—Permanence of Paper
for Printed Library Materials, ANSI/NISO Z39.48-1992.

By three things is the world sustained:
By justice, by truth, and by peace.

—The Talmud

Contents

Foreword

Memories of My Grandfather

Roderic Ai Camp

M Y FIRST MEMORY of my grandfather occurred in 1950, when my brother and I were five years old. We were walking along a beautiful section of Laguna Beach, California, each of us holding his hands, when a female stranger complimented my grandfather on his young children. Not wanting to take away from this woman's compliment, he went along with her erroneous perception. When we were older, he often joked about this incident. Family members or acquaintances typically observed or implied that he was handsome and young for his age.

One of the mysteries that plague most genocide survivors is the central question they repeatedly ask themselves: *How did I survive?* Many years later, an older cousin suggested to me that he believed my grandfather's personality, both charming and modestly charismatic, may have played a role in his survival. Whatever role his engaging personality played, to my mind his knowledge of multiple languages, including Arabic, Turkish, Armenian, and English, unquestionably allowed him to impersonate a non-Armenian, surviving for some time in a labor camp in Turkey, along with prisoners of war, during World War I.

Subsequently, my brother and I spent a great deal of time with our grandparents, first in Los Angeles; in Cloverdale, in northern California along the Russian River; in Fresno, where thousands of Armenian immigrants and other relatives settled in the early twentieth century; and, finally, in Santa Barbara. Our grandfather distinguished himself with his avid interest in world affairs and American politics. For many years, he subscribed to *U.S. News & World Report,* storing dozens of back issues in large stacks, which he encouraged me to read. His seriousness about intellectual matters offered a role model for both of us, and we both pursued careers in higher education.

I also learned that my grandfather had begun an equivalent experience at an American Missionary College shortly before his family was deported. He also was interested in poetry and intellectual activities among budding Armenian intellectuals of that era. When I was in high school, I asked him why he hadn't continued his college education after arriving in New York. He explained to me that he could not concentrate adequately in a classroom setting because of his genocide experiences, and therefore, sadly, he gave up his dream of teaching. His explanation made me more fully aware of the psychological consequences of his horrific memories. My greatest satisfaction in my relationship with my grandfather was learning that in his nineties, the University of California at Santa Barbara (UCSB) asked him to teach a course on the Armenian language, and he did so at his home. At that time, he was told that he was the oldest instructor teaching at UCSB.

As I began to read more about the Armenian genocide, as well as numerous books about the Holocaust, I grew increasingly angry at what had taken place in Turkey—specifically at the irreplaceable loss my grandfather had suffered, leaving him with only one surviving sibling from their forced deportation, a sister. Yet my grandfather taught me a wonderful lesson, which tempered my earlier response to his experiences. In January of 1973, Gourgen Yanikian, an Armenian who had lost numerous members of his extended family in the genocide, assassinated the Turkish consul general of Los Angeles and another consular official in Santa Barbara. Before killing those officials, he published a letter in an Armenian newspaper advocating that Armenians attack Turkish representatives. In a letter to the *Armenian Observer,* my grandfather strongly condemned the murder of the two diplomats; consequently, according to other relatives, a number of individuals from the Armenian community criticized his position. Thus, what I learned from my grandfather was his principled belief in forgiveness and his equally strong belief in nonviolence. It has been a lifelong lesson for me; if he could reject violence as a solution, how could I, as his grandson, who never shared any of these personal experiences, justify a different attitude?

Our relationship with Grandpa John, as we called him, as well as with my grandmother, was one of fondness and deep affection. Together, they aged physically, but they never aged in terms of their joyful interactions with dozens of friends and family. They both were characterized by a wonderful sense of humor, they were outward oriented socially, and thus they counted many younger people as friends. As I approach their age today, my wife and I remember those admirable qualities and try to apply them in relationships with our grandchildren and friends alike.

Introduction

Anoush Baghdassarian and Wendy Lower

The fire of hatred had spread all over the world, consuming everything that was noble in the human heart. The world lost its equilibrium and reversed all the values of life. Truth lost face, criminals became heroes, and liars, patriots! Demagogues' shouts silenced the wise. People in power become gods and their followers dance to the tune these gods play. In a whirlpool of motion we have lost all reason.

—John Minassian

MORE THAN ONE MILLION Armenians were murdered by Turkish perpetrators and their collaborators between 1915 and 1923.[1] In fact, the decimation of that ancient community and culture was so extreme that it gave rise to the concept and crime of genocide. Today, mere traces of Armenian culture survive in eastern Anatolia (the former Armenian-inhabited region of Turkey), and published testimonies of the murdered and the survivors are rare.

In 1916, the British Foreign Office compiled and presented eyewitness accounts in a Blue Book report.[2] Similarly, the American consuls in Turkey collected accounts that can be found in the archival records of the U.S. Department of State. Not until the 1970s and 1980s were hundreds of Armenian survivors interviewed, their stories summarized and interpreted in various publications.[3] Fewer published memoirs. Survivors in Turkey were silenced by official and local denial of the genocide. Those who

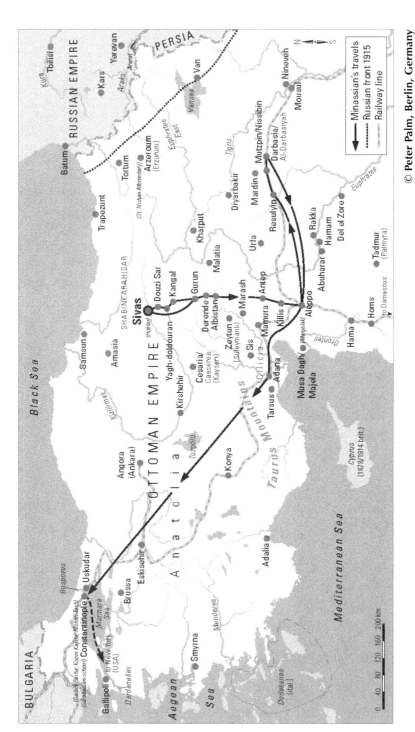

© Peter Palm, Berlin, Germany

lived as refugees in neighboring Syria, Greece, or the Soviet Republic of Armenia were not encouraged to speak out in the manner that Holocaust survivors did in the late twentieth century. John Minassian (1895–1991) was one of the few to have lived through the genocide, immigrated to the United States, and in his retirement recorded his story, transcribed it, and then edited it for publication in 1986.

Now, thirty years after he first published his account, scholarship on the Armenian tragedy has become a major subfield in genocide studies in spite of continuing official Turkish denial. The growth in research and attention to this history make this new edition of Minassian's memoir possible and necessary. Besides being a compelling, illuminating—and, at times, gut-wrenching narrative—it is a powerful educational tool and weapon in combating the deniers.

Minassian's intended audience, however, was not the deniers. Rather, as he stated in the first edition, he wrote his memoir for those who were murdered, especially his mother and father, who ensured his survival and whose deaths haunted him. From their tragic fate, we could learn from the past and "save tomorrow from prejudice, hatred, ignorance, and meaningless traditions." Out of the darkness of his grief and loss, Minassian envisioned a more civilized future. His story is one of hope.

This new edition contains explanatory notes that corroborate Minassian's statements and historical experiences with additional documentation and scholarship that has become available these past decades. It provides critical comments that help point out the prejudices of the era as well as literal translations of specific cultural references and terms. The map traces his journey from his hometown of Sivas to Aleppo. Further, Minassian's grandson, Professor Roderic Camp at Claremont McKenna College, helped us bring the memoir back into print by sharing the original manuscript, private family papers, and photographs that were not included in the first edition. Camp's determination to publish the memoir and his written tribute to his grandfather demonstrate the generational transmission of this history in the deeds and words of a survivor's descendants.

It is remarkable how sharp Minassian's recollections of events were. The level of detail seems to support cognitive theories about the deep imprint of traumatic events, especially those experienced as a young adult. Minassian was twenty years old when the genocide began. His story starts at his birthplace in Sivas, Turkey, where he describes his pre–World War

I schooling by American missionaries in Gurun and the coming of the Great War that interrupted his college education. It ends with his arrival in the United States in 1920.

Born in 1895, Minassian came of age in the era of great power rivalries, imperial crises, and, ultimately, the final days of the Ottoman Empire. The genocide of the Armenians occurred in the context of the First World War, but prior to that, Armenians had suffered discrimination and violence at the hands of Ottoman rulers and the Turkish nationalists. By the 1870s, Armenian leaders (influenced by Western human rights ideas and liberal nationalism flowing from the French Revolution) began to urge political reforms and called for an end to discriminatory practices, such as increased taxes based on religious differences. England, France, and Russia were involved in mediating the situation and pressured Sultan Abdul Hamid to reform, which exacerbated the situation by humiliating the sultan. In explaining the root causes of the genocide, Turkish historian Taner Akçam stresses the sultan's resistance to reforms, the humiliating loss of territories (Greece, Serbia, Montenegro, Romania, and later Bulgaria, Bosnia and Herzegovina, Libya, Albania, and Macedonia) and the encroaching power of the czarist empire, which altogether threw into question the sultan's legitimacy. Internally, nationalism among the Young Turks and revolutionary movements including those led by Armenians seeking autonomy created cracks in a centuries-old system that was economically and politically resistant to modernization. One response to these pressures was violence: first the Hamidian massacres; then the coup that brought into power the Young Turks and the military elites (the Three Pashas); followed by the decision to join the Central Powers in the war against England, France, and Russia. The tool of violence to suppress internal discord, usurp rule, and expand power through alliances and warfare proved a blunt instrument wielded by a weak state.

The failure to reform, the demands of minorities seeking rights and of nationalists pushing to secularize against the authority of the sultan became the dry tinder (among other combustible forces) that led to the genocide and collapse of the Ottoman Empire. Central and local Turkish and Kurdish actors ("Muslim religious leaders, student and brotherhoods")[4] murdered several thousand Armenians and other Christian minorities in 1894 in what was known as the massacre of Sasun, followed by the Hamidian massacres (1895–1896) in which an estimated one hundred thousand were murdered in gruesome pogroms, leaving at least fifty thousand children orphaned.

John Minassian was an infant at the time; his parents hid with him, fearing for their lives as hunted "gavour," or infidels.

In 1908 the Young Turks drastically curtailed the powers of the sultan and guaranteed the Armenian people basic rights. Then, in 1913, in an about-face, they seized full control of the government and abandoned the rights cause altogether, pursuing just the opposite campaign of Turkism based on exclusion of minority cultures and religions. The Three Pashas—Minister of Internal Affairs Talaat Pasha, Minister of War Enver Pasha, and Minister of the Navy Djemal Pasha—ruled during the Great War. They sought to unite all Turkish Muslims and expand the borders of Turkey into Central Asia, thereby creating a new Turkish empire that was ethnically cleansed of "internal enemies," starting with the Armenians who were the largest Christian minority in the eastern Ottoman provinces. The Three Pashas embarked on these sweeping campaigns to solve the so-called Armenian Question shortly after the war started, and their intentions were not kept secret. German military commanders soon learned of Turkish plans to Islamicize non-Muslim communities "by force, or failing that, eliminated."[5]

In early 1915, only a few months after joining the Central Powers in the Great War and a humiliating defeat by the Russians at Sarikamish, Turkish leaders issued a salvo of orders and actions against Armenians, which viewed in hindsight were clear warning signs that something disastrous loomed.

It started in the provinces. Armenian soldiers in Turkish armies in towns such as Erzurum and Marash were disarmed and placed in labor battalions. In March 1915, the arrests and deportations of Armenians expanded to different regions of what is currently eastern Turkey, including Zeytun, Iskenderun, and Dortyol. Armenian leaders from many of these villages were removed. Mass hangings in the centers of towns frightened most Armenians into compliance and inspired others to form resistance movements (for example, in Van and Zeytun).

Then, in April 1915, the exclusionary policies and violence reached Constantinople. The leading Armenian newspaper, *Azadamart*, was shut down; and on April 24, 1915, Ottoman authorities rounded up 250 Armenian intellectuals and leaders. On May 27, the official Edict of Deportation was issued. The mass arrests and violence spread throughout the entirety of the Ottoman Empire. Entire communities were rounded up and forced onto death marches, robbed, tortured, and brutally killed in the open. Those who survived the assaults on the death marches were led to the Der-Zor desert in Syria, where many perished from famine-related illnesses.

Among the few outstanding acts of international intervention and aid was the rescue of some four thousand Armenian men, women, and children near Musa Dagh (Mountain of Moses). Armenian fighters and their family members resisted Ottoman eviction notices and deportations by retreating to the mountains above the Mediterranean coast near Alexandretta (today Iskenderun) and holding out with a few hundred rifles and foodstuffs for fifty-three days between July and September 1915. French naval vessels patrolling the coast spotted them and ferried them to a refugee camp at Port Said, Egypt.

However, under the cover of war, the Young Turk dictators continued to carry out their genocidal policies. In 1916 the Turkish government ordered the extermination of any Armenians surviving in the Der Zor desert of Syria, exiled the Armenian patriarch of Constantinople, and repealed the Armenian constitution of 1863. New developments among the key actors in the Great War, such as the United States' declaration of war on Germany and Turkey's subsequent breaking of ties with the United States, gave Armenians some hope and allowed for another notable moment of international support.

In January 1918, in point twelve of his Fourteen Points, President Wilson declared that nationalities under Turkish rule should be "assured an undoubted security of life and absolutely unmolested opportunity of autonomous development."[6] Armenians fought for their autonomy once again, but this time they succeeded. Reinforcing their sovereignty and independence, the Armenians defeated the Turks in the battle of Sardarabad (May 21–29, 1918) and formed the independent Republic of Armenia in the Russian Caucasus region on May 28, 1918. Yet many of the historic territories Armenians had inhabited in Anatolia were not part of the official Republic of Armenia.

The November 11 armistice that ended the Great War did not mark the end of conflict in the Ottoman Empire. During 1920 Turkish nationalist armies battled with the Soviets over Turkey's northeastern borderlands; and in December 1920, Armenians sided with the Soviets as a bulwark against Turkish nationalism and Islamicization. The Soviet Republic of Armenia was mostly safe from Turkish attacks, but other areas of Turkey were not. While Anatolia had been "cleansed" of Armenians between 1915 and 1918, in western Turkey areas such as Smyrna (Izmir) waves of deportations and massacres continued into the early 1920s, eliminating Armenians from that region as well. It is clear that the genocidal and discriminatory policies of the Turks against the Armenians spanned at least seven years, from 1915 to 1922. This begs the question: How was this genocide possible?

Historians have offered several explanations. According to leading scholar Ronald Suny, toward the end of the nineteenth century, "a pervasive fear triggered a deadly, pathological response to real and imagined immediate and future dangers," and this affective disposition—"an emotional understanding of who the enemy was"—spread from the leaders of the Ottoman state to individuals across Ottoman society.[7] Historian Donald Bloxham concurs that anti-Christian chauvinism was widespread and decisive in causing the enormous scale of suffering and deaths. For centuries, Christian Armenians had lived as neighbors with Muslim Turks—working in the same villages, practicing similar trades, and participating in daily life in the Ottoman system. Yet the Armenian minority became more visible and vulnerable as it led in trade and business ventures, despite the excessive taxes and other discriminatory measures they endured as the *dhimmi* (non-Islamic residents who lived under the protection of the Islamic state). Like the Greek, Assyrian, and Jewish minorities, Armenians often were conspicuously different in their dress and the architecture of their homes. Some gained influence in government and the community; their Ottoman neighbors began to feel "deep feelings like resentment, fear, anger and hatred . . . which were integral to the mental universe of those constructing the Armenians as deceptive and treacherous."[8]

But fear alone, or destructive currents such as jealousy and greed, could not cause genocide. It required the mobilization of diverse sectors of society, indifference of bystanders and witnesses, and the allocation of resources to implement the killing in a systematic manner. It took the steely, determined rule of the Three Pashas, acquiescence of the Turkish military, popular support, willing collaborators, and myriad social and cultural factors including peer pressure, opportunism, and anti-Christian prejudices.

In Minassian's memoir, he places himself in this historical maelstrom by referring to political developments in Constantinople—the great battles at Gallipoli, for example—often drawing from information he had read after the war. He interweaves his childhood memories with his reading of the history as an adult. He does not offer a comprehensive explanation for the genocide. Instead, the great historical contribution that he makes to our understanding is not in answering why it happened, but in opening a window into the who, where, when, and how such a tragedy is experienced from the ground level of events and the standpoint of an orphaned victim.

We learn what happened to him, his family, and community, and what life was like for an ordinary, rather integrated Armenian family before, during, and immediately following the genocide. His vivid memories open up lost worlds and restore life before the destruction. We learn about prewar society in Sivas and Gurun; the interactions at the marketplaces, church, school, and the intimate interiors of the local bathhouse with its dim lights and moving shadows of women; of mothers such as Minassian's, who dutifully scrubbed their children with coarse Turkish cloths.

Minassian describes himself watching the naked women in the bathhouse through the eyes of a pubescent boy. Here and elsewhere, Minassian's chauvinism leaps off the page, and although eyebrow raising to the sensitive reader of today, it manifests sentiments of his generation that should not be dismissed out of hand but understood more critically in this historical context of a patriarchal society and culture where notions of women's rights and equality were largely absent.

Minassian recounts aspects of the genocide and the First World War that are missing in standard historical accounts. For example, scholars have recognized the importance of American and German missionaries (focusing on Johannes Lepsius) as witnesses to the genocide and as rescuers.[9] In Minassian's account, we meet similar, less-prominent individuals who provided critical care and shelter at the orphanages and schools where Minassian found refuge and work. He presents Kurds as collaborators, the sexual slavery and violence against girls and boys, and the widespread exploitation of slave labor. We can better understand the interactions of German and Turkish officials in waging the war economy by employing Armenian refugees and Indian prisoners of war in construction and railway work.

The pauperization and plundering of Armenians stand out as major elements of the genocidal process. The Minassian family was forced to trade its entire store of household valuables for the donkeys that would carry them to their deaths. When John, his parents, and three siblings departed from their hometown, "the Turkish population opened their doors to watch us go, gleefully cursing us for wasting the things we took along for such a 'short trip.'" Similar to the Holocaust, the behavior of greedy neighbors is striking.

The perilous moments and unfathomable traumas of the victims are described unblinkingly. As Minassian recalled, on the third day of the family's expulsion, exhausted by the climb and weakened by lack of food, water, and sleep, they arrived between two peaks in the Taurus Mountains with a river winding eight thousand feet below. They were trapped. At this moment, Minassian found himself on the precipice of his and his family's life:

> I smelled something strange. It seemed to be gunpowder, but we heard no gunshots. By this time, I had become separated from family—I often walked ahead of them so that I could warn them of danger, and so that I could look for water. Slowly, carefully, we reached the summit where the road widened and exposed to view the hill and valley below us. People were running helter-skelter, grabbing whatever animals they could, shooting and killing with whatever weapons were at hand—knives, hatchets, and guns. Some rolled burdened donkeys downhill. I left my donkey and proceeded slowly. The acrid odor of burning flesh and the cries of a woman filled the air. I stopped a moment to decide what to do but saw that it was already too late.

The odyssey of Minassian's survival, starting with this first blow of losing his parents and siblings in the slaughter, is nothing short of miraculous. Hunted and then cast out in the desert, orphaned, famished, and alone, Minassian remembers wandering "without an apparent end," talking to himself, and even singing the Armenian national anthem while praying to God. He arrived in Aleppo as the war concluded, caught in the crossfires of Arab civil wars and under British occupation. He witnessed the chaotic creation of the modern Middle East in the wreckage of Aleppo, a ground zero of political struggles. Refugees such as Minassian streamed in from all parts of the collapsing Ottoman Empire, fleeing conflicts and revolutions, seeking a home and a future.

Minassian reunited with his younger sister in an Aleppo orphanage but decided to leave Turkey and immigrate to America, the land of his dreams. He arrived in New York City in 1920 and later married Mary Eknoyan, xxii	Surviving the Forgotten Genocide

another Armenian survivor. Minassian worked for the New York City welfare department, obtained U.S. citizenship, relocated to Michigan to work at a Ford factory, and then continued westward to California, where he sold men's clothing and shoes for many years at Macy's department store. Later, he and his wife ran a small motel in Cloverdale and then Fresno, California, before retiring in Santa Barbara. The war years had disrupted his education, and he was unable to resume his studies in America. He also married rather late. He raised one daughter and had two grandchildren, a small family that would have been unusual for his Armenian ancestors.

In Holocaust studies, victim narratives such as this one have been characterized collectively as acts of bearing witness. They come in various forms—letters, scraps of papers thrown from railway cars bound for Auschwitz, engravings on the interior walls of ghettos and prisons, diaries and post-genocide affidavits, audiovisual testimonies, and oral histories. Survivors as witnesses seek to speak the truth of what happened on behalf of their murdered relatives, to educate the public, and to combat genocide denial. Compared to the Holocaust, Armenian accounts are much fewer and not as varied in form. Thus, each one demands our extra attention, study, and wider dissemination.

Minassian documents his determination to survive; to climb out of the pits of hell that he was thrown into; to tell the world what happened to him, his family, and fellow Armenians. His decision to relive these traumatic events of his youth by writing this text is yet another noble demonstration of his determination to rise above the past by documenting the horrors that befell his kin. Reflecting on his experiences, Minassian wrote in his memoir, "There are few stages in life: some crawl; others coast; but only a few choose to climb."

SURVIVING THE FORGOTTEN GENOCIDE

Preface

EVERYONE WHO WRITES A BOOK has a very good reason: some for fame and some for fortune. At my age, neither of these interests me any longer. Obligation, I feel, compels me to write, and I hope my story will be a great hope to the next generation. I say "next" generation, because my own generation has been wandering and aimless, foolish and selfish, always searching for new victories, creating new, foolish conflicts. Though it might seem that I am a little late in accomplishing this work, I chose this time because the maturity I have reached will lead me to make fewer mistakes and find me with fewer prejudices, mellower in nature and more tolerant of everything and everyone. These fruits are the gifts of nature in autumn.

I must express a word of gratitude to the many people who are responsible in so many ways for helping me accomplish my aim, people whose memory I have cherished, and will cherish, all of my life:

My school principal who, by his heroic efforts, encouraged many like me to go ahead regardless of what may come. A great disciple of Christ, a minister, and an angel from Germany, who fought tirelessly for the salvation of many children. The American consul in Aleppo* who met the

---

*Jesse B. Jackson (1871–1947) was the American consul in Aleppo, central hub of mass deportations, spoliation, and killing of Armenians, from where he observed that "wartime anti-Armenian measures" were a "gigantic plundering scheme as well as a final blow to extinguish the race."

challenge of being human when it was very hard to do so.[1] The American ambassador in Constantinople (Istanbul),* whom I never met but who was instrumental in bringing awareness of the Armenian tragedy to the New World;[2] the Jewish railroad man who told me I was his responsibility and who saved me from being captured as a runaway from Turkish authorities; the Hindu prisoner of war who one moonless night helped me escape from being butchered by his Hindu compatriots; the Turkish sheik who stopped reading his Koran to tell me that I, too, was his son. And the Turkish policeman who said, "God is great, may His grace be with you." There was the little boy who allowed me to take the place of his lost father; a student in the Turkish prison who said to me, "We may not survive, but your generation has a call and a duty." Many more, in their way, helped me to survive. If they could talk to me, they did; if they could not, they smiled, whispered, or touched me in sympathy. A strange unknown woman visited me in my sickbed and fed me every afternoon until I was on my feet again. And then, my father, a man among all men; and my dear mother, who blessed me and stopped me from joining her in flight so that I might be saved.

These people have compelled me, induced and haunted me, to publish these memoirs. We don't progress until we improve, and we don't improve until we learn from the past. This book may help to save tomorrow from prejudice, hatred, ignorance, and meaningless traditions. The terrible mistakes of the past have made the present so chaotic.

If we get out of our present dilemma, we may have a new world. We owe the effort to the next generation so that they may build on the mistakes of the past a more civilized future.

---

*Ambassador Henry Morgenthau Sr. (1856–1946) served in Constantinople from 1913 to 1916 and was instrumental in communicating the severe plight of Armenians, confronting Ottoman leaders about their role as perpetrators, and saving some deportees.

WHY THIS BOOK? - CLIPPINGS FROM YESTERDAY

Everyone writes a book for a very good reason. Some to make fame
will
some to make a fortune. Now at this age, ~~nothing~~ neither interests
me ~~any more~~... but the obligation, I feel, ~~im~~ compels me to do so...
with a great hope for benefit to the next generation. I say next
generation because my generation is a wandering generation -- foolish
and selfish -- always looking in search of new victories... creating
+ new, foolish wars.+ It looks as though I am a little late in my efforts
to accomplish this work. I chose this time because maturity of age
make one ~~make~~ less mistakes...less prejudice, mellow in nature and
toleraht in general. Fruits are the gift of nature in autumn.

I have a word of gratitude to so many people who are in so many
ways indirectly responsible for accomplishing this work...whose memories
I have cherished all of my life. First to my school principal who, with
his heroic effort, encouraged many like me to go ahead regardless of
what may come. On my way to deportation, the greatest disciple I ever
saw of Christ, an angel from Germany whose everlasting fight for
of   *american*
salvation ~~helped~~ so many of us -- and children. The ~~XXXXX~~ ~~Armenian~~
Consul in Aleppo who met the challenge of being human when it was so
hard to do so. The American Ambassador in Constantinoplæe , who I
had never met ~~before~~, but who was instrumental in bringing ~~maxia~~
awareness of the tragedy to the New World. The Jewish railroad man
who told me I was his responsibility who saved me from being captured
as a runaway from the authorities. The Hindu prisoner of war who,
one moonless night helphed me escape being butchered by his Hindu
call
friends.The Turkish sheik who stopped his Koran to ~~tell~~ me ~~I was~~ *my*
~~his~~ son. The Turkish policeman who said, "God is graçe, son, and His
grace be with you." ~~The~~ little boy, who allowed me to ~~fat~~ be his
father.

1

Sivas

I N 1914, AT THE AGE OF NINETEEN, I was ready to enter my second year in college. One morning, late in August, I prepared for the three-day horseback ride from my home in Gurun* north to the American college† at Sivas (Sepastia) in central Turkey (see figure 1.1).[1] My family had been up since early morning, both excited and upset because I was leaving. At breakfast, Father, with great serenity, graced the table and asked God's guidance for my safety. My mother wiped at her tears and suddenly looked at me full of love and suffering.

"You take care of yourself, son," she said, "God will be with you." I promised, with an artificial smile, acting brave; inside, I was sad and afraid. But I was happy, too. I was one of the fortunate few who could go to college. It was a great adventure to learn from teachers who had already been out and abroad.

Several men came to the door with four donkeys. My father introduced me to Hagop-agha,‡ who took my belongings and suitcases. Father talked

---

*A town in historic Lesser Armenia, still known today as Gurun.

†The Sivas Teachers College, which was founded in 1912. Sivas became a center of American missionary work at the end of the nineteenth century.

‡Traditional Ottoman culture used the honorific term "agha" to signify a person of distinction, as in "Sir," hence, Hagop-*agha*.

FIGURE 1.1
Postcard of Armenian American Teachers College, Sivas

to him, entrusting me to him and wishing us good luck. Mother insisted that I write often. I jumped on the donkey's back, to show my parents my ability to take care of myself and how grown up I was, and we started. One more backward glance—I saw Mother using her white handkerchief.

Each door we passed on our way out of town was open, and in each was a blessing for me. I smiled to each of them, and each wished me a safe return. I felt like community property. One woman said, "What a teacher he will make." Another: "He's going to be a minister." We turned the corner of my block, and my home disappeared in the distance. As we moved away, I was more at ease. Some still greeted me, some nodded, and others waved, for many were sad; these were considered bad and dangerous times for Armenians living in Turkey.[2]

We finally passed out of the residential part of the valley, past the main fountain, where devoted Muslims washed their faces and hands as part of their ritual cleansing to thank Allah for His blessing. It was too early for noon prayers and too late for the morning ones.

We took the main road, a gravel one, moving up the hills and leaving behind us the town of Gurun, which we could still see, getting smaller and smaller as we went around the crest. We must have looked like small specks to the people down in the valley. At this moment, I thought, the townspeople would be bidding their last good-byes, closing their doors, and kneeling down in their favorite corners to pray to their God for the guidance of their loved ones.[3]

Lively and full of high hopes, we moved a few miles downhill. Hagop-agha moved us to the right, avoiding the main road. I had made this trip a year before, and I remarked to Hagop that we were taking a much longer route this time. He gave me a kind smile, implying that I was wise to have noticed but foolish to question. "We are not interested in reaching sooner but safely. We are trying to avoid army recruiters. They will take our donkeys, and—who knows?—perhaps even you and me."

At noon we stopped, unloaded the donkeys, loosened the saddles, and hung the feedbags over the animals' heads, turning them loose to munch on barley and oats. We spread some cloth on the ground and opened our lunches. My mother had provided food for the three-day trip and had instructed me what to eat each day. First, a hard-egg omelet, spread between two layers of thin *pita* bread (the powdered sugar made it easy to eat). She had made us some hamburger *kefta** and *halva*† for dessert. Hagop-agha and his two comrades crossed their hearts in a short grace. I didn't. They looked at each other in dismay. Hagop made a face, and they got the message.

Then we started eating our lunch. While we ate, Hagop made a plan. Though we could reach Manjelak before dark, he didn't want to enter the village, a stopover for all travelers: postal earners, official travelers, and the Turkish army—groups he wanted to avoid. Hagop stretched out on his back as he chewed his last bites and looked up at the clear blue sky. At any stage of life, a man who looks up and enjoys the sky is, to me, a poet. Finally, with great authority, he turned to us and announced, "We are not going to have any more rain."

I lay down to rest and thought about my happy state. Soon I would graduate, return home to Gurun, and teach. My father would be very proud of me, and my mother would thank God for such a learned son. Old friends would tell one another, "We knew he would be somebody, we knew it." No more than two dozen boys from my town were able to go to college. Some

---

*Also spelled Keofté. This is a traditional regional food containing spiced ground meat baked in layers or boiled in shells of cracked wheat (bulgur).

†Traditional Middle Eastern dessert made with stirred flour, butter, and sugar.

went to Kharput,* and a few like myself to Sivas. Both Kharput and Sivas boasted of American colleges, which had great prestige.

So my thoughts went. I was very comfortable after lunch, drinking some cool *tahn*, a mixture of yogurt and water. I thought of my mother and was lonesome. Why would anybody want to be separated from a home like mine, where the family ties were strong and so tender?

Mother had been a very young girl in the 1870s, when her parents decided to leave the town of Shabinkarahisar.† Her father, Sarkis-agha, had become a Protestant, not a popular idea with many Armenians. To them, becoming a Protestant and disavowing the old Apostolic (Orthodox) Church was a denial of one's identity as an Armenian. They looked upon Sarkis-agha as one who had drifted from national unity and, even worse, as a Westernized traitor to the faith of his people. So my mother's family moved to Zara, a small town half a day east of Sivas on horseback, about thirty miles.

My father, Bedros, was born in Gurun in the 1840s. In his youth, he had been an altar boy and hoped to become a minister. But he had never entered school—there were none. Nevertheless, he learned to read and used his talent as much as possible. He knew all of the church rituals and helped in the grand mass in the classical language of Kerapar (Grabar).‡ He became a merchant and moved to Sivas, looking for better business opportunities. Sivas, however, was too small and did not satisfy him. He decided to try Constantinople. Because of the long and risky journey, he left his first wife and four sons in Gurun, planning to have them join him when he had settled.

In Constantinople, Father, then a member of the Armenian Apostolic Church, began attending the missionary board meetings for the newly organized American Protestant Church, the Congregationalists. Newcomers in Constantinople, the American missionaries showed Father different meanings in the Bible and a new religion that was simple and understandable. They used a Bible translation in plain, spoken Armenian. This spoke

---

*Also Karpoot, Harput, or Kharpert. A part of the ancient Urarutian kingdom and the historic Armenian province of Tsopk. Currently, it is known as Elazığ in eastern Turkey.

†Also Shebinkarahisar or Shabin-Karahisar, a northwestern district of the former province of Sivas.

‡Kerapar (Grabar) is the classical Armenian language. All current dialects of Armenian stem from this language.

to his belief that the church should serve its people, and he decided to become a Protestant.

He was grateful for the missionaries. He felt they were bringing light to his people. "Although we were Christians before," he said, "the way these Americans explain the Bible gives it more and greater meaning."

Filled with the happiness of this new religion, Father bought some merchandise and planned a return to Sivas; but before he could start, he learned of his wife's death. He stopped in Zara, where he met other Protestant converts. One day he was invited to a prayer meeting at Sarkis-agha's house. Father spoke as a new convert, full of his experiences in the capital. After the meeting, Sarkis-agha thanked him for his short speech and called him Brother Bedros; thus began a close friendship.

And thus, too, my father met my mother in the early 1890s. She was then in her early twenties and very attractive, with light skin and blue eyes. Many young and wealthy men were anxious to meet her, to ask for her hand, but she had turned them all down. They seemed too shallow, not like her father, Sarkis, or his new friend, Bedross-agha; and their knowledge of many things, especially this new faith called Protestantism. To my father's amazement, she agreed to become his wife.

Armenia Under Turkish Rule

In 1520, incoming Turkish hordes under Suleyman[4] conquered much of what is now Eastern Europe, the Near and Middle East, and North Africa, establishing a new and greater Ottoman Empire. As part of the process, the Turks defeated the Armenians, a nation of people that pre-dated the birth of Christ. The Armenian civilization, situated to the south and east of the Black Sea, derived its name from Mount Ararat, upon which Noah's Ark is supposed to have landed after the flood. The Turks deprived the Armenians of their civil rights, drove them from their homes, and took their property, including their cattle. Thousands, of course, were left homeless.

In the late nineteenth century, the Armenian Revolutionary Federation[5] was formed to protect the population from murder and the kidnapping of young girls and the burning of homes. In order to attract the attention of the Western powers, the Armenians protested in the Turkish capital of Constantinople, where European governments maintained embassies. In 1892, a plot to assassinate Turkish sultan Abdul Hamid failed, but the European countries were aware of the suffering of the Armenians, who always believed that their Christian brothers would respond to their suffering. But the Armenians were given only promises that were never kept.[6]

Sultan Abdul Hamid, to subdue and instill fear in the Armenian population, ordered officials in the interior cities to massacre the Armenian infidels. The orders reached the territorial governors in the autumn of 1895, when I was six months old. Houses were burned and people were killed, regardless of how peaceful they were. Churches and stores were looted. By the time the news reached the European embassies in Constantinople, more than one hundred thousand Armenians were dead and thousands upon thousands were left homeless. Children were orphaned and wives widowed and left in hopeless despair. Some embassies demanded that the massacre and ravages be stopped.[7]

My father's store in the Sivas *tash-khan* (shopping center) was left intact because it had stone walls and iron gates—the only one of its kind. My parents hid with the newborn baby they had named Hovhannes, after John the Baptist, the martyr who was beheaded because he told the truth. A few weeks after the massacre, the *tash-khan* gates opened cautiously, and Father opened his shop. Sheik Haji Medj-Meddin was his first customer. The sheik entered Father's shop very thoughtfully and greeted him: "Salaam alaikum," he said, bowing his head wrapped in a heavy green turban. "I prayed for your safety, and God answered me. God is great," he concluded and left.

A few years later, Mother took me to the American missionary kindergarten. Miss [Mary Louise] Graffam, who opened the American school,[8] introduced us to the teacher, Miss Rosa, who wore a pure white starched dress that hid black shoes. She greeted my mother warmly; they knew each other from church. Each morning my aunt would hold my hand, and we would go to school. She sat me next to a girl named Alice, whose pierced ears smelled of medicine. I still remember the smell. With Miss Rosa's help, I learned the Armenian alphabet. We learned how to play maypole;* round and round, under the ribbon, we would clap our hands and jump.

---

*A ceremonial folk dance typically performed in the spring around a tall pole garlanded with greenery or flowers and often hung with ribbons that are woven by the dancers into complex patterns.

I learned to sing to the organ. What a strange sound came from that box by the magic touch of Miss Rosa. I led the group playing mailman, singing a solo in Turkish to the tune of "Yankee Doodle." The group would sing, "Here comes the happy mailman with a whistle." Then I would sing, "Here I come, a letter from your parents and from your friend, but now I must go." The singing made me popular with the children and their parents. Everyone would say, "Here comes the mailman, Hovhannes."

After some poor business dealings, my father gave up his partnership and with very limited capital went into a wholesale kerosene oil business. He rented a warehouse and waited for the winter, when there was no more oil importation from Russia. Soon he started selling to dealers and shopkeepers. For each five-gallon can, which cost him between eleven and twelve piasters each, he received eighteen or twenty piasters.* Sivas, in central Turkey, is a cold place in the winter, and Russian goods were slow to arrive. Their cargoes had to be transferred from boat to horseback and carried from Samsun on the Black Sea coast to Sivas. In the wintertime, when the snow was knee high, kerosene was scarce. The price went up to twenty piasters a can. The next summer, when oil prices dropped, Father sold the few cans he had left and closed his shop.

The following year Father specialized in wholesale burlap—his least successful commercial venture. But he was a church elder and had varied ventures in his community. He was a member of the National Armenian Hospital; there were no city or state hospitals in all of Turkey.[9] As a trustee of his church, Father visited the central jail to talk to political prisoners and others, accused of crimes, who had been locked up for years without trial. One had to provide one's own food and bedding; the guards sometimes would forget to bring dinner.

Garbo Varjabed, a teacher, was one such prisoner.† In the 1895 massacre, he had tried to protect his house from Turkish looters; in self-defense, he had shot a Turk. When the looting and killing ceased, Varjabed was arrested for murder. He had no defense, and the Turks sent him to the Sivas state prison to be tried. Father heard of this, and though he was not

---

*A monetary unit of several Middle Eastern countries, equal in 1910 to one hundredth of an English pound. *Summary of Foreign Commerce of the United States*, vol. 3 (Washington, DC: Government Printing Office, 1911), 1614.

†The word *Varjabed* itself means teacher and was not his surname.

a lawyer, he somehow managed to meet a high court judge—almost all judges in Turkey were Turkish, and the law of the land was based on the Koran or wisdom of Islam. First, Father consulted with his friend Haji Sheik Medj-Meddin. He asked the sheik's advice and explained that he was sure Varjabed didn't intend to kill anybody; he was merely protecting his home from thievery. Medj-Meddin slowly counted his string of amber beads. Without raising his head, the sheik said, "But a faithful Muslim has been killed thoughtlessly."

"Haji," replied my father, "Varjabed did not ask this man to come to his house. Believe me, I am not trying to protect a criminal. I am sure you would do the same if you were in my place." A few days later, Father had an appointment to see the high court justice, a very eminent judge of the state, at his residence. A doorman led Father to the judge's private room. Father entered the room reverently and waited until the judge asked him to proceed. He was invited to sit by the judge. The judge told Father of his respect for Medj-Meddin and his trust in him. My father argued in Varjabed's defense for half an hour, reminding the judge that this man, an Armenian, was a respected and humble man, that he had upheld the law and was a good man, God-fearing and mindful of his obligations as a citizen and as a father.

"Have mercy on his children, your honor," my father pleaded. The judge asked Father if he was related to this Varjabed. "No, your honor," he said. The judge was moved. With a heavy dignity, he said, "You came to me through a very dear and honorable friend. Justice will be done." Father thanked him and left. A few weeks later the case was reopened. Father got permission to enter the jail and visit with the prisoner. Varjabed's death sentence was changed to life, and in a few years he was released. On Sundays, Father would often come home late in the evening. Following the morning services, he would visit the sick in the hospital. On Thursdays, he went to church and prayer meetings, and he would come home when it was very dark.

Visits to the boys' and girls' orphanages were also on his schedule. He was a trusted friend of Miss Marie Zenger, a lady from Switzerland who opened the girls' orphanage, and a close friend of the American missionary. Mr. [Dr.] Ernest C. Partridge, the American College's principal, often came to our house for prayer meetings and visited us at Christmas and Easter. Mr. Partridge spoke Armenian well, and Miss Graffam, Partridge's sister-in-law and founder of the girls' college, spoke child's Armenian—stop and go. We admired them all for their personal sacrifices and welcomed them. Father told them that we did not need gospel preaching as we Armenians were already Christians, even before the discovery of America.[10] Teaching and scholastics were needed, and we were grateful to them for these.

Father's business slackened as his activities in social work increased. He used to say, "There is so much to do for orphans and widows, how can one sleep comfortably?" He was always troubled by the troubles of others, and more so when he couldn't help them. At times he would reach in his pocket, bring out a coin or two. "Maybe this will help you."

He was worried about my future because the political situation looked dark and was getting worse. He would often say that Christian nations forgot us. "No hope," he would say. "They won't help us anymore." He wrote a few lines to Dikran Kabakjian, who had taught in Sivas high school and was now studying science in America. Kabakjian answered that Father was too old for the New World, and that he would feel strange in a foreign country, particularly because he did not know its language. Friends in Gurun, his hometown, got panicky. Sons by his first marriage insisted that he go to his old home to spend his remaining days happily, now that he was getting old; Haji Medj-Meddin suggested that he share space in his store.

Father agreed to start a coin collectors' business for the convenience of gift buyers. Coin collectors could do business with small capital; no work was necessary. But he was never satisfied. He wrote to his youngest son from his former marriage, who lived in the United States, but Father did not receive any answers to letters from America. He was old, yet had brave and young dreams: If he could only bring us to a better life in a civilized, Christian country, with kind people such as the Americans. How could he do it? This was his dream for a New World.

Finally, he gave in to the pressure from his first family and returned to Gurun, where he had been born, raised, and married, and had raised four sons, married them into choice families, and where he had relations and friends. He consulted Medj-Meddin about his plan to return to Gurun. In his sad voice, the sheik said, "I wish you wouldn't move out of Sivas, because, in case of need, I want to be near you." The sheik's meaning was not clear until a few years later. We moved from Sivas to Gurun in May 1908.

It was evening and getting late. Hagop-agha stopped and looked around. We spotted and soon reached a nearby farmhouse in a small

Armenian village. It was time to relax. We unburdened the beasts and got ready for our big meal. A lady came from a nearby house and asked if she could give us some cool water to drink. Seeing me, she exclaimed, "How did it happen that your mother let you go, a young boy of your age?" In the evening we covered ourselves with whatever cover we could find and fell asleep under the stars in a clear sky.

Next morning, refreshed, we continued on our journey to Sivas. Hagop-agha wanted to know if I was all right and enjoying my tea. He suspected my mood, because I was very quiet most of the time, carried away by my thoughts of the past and the mysterious and unknown future. I thanked him for his concern and followed him on horseback, still with my thoughts.

The Young Turks

Members of Turkey's new generation, educated in Europe, mostly Germany, formed an organization to oppose Sultan Abdul Hamid's unlimited powers and to institute progress for Turkey. They organized in Europe and extended their fellowship to the interior of Turkey. They called themselves the *Etiyaht* (Ittihad/Young Turk) party and asked the persecuted Armenians to cooperate as they tried to build a new Turkey and to support a new program, which called for constitutional changes. The Young Turks' motto was "Freedom, Equality, Justice, and Brotherhood for All."

On June 24, 1908, the Young Turks overthrew the sultan and exiled him—against the wishes of many Turks who believed that the Turkish sultan was also the caliph, the head of the Islamic faith.[11] The air was filled with joy of newfound liberty and happiness. For the first time in centuries, Armenians, treated as equals by the Turks, had a new life. They built new schools, where they could teach the Armenian language in the open; and assembly halls, where they could speak to the public and admonish Armenians to be good citizens. "We are friends and brothers now to our Turkish neighbors. No more persecutions, jails, or injustice. We are equal and free."[12] Few nations have had the privilege of enjoying the happiness we knew then, particularly after the sacrifice of so many thousands of Armenian lives.

Many old people couldn't believe that the revolution had occurred. Only a few years before, the Turks had massacred innocent people. This seemed impossible. But it was true. All Turkish officers, governors, mayors, and heads of the armies and police put their hands on the Koran, taking an oath God would witness that they would carry out the new constitution with equality, justice, brotherhood, and freedom for all. Cities acquired a new vigor. In the villages and towns and up in the hills, one could hear music and singing. Plowmen and shepherds in the field were not afraid. Magazines and daily newspapers returned in a burst of energy. "Mother Armenia wept no more; but like a phoenix, arose from the ashes." The promise of a new life, which Armenians had dreamed of for centuries, made life sweet, bright, and full of hope. "Freedom, equality, justice, and brotherhood" were inscribed on the new coins, the most valuable of all coins. Very few nations were as privileged as the Armenians who experienced freedom and equality after having been under the yoke of slavery for centuries. They took a deep breath and set to work for progress from city to city. Commerce flourished. Even some Turks liked it, as they were relieved of the burden of their hatred.

I had my share of the joy, too. It would be easy now to go to America and become a man of importance, like the Americans whom Father and I loved so much. I learned about George Washington, that truthful boy—and respected the best flag in the world—the one that was flying over my kindergarten. I thought, *That's what I will do. When I'm older, the first chance I have, I will go to America.* I would prove that the people who had had faith in me weren't wrong and become a good teacher like Mikhail Frangulian, Rupen Rakupian,* or even like Mr. Partridge, Dr. Clark, and that young man, Mr. Henry Holbrook, who was shot by the Turks because he was taking pictures of a Turkish woman. Wait until I grow a little more.

About 1911, I first tried to execute the plan. I told Father that the local school had nothing new to offer me and that I wanted to go to America. ("I am going away to a new country a lovely country, indeed.") Instead, my parents agreed to send me to Sivas Teachers College. Father was convinced, but Mother still cried to see her son going away to a new, lovely country, miles away—perhaps never to return again.

Gurun couldn't provide enough schooling for my ambitions. So, Father wrote to Mr. Partridge at the American teachers college in Sivas and consulted with Mr. Rakupian, head of the faculty there. I was accepted for

---

*Both Professor Frangulian (Frengulian), a graduate of Oberlin College, and Professor Rakupian (Racubian), with postgraduate studies at Columbia University, were murdered during the Armenian genocide.

the 1912–1913 term. Now I was on my way back for the second year, and toward adventure and the privilege I thought awaited me. Our journey was ending, as we climbed the hills of Ulash from where we could see Kuzeler-mak (Kizil-Irmak/Halys/Red) River and Sivas—the morning air was cool with the hope and dream of progress, making us strong and happy.

We arrived in Sivas late in the afternoon, tired and dusty from our walking and riding. At last, I was near my goal. Hagop-agha took me to my distant relative's store where Turkish towels were sold. He was surprised that we hadn't let him know of my arrival. We lived in a country where mailmen delivered only once a week; there were no telephones, and telegrams were too expensive.

My traveling companions took down my belongings and wished me good luck. Hagop-agha was to be in Sivas for a few days, and I promised to give him a letter for my father before he returned to Gurun. My relative took me home, surprising his wife. She graciously prepared our dinner, and I gave them news of their friends and relatives in Gurun.

The next morning, I put on clean clothes and my new shirt, polished my shoes, and started out for Hoktar. There the teachers' college sat high on a hill with the American flag flying—spreading hope and confidence. We were all somehow related to this flag, because we were closely knit to these wonderful people who came to live in our strange city, among a strange people, and to work, help, heal, and to teach or maybe to spread the Gospel and to bring love, service, and sacrifice. The Americans represented a people of the greatest moral understanding, above all other nations, even the English, of whom we knew so much.

I passed Hoktar fountain where Mukitar Appa (Abbot Mekhitar) had been born many years before. Through his learning from Jesuit missionaries, Appa went to Venice and translated into Armenian masterworks from many other languages. His was a village of scarcely a few cottages. But from one of these humble shacks came this great man, destined to be the backbone of future Armenian literature.[13]

A few more steps, and I was on college grounds. To my surprise, they had started a girls' college nearby. Next year, I told myself, we'll see girls more often than ever. How lucky can you get?

I saw the gardener and asked for Mr. Partridge. Mrs. Winona Partridge came out and greeted me as though I were family. "Hovhannes, you are here, how are you?" She asked about my father and mother. Mrs. Partridge had taught me English the previous year.

We entered Mr. Partridge's private study. We shook hands, and he asked about Father. I had recited to myself some chosen Armenian words to prove that I was already a scholar. This trip, I said, was necessary for me to take if I was to be prepared for the entering courses next semester. This is why I came early. Mr. Partridge could see my enthusiasm and that I was a young man full of dreams and ambition.

As soon as I finished speaking, Mr. Partridge said, "But I sent a telegram to Gurun just a few days ago, informing you that we would not have school for out-of-town boys this year. Considering the mood of the country, we think it is best that you young men stay with your parents."

All of my dreams came tumbling down, crumbled. Mr. Partridge knew what the school meant to me and said in his best Armenian, "You know, Hovhannes, we always thought you were one of our best students, and the faculty and I have great hopes for you, regardless of what may happen. And we feel certain that someday we shall have cause to be proud of you. On your return to Gurun, convey our love to your wonderful father and mother."

So close to the fulfillment of my youthful dreams, yet suddenly so far, far away. It was a bitter disappointment. I was faced with failure. The mold was cast then and there. Whether I liked it or not, my destiny took a different turn than the one I had anticipated. I couldn't go to school this year; maybe not next year either. The next day I informed my relative of my plan to return home. Before leaving, however, I went to see a friend, Toross Baronian, at Sanasarian University,[14] which had just been moved from Arzeroum (Erzurum) to St. Nishan* Monastery (this is said to be the place where the Armenian king Senekerim's crown lay buried with his gold throne and scepter and his palace treasures). Acres of wheat fields, which the monks tended for their modest living requirements, surrounded St. Nishan Monastery. I watched strange activities going on before I entered the gates. The monastery's forest was full of horses tied to trees. At the college, Toross told me that these horses had been confiscated by the army from the peasants and nearby farmers, and that they were kept there for a long time without food. The hungry horses ate the tree bark. Conscription

---

*Also spelled Nshan, meaning St. Mark or Holy Sign.

had made it legal for the army to confiscate all kinds of necessities, but the horses were left to starve. They had neither food nor shelter. One could sense a defeated Turkish army before the war had even started.

Toross, orphaned in the 1895 massacre, was supported by a wealthy relation. Now, near his graduation, he faced the draft. He urged me not to lose time but to hurry back home before it was too late. Soon it would not be safe to travel, he said; he asked me to convey his regards to his relatives, who were neighbors.

Mother had asked me to visit some friends while I was in Sivas, and so I stopped at one of our neighbors. I pulled the cord that rang the bell. As I waited, I looked around. Across the street was a beautiful two-story building. When I was young, I used to read on the building large letters in gold: Garabed Peranian 1905—a local merchant from Gurun. On another corner in a stone building, one of the best ever made, was the candy maker Avak. A few blocks away was the Armenian hospital, supported solely by Sivas's Armenian community. Nearby was a boys' orphanage, supported by the Americans. Then there was the Topbashian residence, one of the local merchants, also from Gurun; Tomajian, a very successful merchant, who years ago had been my father's partner; and Murmurian, whose son was my school chum not long ago and who lived down a block. Sivas was a center of Armenian culture and commerce. Many schools supported by the Armenian community had been built there. I was curious to see the fountain where I used to carry home drinking water when I was very young. It was called the Balaksokhak Fountain. Nearby was an Armenian girls' orphanage, headed by the Swiss lady, Miss Zenger—rosy-cheeked and devoted to her work, educating young girls orphaned in the massacre of 1895.

Life in Sivas

The Baths

Not far from the girls' orphanage is a big building with a church dome. It was the bathhouse where, as a child, I used to go bathing with Mother every other week.

We enter through a dull, heavy, wooden door. Unpleasant odors hit us as we descend a few stairs. Up on a balcony sits a tough-looking woman who stares at me, then gives Mother the nod—it is all right for me to enter with her. Mother places a copper coin in the hand of this ugly woman, who then directs Mother to an available compartment in the middle of a large room. A noisy fountain with a circular base shoots up water, which cascades down, making melodious but monotonous sounds.

We undress in our compartment, which has been assigned to us and our partner's family. The partner's son waits for me so that we may go in together with his mother and sister. Women wear silk wrappings below their waist, which gave them the appearance of statues when wet. We boys under fourteen, nude, as children are, run around carefree and innocent among all of these women and girls. Then we approach another heavy door that hardly wants to be opened, perhaps unwilling to reveal its secret treasure of the most beautiful maidens in the nude. This is the entry to the outer chamber.

As we open the door, steam rushes out to welcome us. We can hardly see anything, but the warm glow envelops us as we feel our way toward the center. We follow the moving shadows of the women around us. A dim light from a high-up dome, which passes through crystal glass and breaks into fanciful rays, is no help to see by. An oil lamp contributes to the already heavy-laden atmosphere. We continue our search for the center marble area. We pass booths assigned to each family, each with stone sinks, above which extends a wooden spout from which runs the water from the main water storage, which is heated to boiling by a fire burning day and night. Each spout is packed with a rag to block the water until needed.

Finally, we reach the center circle—the marble top of the hot, boiling water—that serves as a steaming gathering point. More people pour in. We have fun sliding down the slippery wet marble as we take our steam baths. The incoming women, wearing wooden sandals with golden tassels, add to the noise.

Eventually our mothers come to take us to the "torture chamber," where they rub us with coarse Turkish cloths, scraping our bodies.* My skin reddens, and rivulets of sweat and water roll down my body. Mother says, "See how dirty you are. Keep quiet." Then comes the combing of my hair. I feel the pressure deep beneath my skull. We holler in protest against further torture—more soap, more hot water. We've had it and are

---

*Turkish baths (Hamam or Hammam) use coarse rubbing cloth to exfoliate the skin.

anxious to escape. But we have to wait until our mothers are ready to take us out, for the floor of the bathhouse, slippery from the overflowing water mixed with soap and clay, is dangerous to walk along. The place looks like a temple to some goddess. All are nude and beautiful. Indeed, Asdig,[15] goddess of beauty, had sent to earth her gift to the Armenian maidens—beauty and fertility—with the promise of happiness if they kept their purity, chastity, and fidelity (their belt of virginity).

The noise of the bathhouse is confusing with the running water and the echo of the high crystal dome. Our semicircle of marble was occupied now. The bodies of the women were spread all over and their wrappings discarded. They lay flat on their faces, hugging the hot marble floor and dreaming the dream of motherhood and the night of the bath. With the help of the steam and clay, they become the queen of their chambers, with everlasting charm.

The small holes in the crystal dome shed beams of light through the steam-filled bathhouse. The women's hair is loose now and spread over their bodies to their ankles—pink adorable bodies. Once in a while, they shake from the cold drippings of the sweat from the dome. Stars above, and angels all about us. Then, one by one, they wrap a towel around their bodies, carelessly leaving their breasts exposed for cooling. They rush to the outer chamber, holding their copper pans, where they place their belongings and leftover soap, coarse cloths, and combs made of birch in a small bag made of hemp or linen. They enter the outer court, where the fountain has lost its charm. Pink and red, rosy-cheeked, it is as if they had been soaked in the very essence of roses. Feeling good, clean, and happy after their bath, they rush to their balconies, and in this happy mood, approach the outer door with the eldest leading the family. The ugly woman looks uglier as we leave the bathhouse, but, alas, time has taken away all of this from us, replacing it with sin and sinners. Christianity has robbed us of the past glories and beauty of our pagan ancestry.

The Market

Before returning to Gurun, I thought I might as well visit some of the old familiar places of my childhood. To see once more the marketplaces, the stores and shops, then on down to the residential district, called *bezeerjy ard.* I followed the same path as in my childhood when I was going to school.

You cross a big vacant lot, going from the residences in toward town, then another vacant lot appears near the English consul's residence, and across that is the Catholic school, supervised by the Jesuit brothers. Just above is a large building, called *Karnedogenk.*

A wild river runs along the side of this street, which is covered by heavy pieces of lumber. Sometimes a plank piece, which has fallen, makes you walk carefully, or you may lose your shoes. The river sways right, making a curve to the corner. A few homes down is the Kabakjian house. Mr. Kabakjian lectured us about X-ray in the year 1906. His wife was sick, so he connected some magic wires to the church windowpane and told us that when we sang in the church, his wife heard us and shared our music in her bedroom. She passed away, and Kabakjian eventually went to America to study science. He was replaced by a young man named Payelian, the only person who had a bicycle.

Then I visited the old church school I had attended in my boyhood days. Katchaturian, Teghnazian, and Zarifian had taught me well. We would have a prayer meeting every morning, with interesting Bible stories. Before I could graduate from high school, we had moved out of town.

Across the street was a mosque where Turkish boys were taught religion. Next to it was a Turkish bakery, and next to that a small shop run by Khalil-agha. We all liked him, even if he was a Turk. He would fuss about if we wanted to buy a pencil or a pen point or a Turkish reed writing pen called a *kamish.* He would open up the reeds, very carefully splitting the middle of each to shape the point. Often, we would ask our teacher to do this for us, as he always had a sharp pocketknife handy.

The church school was attended by Protestant and non-Protestant children of all classes. Upstairs, where the church meeting took place on Sunday, school was held from Monday to Saturday noon. From a small platform, Rev. Mihran Kazanjian would preach each Sunday morning. On his left side would be seated Mr. Perry, who visited Father often, but I could never get used to him. I thought that at six feet tall he was too large a man, too big to be a missionary. He wore a graying goatee and spoke Turkish because he was the acting American consul in Sivas.

To the right of the reverend on the platform would sit another tall, but shapely, young man: Ernest Partridge, our school principal. He was sent from the American missionary board. Mr. Partridge was warm, energetic, and, to top it all off, spoke Armenian with both an English accent and a slight drawl, choosing his words carefully and speaking slower than a native Armenian. Of course, we were happy to hear a man of such importance speaking our mother tongue (indeed, it was illegal in some parts of Turkey to speak Armenian previous to the revolution of the Young Turks in 1908). It is only human nature to feel close to someone who understands you.

The girls' chorus would sing in church, led by Miss Zenger from the orphanage. Miss Graffam would lead the choir from the organ. The girls who didn't sing would sit in the balcony under the careful discipline of Maritza-Hanum, Kabakjian's mother-in-law, who had charge of the girls' boarding school. When she entered, as if by magic, all young men would turn to view the entrance of a very attractive young lady dressed in American style. Her name was Shenorig.

The one-hour sermon by Reverend Kazanjian ended with singing and a benediction. The people would rise, and my father would take his position at the head of the stairways with the collection box. The collection box for the poor was under his jurisdiction. He would say, "May God bless you," suggesting that whatever you gave you would get back many times over, so why not give more? "Remember the poor, God bless you." Nobody helped him count the money; he kept it and used it for the poor.

Mother would proceed with the people to the yard, down the stairway where the shoe shelves were kept. Katchig Ammy, the school caretaker, greeted us proudly. With his help we would find our shoes. People would greet my mother, who wore a special handmade silk dress, a black shawl with red roses over her shoulders, and attractive earrings imported from Aleppo[16] gracing her ears. She wore handmade patent-leather boots. Father would join us after he got through counting the money. He held my hand, and we would go home.

On the way he would ask me if I remembered what Reverend Kazanjian had been talking about, whether I understood any of the stories or the sermon of the day—or anything at all. That is why, at the age of seven, I would jump on a chair at home and, in a loud voice, mimic our minister. My parents were proud of me when I preached the sermon of the Sunday before.

On Sundays, we would often have a midday meal, after which Father would leave to attend the young men's prayer group. He was not young, but he was interested in young people. When I was older, he would grab my hand and snatch me from my aunt to take me with him to these meetings. They would sing, after which Father was expected to say a few words. An artisan there was famous for his cutlery. He would get up and with his slow, impressive bass voice start praying, often using the same words, "Our God Almighty, gracious Creator of the world . . ."

Sometimes, depending upon the prayer, his voice would crack, and he would break down and start weeping. We called him Brother Hampartzum. He had deep smallpox marks all over his face.

As you leave the old church you come to the Tokma River,* flowing swiftly out of the town. As you follow it along its course, you come upon St. Kevork School, next to a Greek Orthodox Church. I lived on this same block for about two years. This street had no name. Our streets were not named or numbered; an "address" would be referred to as being next to some building or maybe next to the fountain that the Turks built (the Turks liked to build many fountains, probably to help passersby quench their thirst, or for the faithful to wash at before entering the mosque— most fountains were next to a mosque).

At the end of this street is Pasha Bostan,† the Governor's Garden, where the Sivas governor resides. Sivas is the name of both the state and the capital city. In our childhood, we would wait on the street corner for the governor to go by. As the fast-running coach horses passed, he would glance at us and return our salute. We would rush home and tell our parents how thrilled we were that the pasha had recognized us and even returned our salute.

In this neighborhood lived Aziz, the only Turkish student in our college. I had met him the year before in school. He was a lonesome boy but so outgoing and warm I was not ashamed to call him my friend, even though he was a Turk. I was not only polite, but genuinely interested; we had long conversations. He was very thoughtful, polite, and a fine boy. He was about my age. Aziz attended the college specially to learn English, but he also wanted to speak Armenian, if I would help him. I was pleased to do.

The atmosphere around Aziz was cold; he was a Turkish "outsider." There was a gap of centuries between our religion, culture, history, and language. He was proud of being an Osmanly,‡ a member of the Ottoman lineage.

---

*The Tokma Su (River) meets the Euphrates River in the Buyuk Vadi (Big Valley).
†"Pasha" is an honorific title for a highly ranked Ottoman official.
‡Descendant of Osman, Turkish emir who ruled from 1299 to 1326 and laid the foundations for the Ottoman Empire.

And though I considered myself slightly Americanized, I was proud of being an Armenian—proud of my background, ancestry, and language. I never argued with him as I often did with my Armenian classmates, especially the seniors, about subjects I wanted to be informed about. I would often talk to Aziz in Turkish, and in return, to flatter me, he would proudly throw in the Armenian meaning of the words. When school closed, we parted as close friends, with the hope of meeting again the next year. I wonder what he is thinking about me now. Does he still regard me as his best friend? It is too bad! I had promised to visit his home and had a secret desire to let him sneak into our big Armenian Apostolic Church and hear the Mass. Not a Protestant Church, which we called the meeting place, but the Mother Church. Although I never saw him again, he made an impression on me that I shall never forget. I was not as hateful of the Turks as were others because I had known Aziz. I thought of how easy it could be to love any Turk if he were like Aziz. I wonder whether he thought the same about me.

Now you enter the shopping center in greater Sivas. On your left is the Yeilduz Fountain, across from the great mosque. You follow the crowd and cross a small street where men are walking in all directions. There are a few fruit stands. The hammering of brass bars informs you that you are passing vendors roasting coffee and making powder close by. The aroma of coffee filled the air. Then you see a big man with a large iron bar hammering away at fresh-roasted coffee in stone tubs. You pass the *tash-khan*,* where only choice merchandise is sold, and where my father's shop used to be. There is the bakery shop with a dozen dogs begging for pieces of bread from the customers—Turks favor dogs. The dogs have a hungry, pathetic look in their eyes, hoping someone will have mercy; they follow you around, and if you aren't watching the long, braided bread hanging from your arms, the dogs grab the bread and disappear fast. You can't do anything about it; if you hit a dog, the Turks will hit you back, for they believe the reincarnation of a soul might be in a dog.

Next, you see small shops of all kinds and the Bon Marche, the only variety store in the town. Here begins the street of the knife makers. You can smell the unpleasant odor of the warmed goat's horn from which these people shape a handsome handle. They make the most beautiful pocket-knives you will ever see. They are artists. With their hammers, they shape

---

*A shopping bazaar.

the steel and iron. People come from all over the region of Sivas to buy these knives, for themselves, for resale, or as gifts for friends. They say, "This was made in Sivas."

A few blocks away are the shoemakers, where shoes are all made by hand. All of the most important shoemakers are Armenians. They take your size, and within a month, you can call to claim your new shoes. If they do not fit, the master boot-maker's force would make them fit. "It will stretch," he says. "It might be a little tight now, but it will give soon." In the winter when everything is frozen, the shoes are about two sizes too small. You recall what the man told you, and you think, maybe your feet grow fast.

Here and there you find a Turkish shop making cigarette holders, from two inches long to a foot. With their primitive tools, like a violin bow, and with the help of a chisel, they shape the wood, scrape, drill holes, polish, and sell it. Each Wednesday, early in the morning, before the stores open, women from neighboring villages bring men's socks they have woven from brilliantly colored wool. That is why this place is called Chorab Bazar, market of socks.

On the left opens a semicircle that divides the streets left and right, and in the center is a *kan*, or inn. There people with horse and carriage stop overnight. They are provided with a room for the night. Each *kan* has a stable below. Rooms usually are surrounded by a circular balcony looking out onto the ground floor. The innkeeper is called *Kanjy*. He feeds your horses and waters them. He also keeps a two-foot-by-four-foot place with a slow charcoal fire in which to prepare Turkish coffee.

Merchants are very complimentary to their out-of-town buyers. When the bargaining begins, the shopkeeper, at his wit's end, hollers for the coffeemaker, to relieve the tension building up within him. The customer will soften up under the aromatic fragrance of the delectable warm coffee and will sit down again on a raggedy woven-reed chair, where the merchant would place a soft pillow to further mollify the customer. He provides all kinds of comfort, then will start bragging about his merchandise, "The best of its kind," he might say, or, "I'm losing money selling it so low," or, "Because you are my best customer, God willing that you remain such."

The buyer sits waiting and hoping that his coffee will soon appear, but the man with the pot of coffee never comes. The shopkeeper notices that the customer is getting restless and that he might lose him, so he hollers again for the coffeemaker, who is not in sight. The buyer weakens; and the merchant, now with hopes high, assumes a scolding tone to get the coffeemaker to come quickly. The coffee vendor finally appears, apologizing for his late arrival, then pours from a special container, called a *jezveh*,* one small demitasse cup for the customer and another for the shopkeeper. He pulls a worn piece of chalk from his filthy apron pocket, marks a tally line for each purchase on some hidden boards to be counted up at month's end. Nobody doubts his counting and nobody touches his marks until he gets paid, three paras† for each cup. The buyer can't resist this Oriental hospitality. He drinks his coffee, closes the bargain, opens his dirty moneybag taken from his pocket, pays, and thinks the deal has been made with his blessing.

Then I stopped at one of the shops specializing in Turkish towels, the largest in town. The owner had married my cousin, and he was my host. He noticed an ice cream vendor resting across the road, who, in his own peculiar voice, was advertising his ice cream as the best kind, made of pure cream and delicious sour cherries, all for a copper piece, ten paras. At the behest of my host, the vendor filled a dish to the top from a can where he kept his treasure. There were two cans, side by side, each with a different flavor. The two cans were artfully decorated with tassels, and bells jingled each time he would hoist the two cans that hung on the bow-like stick across his shoulders. A butcher nearby in a close, dark corner shop hollers that he has just killed a young lamb.

From that corner you turn to the left "till sunshine and blue sky greets you once again." Across the street from this shop is the sheik Haji Medj-Meddin's shop. This was my father's last shop in Sivas. His was the first shop in the line of coin collectors, which carried coins at all prices and for all occasions.

This was on the main road that took you to the central bazaar, where large quantities of wheat were sold to locals for year-round use. Some of it was ground for flour, some for bulgur (cracked wheat), which is one of the famous products of Sivas. Sivas produces many beautiful Oriental rugs made by young Armenian girls. Many villages are spread around Sivas, hundreds of them, and most of them with substantial Armenian commu-

---

*Usually a ceramic or copper beaker with a very long handle, meant for hot beverages.

†The "para" was an early form of pure silver currency of Ottoman Empire Turkey and Egypt. Pamuk Sevket, *A Monetary History of the Ottoman Empire* (New York: Cambridge University Press, 2000), 96. In this case, however, it seems to have a much smaller value, such as a piaster.

nities. Many date from the time of King Senekerim.[17] Sivas is considered the center of Armenian commerce and culture. Yes, Sivas always has been considered the center of culture for Armenians and commerce for all. I returned to my relative's store, where I left a message that as soon as Hagop-agha was ready, I would return to Gurun with him.

Douzi-Sar

Hagop-agha, convinced by friends that the Turkish army might take his horses, had sold them and bought three donkeys at a secret bazaar. They gave me a donkey to ride that didn't want to walk, so instead of riding him, I had to walk some seventy-five miles back home with him. I never liked donkeys. Horses are beautiful and gentle and one can ride them and tell them to run; one can't do anything with a donkey. They are conservative creatures. They won't rush; in fact, they hardly move. Nothing about a donkey is beautiful, except perhaps its dark eyes and long lashes, mellow, sad, but beautiful, and the way they hang their heads when they are thoughtful. You can't command a donkey as you travel; they don't listen—they will go near water whether or not you want them to. They compel you to go in their own sweet time, in their own sweet way. In the end, they're always exhausted. They are not like horses.

We packed our things and proceeded on our way back to Gurun. The hills were still covered in green. Below, we could see the people wielding their sickles, harvesting the wheat. The women cut the wheat with their hands, while the men carried in the crop and piled it mountain-high next to the thresher. A man with an ox threshed the wheat on a board with chips of flint stone underneath to crush the straws of the wheat. Another man with a partner would throw the crushed straws to the wind and, with the help of a little breeze, would separate the straws from the wheat, the golden, life-giving wheat. They seemed to be in a hurry to finish. They paid us no attention but thoughtfully attended to their work for fear the rain might overtake them before the crop was in. When winter came, they would need their stores filled, plenty of flour for their bread and bulgur for their table. They would pay their 10 percent tax on their crop to the government collector, another percentage to the church, and some to the widows and the poor and for the newly built school. This year, they would have better clothing for their families.

The winters in central Turkey are very severe. The families would kill a few lambs to provide themselves with meat for the dark, cold months. Their chimneys always would have smoke when babies would be born, as the women were as fertile as Nature; when spring rolled around again they would be ready and able once again to help the men with their seasonal chores.

Nearly twenty years before, they had been robbed and their houses burned by marauding Turks; the men were massacred at the order of the sultan.[18] But since then they have returned to work, minding their orphans and supporting their widows. They build during their winter and work the fields in summer. The village has come alive again with the help of the few young men who managed to escape to America. They built a sizable school for the children so that they would learn to read the Bible and to write, so that they could communicate with their separated brothers and fathers. These noble peasants, the villagers, had an inborn urge to live and build.

The shepherd dogs stopped us as we entered the village. They looked as big as calves and wore neckbands with spears with which to attack wolves when necessary, and their bark was an angry sound, like thunder. A man came on horseback, saluted us. He wanted to know where we intended to go. Hagop-agha gave a friendly answer and asked him if he knew where we could lodge, water our animals, and take care of the young man (pointing at me), and if there were people who would shelter us overnight. The man jumped off his horse and asked me my destination. I told him the sad story that, on account of the war, I had to return home

"Well," he said thoughtfully, "you are welcome to stay in my house with us tonight. It will be our pleasure to have you with us, Baron Hovhannes." (Baron is a title of respect for a man who was "somebody," and I guess I was "somebody.") I was separated from the group and followed Sarkis-agha. As the head of the village, he represented his people when government cases came or when it was a matter of settling taxes. He was responsible for the operation of the church and the school, and he acted as both police and judge for the villagers. He would be fair and good to all of his people as his father had been before him, and they respected him as they did his father. He would tell his people of their duty and obligation to the church and that they were blessed by God; and he also reminded them of their obligation to the deprived widows. He would recommend marriages and assist in building new houses with the help of all able-bodied men in the village.

We stopped at an adobe house and entered a room with an earthen floor. It had neither chairs nor sofa, only some goatskins and *kilims,* a type of flat rug without nap, woven by the women of the house during the dark days of winter and made of lamb's wool, usually spun by the elderly women. There were some small saddlebags for the donkey to carry their things in when they needed to shop and journey to Sivas.

Sarkis-agha's wife was about forty years old. She welcomed me as an honored guest, and the preparation of the dinner started. Whenever she walked, there was the jingle-jangle of her bracelets and necklaces and her many small and large gold coins. Her head was covered. After dinner, Sarkis-agha asked me if I would like to see the new village school. We walked a few blocks, and I had the surprise of my life. I had never heard of this village, or its name, but here was a very modern school, built with money sent by the few young men who had been fortunate enough to go to America. They also sent money for the expense of operating the school, to make sure that the children would attend. I had the privilege of signing the school guestbook.

As we were walking back to his home, Sarkis-agha stopped, looked me over, and half pleadingly asked if it wouldn't be great if they could hire me that year as their schoolteacher. "We have no teacher yet," he confided. I was overwhelmed, honored, and challenged. Our college required two years of courses in order to teach, that is, to obtain a diploma. All I knew then was that I had to go home to consult with my father; then I would know.

"Would you do that, please?" Sarkis asked, and we continued to his home. My bed was placed near the stone-built center of the main room— the *tonnir*, a firepot for cooking and making bread. The circular wall of the *tonnir* is made of clay as much as three feet deep and twenty-four inches wide. This is the eating center during the winter nights. In the morning we had our breakfast of freshly baked barley bread. In the Near East, the hospitable way of expressing friendliness is to accept things gracefully. It is also the accepted custom to repay with equal generosity. I left a silver majidia, one-fifth of a golden lire, under my pillow to show how much I enjoyed their warm welcome. You don't give money directly to anybody. It is considered poor manners.

Hagop-agha came to pick me up, and we were ready to leave. I thanked my host and hostess with the wish that I might see them again very soon. I also promised to write regarding their offer as soon as I got home. At that time there were no telephones. But I was surprised upon leaving Sarkis's house and passing through the village that all of the workers stopped what they were doing to greet us and wish us good luck.

The village of Douzi Sar (place of the salt mine) was surrounded by a salt lake, and we walked along on its dry salt bed. Hagop-agha ordered his men to fill their sacks with salt, for the animals were unburdened on our return trip, and, in this way, he could earn a few piasters.

We followed the donkeys at a slow pace until we reached a spot called Yagh-doldouran. Hagop-agha told us that once upon a time, in this same spot, a man and his caravan loaded with merchandise stopped for their noon lunch when suddenly three men on horseback came upon them and commanded him to surrender the load and animals. The man was preparing a dinner for himself and melting butter for his bulgur pilaf; he begged the men on horseback to be his guests and enjoy the pilaf. They agreed, and the man melted more butter, boiling hot, supposedly for the pilaf. The uninvited guests waited nearby, ready to enjoy. The man approached them and, instead of pouring the piping hot fat into the pot, he threw it in the thieves' faces, thus saving his goods, animals, and his own life. Hagop told me this while we were passing through the hills of Yagh-doldouran.

Gradually dusk turned into night, and we relaxed for a long rest on the hillside. The next morning our small caravan, full of vim, vigor, and vitality, proceeded on our journey homeward. Our leader, Hagop-agha, planned to arrive home late. When we finally arrived, the town was asleep. A few dogs in the street barked at us, and some we chased away. We didn't want any welcome at that late hour. Upon arriving at my home, he dropped off my belongings. I thanked him, and he disappeared into the darkness around the corner of our block.

At this time of the year, people slept under the stars, on the rooftops, or perhaps upon an extended wall of the house, with a roof open all around. Children loved it; they had fun jumping around and giggling. There, with happy smiles still on their faces, they would fall asleep. A nearby apple tree might drop an apple or two and wake them momentarily, but they would fall asleep again until the sun sparkled against their eyelids.

The street was quiet when I knocked on the door. To my astonishment my younger brother, one of the twins, was awake. He jumped and woke my parents, shouting gleefully, "Brother is here, brother came back!" Father opened the door and, before he could greet me, Dikran jumped on me and hugged me so tight I could hardly talk to my father. He was three years old then. Father told me that they had been talking about me and that Mr. Partridge had told them about the closing of the school. Then we talked about my trip. Many questions were asked: Had it been safe? Why did it take four days instead of the usual three days? Did I see any troop movements, or anything special in Sivas? Finally, they asked about Mr. Partridge and friends.

Father seemed worried about me. At last he said, "Maybe it is best for us to be together." And we went to bed once again under the family roof. A gentle breeze brought the fragrance of roses and jasmine.

2

Gurun

The Missionaries

AFTER THE 1895 MASSACRE of Armenians by the Turks, the town of Gurun didn't know where to turn for help. A few American missionaries came from Sivas to preach the Gospel, organize an orphanage for the boys, and gather a few families for prayer meetings. They led them, taught and comforted them, and convinced them that all good and bad came from God. "He has a plan for all of us," they would say. Only a few surrendered themselves to these good, unselfish people who came to heal and help the poor widows and orphans.

But others in the community tried by other means to find a way out of their unfortunate lives. They rebuilt their houses from the ruins with their bare hands, cultivated their yards for vegetables for their tables, and worked for a few coppers a day. Gradually, a few learned men got together to organize the weaving of Persian shawls on hand looms. Some would create the pattern. A few holes on a strip of cardboard were turned as a row, which would fall on a bunch of wires. On the head of the machine, threads supported and received support from the main loom. Then the weaver would pass his shuttle through, weaving a design on the loom. By 1908, Gurun was a well-known center for the weaving of shawls. By 1914, it was a beehive of activity.

Manufacturers used Gurun shawls as spreads and to wear as belts. Womenfolk and children prepared the spools for the men. Weavers were paid by the piece, weaving the shawls from cotton or from the best quality of wool imported from Manchester, England. They even created a double-faced design from which one could make a robe without a lining. Islamic high priests and judges wore these shawls proudly. Merchants and laborers wore them as protection against the cold, or to dress up for special occasions. Every Saturday, the weavers would bring their finished work to the bosses' offices, returning the finished goods. They were paid cash for their labor and would go to the market to buy yardage to be sewn into garments by the family's older women.

The average Armenian family in Gurun had only one bedroom, one sitting room, and a small place for a few lambs, a goat, or perhaps a cow. Chickens supplied their daily eggs. Their houses were protected by adobe blocks handmade of clay and goat's hair. They made a large fire in the kitchen, inside the bell-like clay walls of the *tonnir*, which provided heat. The town's widows would work for the more fortunate families. They would heat water on the fire for the laundry. After the laundry was done, they would spread the coals and have a hot *tonnir*. Expertly, the women would stretch dough on a *rapot*, a pillow made for this purpose. They would thrust the dough, like a pizza, against the wall, three or four at a time. Soon the women would take out the bread, which seemed to have rosy cheeks like blushing maidens of the town.

I always liked Saturdays because I was commissioned to take some of this fresh bread to a few of our neighbors. They would thank me and, in return, would bring some of their fresh bread to us when they baked. In fact, widows of the block received this blessing, sharing the good of the fortunate ones whose husbands had not been killed.

When winter came and snow reached the rooftops, neighbors were isolated from one another, but we went to school just the same, always on foot, running so we wouldn't get cold.

In the main room of the house was a small *tonnir*, which served as a table for the food. They would make a charcoal fire outside. Then they would build a low table and cover it with a quilt. This was called the family circle: literally a circle, around which the family gathered at mealtime. They ate from off the top of this table during the winter, and the whole family would stretch their feet under it. There were times when they had to dig me out from under the table while I was reading my lesson by a kerosene lamp hanging over the family circle. When the windowpanes froze, we couldn't get any light from outside. The neighbor's rooster would still herald the arrival of the morning; and the toll of the church bell would announce late evening.

On winter nights, folks would visit one another, but only with advance notice; one of the children might be dispatched to announce an intended visit. When visitors came, Turkish coffee would be served to the elders. Then came the feast of the day: fruit of all kinds, dried raisins, walnuts, and dried white mulberry the color of amber. Thin layers of mulberry juice would be baked and dried under the sun during the summer, yards and yards of it, which would then be folded carefully like a handkerchief and spread with starch powder between the layers.

The Armenian Apostolics were not concerned about our new Protestant denomination. They gossiped, played cards, and enjoyed themselves as well as they knew how during the long, dark winter hours. But we lived the life of the Puritan of the New World: no card playing, no smoking, no drinking. We were taught to be clean and wholesome, to read the Bible, to pray and go to church every Sunday, and to have evening services, too. The faith kept a tight rein on one born and reared in one of these families.

The children of the village slept on the floor. The bedrolls are made each night, picked up each morning and put away in a closet. Usually there were no chairs, but they built a sort of couch from raised bricks, which they covered according to the family's means. Large cushions were made of stuffed straw and placed against the wall on which to lean; the pillows were covered with decorated printed cotton, and covering this was linen, hand-printed with wood-block designs. These long seat covers with the straw mats were covered with *kilims*, a flat tapestry-like material, or with heavy runners.

During the winter many old people would catch a fatal cold and die. There were some marriages, and many babies were born during the winter. Most young people would hold their weddings in the summer, when it was more fun to get married. Everybody would attend then, too.

Thus were the winter nights lived. If one were lucky, one had a grandmother or aunt in the house to tell the tales of Armenian heroes of the past, Vartan[1] or Sourp Sahag,[2] or stories of Moses, Joseph, Samuel, or Jesus. One either became an expert theologian these winter months or a great admirer of the past history of Armenians. If nothing more, it was a pleasant way to spend an evening. A wide gap existed between Protestants and non-Protestants. To the average Armenian of the ancient Apostolic Orthodox faith, we appeared, and were often treated, as non-Armenians. We didn't even eat like the Orthodox did. When the seven weeks of Lent began, we were free to eat meat and butter, but our Orthodox neighbors would fast, and, week after week, watch the feathers on the onion head, pulling one for each passing week of Lent. My mother was considerate; she would fry nothing in butter so as not to disturb our Orthodox neighbors with the smell of fat from our chimney.

In late spring, about April or May, a new life would begin. Children would play with their lambs, the yard would be dug up for the new season's plantings, and there would be cherries, plums, and flowers. Quinces, with their lovely blossoms opening like a cup, would grow again. There were many varieties of delicious apricots. Gurun is famous for its apricots and apples, which looked like the bright faces of young girls and boys.

In the winter of 1914, after I returned from my ill-fated trip to Sivas, the Armenian population in Gurun was about fifteen thousand. We had four churches, two of which were Protestant. The city had four police-men, a mayor, and one empty jail; neither robbers nor army deserters were among the Turks and Armenians. Turks in Gurun behaved remark-ably well and were very circumspect when passing an Armenian resi-dence. There were no disputes, no fights, or fear of any. The Turks knew that the Armenian people would not tolerate lawlessness. It seems the Turks were friendlier in Gurun, where Armenians were in the majority, than in the other cities of Turkey. The Armenians were leaders in com-merce—shopkeepers, shoemakers, pot makers, cabinetmakers, barbers, and above all, manufacturers and weavers.

Gurun had one dentist and one physician. Nobody died of cholera, as in other cities, and we never had a fire! You could count on your fingers how many died during the year. Venereal disease was unheard of, as was ma-laria. People seemed to live longer here than elsewhere. Perhaps that is why we had no need of more than one doctor or dentist; people thrived without them. A barber practiced "medicine" and "dentistry" and kept leeches in a jar with which to treat an occasional patient. His name was Phillip.

Each neighborhood had a midwife, who performed expertly, without charge, just for the prestige and the love of her work. We had no hospital.

The Armenian Apostolic Church built a new church. The Protestant Church was falling to pieces from neglect. Three kindergartens and three high schools were built with donations from each member of the church. The Central Church had built a new high school and residence for the bishop, Koren [Khoren] Timaksian, the patriarch of Gurun, after the 1908 revolution of the Young Turks, when the golden era of the Armenians began.

You wouldn't see a drunkard in the streets. We had no saloons or bars. The solitary town jail was always empty.

Burglary was unheard of. There were no divorces. It was a most orderly town. Everyone took pride in his home and tended it with loving care. We had only one bakery; most seemed to prefer baking bread at home.

Gurun also had a national leader, the head of the Armenian Church, Khoren Timaksian. Armenians looked to him for guidance and leadership. He was regarded as their spiritual leader and head of the church to which they were so devoted. He was fatherly, wise, and deserved their love and respect, a true shepherd of his flock. Timaksian settled complaints among the people. If there were injustices in city hall, he would walk among the people. Shoppers would stop as soon as they saw him approaching. Even inside the shops, people would stand up and bow reverently until he passed. His sole interest was the welfare of his people.

Years before, when the Protestant school in Gurun couldn't support a teacher, my father wisely advised me to go to the Mother Orthodox Church school, and I am grateful for it to this day. Protestant schools didn't teach Armenian history or language as in the Orthodox Church. The Armenian Orthodox Church emphasized the Armenian language and stressed its importance. It was there that I learned who I was and of my people's history and literature, taught by highly intelligent tutors who had never graduated from any school. When the Armenians gained equality and freedom in 1908, they built a new school next to their church, which was to them a great pride and joy.

Gurun didn't have many rich people. The merchant class was the aristocracy at the time, and it contributed money to build a larger, two-story high school. My father, a Protestant, volunteered to support the school and gave his share toward building the school, which I was to attend. When the project was finished, a few outstanding teachers were engaged, and Garbo Varjabed [teacher] was named head of the group. He was well versed in arithmetic, history, and *Kerapar*, the ancient Armenian language.

Varjabed would start the school day with the Lord's Prayer, singing in Kerapar with joy and vigor. The building's windows faced the central bazaar, so that the Armenian music wafted outside, serenading even the donkeys, which would follow us in prayer and join the singing with their high braying notes; and if they didn't, one of us would extend his neck out through the window to awaken them with our voices in song. At the end of the singing, we would recite the words, "Thine is the Power and the Glory, Amen." All of the students made the sign of the cross except me. I felt awkward, cold, and isolated; after a time, I could not endure being with my Orthodox classmates and friends. However, I learned to make the sign of the cross to my face gracefully after prayer.

Varjabed would next make a few announcements and remarks concerning our education, about our obligations to our families and our nation. He told us that we were the hope and the pride of the Armenian nation, stressing Armenian. Listening to him tell of the history of Armenia gave one a sense of satisfaction and pride. It made one feel, "How lucky I am!" He was devoted, sincere, and convincing; he, too, was a good Armenian, and he liked his work, because it contributed to the good of the nation. He loved to teach, for he believed education was the foundation of progress and knowledge. He would tell us that "knowledge is like a sea without a shore, and whoever thought that he had reached the shore was only a fool."

During holidays my classmates invited me to join in their church services. They would kneel down, bow their heads, and cross themselves. I was an "infidel, unbowed and alien." One day we went into the church, and, when it came time to genuflect and make the sign of the cross, one of the boys looked at me coolly, as if to ask, "Are you not going to do it?" I followed him and made the sign; after that I never forgot to cross my face and kneel.

The curtain on the altar would rise, and Timaksian, in his bishop's robe and crown, would come out from the sanctuary holding up the holy sacrament on a silver platter, wrapped in red velvet. As the bishop neared the altar, the congregation would rise, and the choirboys would raise their happy voices and intone, "Blessed is God. Christ is sacrificed and shared among us. Alleluia . . . Oh, taste ye and see how sweet the Lord, alleluia is, praise ye Him . . . Alleluia."

The bishop would pass down the aisle leading the choir, blessing us as he went along. A silver decorated candelabra hung from the ceiling high above; the candlelight, the music, the voices of young boys, and the incense gave an aura of divine mystery and grace. The harmony filled one with the deep meaning of the sacred words, and the music uplifted the spirit. Regardless of your faith, be it Greek Orthodox, Roman Catholic, Buddhist, or whatever, any church or temple in the world will lift one's spirits and make one feel good. If you do not come into contact with God here, you will not find him elsewhere.

Sometimes Timaksian would say a few words in his deep, sonorous voice, serious and with authority: "Children and brethren, we have a great heritage, and our saints prove that we have a challenge of greatness to follow in their footsteps, and that we have a duty to obey God's commandments. His will is that we live in peace. We render ourselves worthy of the past by proving our loyalty to the government, being obedient to God's commandments, and by living in peace. God bless you, God help you, and God be with you. Peace be with you. In the name of God, the Father, the Son, and the Holy Ghost. Amen." All would cross their hearts, women would weep, and above all things in the world they wanted peace.

The winter months of 1914 were trying.[3] Some of the young men had been arrested while going about their business and never came home. They were never heard from again. Some of the older men paid certain taxes in order to avoid being drafted into the army. But many were drafted without consideration of the hardships to their families. These people lived on a day-to-day basis. They had no income or savings—the men were head of the family and its only support. All of the people in the neighborhood who remained took upon themselves the burden of helping the families whose husbands were gone.

On our street, I was the only one who could write a letter, which had to be in Turkish, but the recipient couldn't read it, so someone else had to translate and read it for him. I would use the family code language: "We are all right now, our neighbor, Torsos (Toros), is sick and can't work. We have heavy weather here, can't visit anybody." This meant that Torsos was drafted and that it was not easy to go around because of the situation. Mail often didn't come, and we had no daily paper in the city. The newspapers once came to us from Constantinople, but they had been stopped a long time ago. Professor Kobakjian used to send Father the weekly *Gotchnag* from New York City.[4] This was the only news we used to get, and when it came it was too late to know what in the world was going on. It took a month to get a copy, and everyone in town tried to be informed. Eventually, that stopped, too.

Soon, many young men were drafted, and middle-aged men were picked up; some important people were called to city hall for questioning. It went something like this: "We think that you are friendly with us, with the administration, and we are sure you will help us. We have information that some years ago guns and ammunition were shipped here. We want you to supply the names, and we are quite sure you can do this. We'd like to hear these names from you."

If he refused to cooperate, he would be thrown into jail "until he confessed or refused." If he refused, he would be punished in public in front of the city hall. Kamil Efendi was the head of the gendarmes. They would beat the man with heavy sticks, ten to twenty strokes until the man pleaded, "I will confess." If he didn't, the strokes would continue until he fainted, then they would throw him in jail for the next day's torture. The gendarmes would descend upon anybody's home, at any hour of the day, to pick up men for questioning. They would accuse them of having ammunition or guns, but they were intent upon bringing in the head of the family to city hall for questioning. If the unfortunate person happened to have had a hunting gun, or any type of firearm, they would ask for more. If the victim swore that he never had more than the one they found, they would punish him so badly that he finally was compelled, in order to satisfy them, to promise to bring the other one.

As soon as he was released, he would go to a Turkish friend or a neighbor and beg for a gun, which he would buy, to keep his promise and satisfy the authorities. Taking advantage of his desperate situation, the neighbor would pretend to sympathize with the unfortunate man but charge a large sum of money for the gun. The neighbor would add that he also had the bullets if he needed them. The man, not having had any experience with a gun, would pick up the gun and the bullets, thinking that he would show the authorities his loyalty. Kamil Efendi would examine the gun and the bullets and discover that there were many different kinds of ammunition. The man learned that his neighbor had given him a mixed assortment of bullets when the authorities insisted that he turn in all of the guns that fit the bullets. Prisons, churches, and inns—all available places were filled with this kind of unfortunate prisoner. All of the prisoners eventually were sent out of the city, maybe to be tried in the state capital, charged with conspiracy and underground secret activity. They never came back, nor were they ever heard from again. Families waited in vain for a long time.

The church was not far from our house. We could hear the gong each afternoon, calling people to prayer. We could see the steeple, over rolling hills, and the brook running behind, bringing life and happiness to neighboring orchards as it flowed on to the river of Tokma. But now the church served as a jail, for the downtown buildings quickly filled with prisoners. Hundreds upon hundreds—merchants, carpenters, laborers, teachers, anybody and everybody who could walk—were being picked up. They were imprisoned temporarily and then sent out. Nobody knew where.[5]

One day they arrested Vartan in his shop. He was a handsome man, perhaps the tallest in town, well built and well educated. He had been married just a few months earlier. He was charged with being the head of a secret organization; and they demanded that he supply the membership list, tell them where ammunition was hidden and where they could find the organization's plans. Vartan denied knowledge of any kind of plans and told them he had no guns. Every afternoon I could hear the cruel strokes of the stick on this man's back, his terrifying cries, shouts, and pleas. "I do not know, I do not know . . . ," he would plead pitiably, like a dying calf at the slaughter, until I didn't have the stomach to listen any longer and would run into the house. Vartan did not confess. When the gendarmes got tired of torturing him, they decided to make a special case of him and continued to torture him, moving him to the city hall jail.

My father happened to know Kamil Efendi; he was a very close friend of one of my brothers. Father also knew the mayor and the chief of police. But times had changed; you never knew for sure who were your friends, or whom you could trust or depend upon or ask favors from. It was different now. In time, our Turkish friends and neighbors had turned cool, very cool, and grew cooler all the time. Very few people would greet one another or say "Salam" to my father as in the past. When they stopped to talk to one another, whispers spread among the high Turks about a conspiracy brewing, conceived by the Armenians to overthrow the government, with the aid of foreign powers, especially Russia. The average Armenian did not even know on which side of Turkey was

Russia. However, there couldn't be any charges if there weren't so many provocations and alibis for persecution. Nobody was put in the witness chair; there was a charge, and they stuck to it.

Father was permitted to visit Vartan in the jail. He was on the bare floor. My father couldn't see anybody, but he heard a sound of choking and snoring. He saw a pile in the dark, which didn't move. He turned to talk to him, but Vartan did not answer him. Finally, he got closer to him and saw that he was shackled. He was beaten so badly that Father couldn't recognize him. He tried very hard to talk to him. Slowly, he told him who he was; he could hardly recognize my father. After a long period, he pulled himself up to a sitting position, and with the help of his finger on his throat he whispered in a very low sound, "They tried to kill me and put a knife to my throat because I wouldn't confess." Then he went on: "Now they know I can't confess." His throat was slashed, and they couldn't force him anymore; this gave him a glimmer of happiness. He said that he was happy that he wouldn't be "weakening" anymore. He was not afraid to die. He collapsed, and Father left. He asked one of the guards if he could see Kamil Efendi. He was told that he was not available.

By this time, our distant cousin who owned the Minassian Khan and other estates in the town was summoned for a report and to surrender his guns. He was the son of a great man who was generous and led the aristocracy. Kamil Efendi knew him well, for he had been invited often to his home. The story is that when the Young Turks had wanted to overthrow the sultan's power, they asked the Tashnag party[6] if they could help them create a new party called the Young Turks. They agreed because Armenians were anxious for a new reform that would better their lot; therefore, it was no secret among the few Armenian leaders that guns had been brought in from out of town for this purpose. This was showing faith in the revolution, and that was good. But now times were different. The Turks charged that the Armenians were going to revolt and help European countries take over the country; they were called unfaithful, disloyal, and saboteurs—they were not to be trusted. But Kamil knew that the Armenians did not have a chance to use their guns because the revolution of the Young Turks was sudden and successful. The population had no need to revolt.

Just shortly before this, the Turkish Parliament, and a few members who were Armenian, objected to the war because the country was too weak to fight against the great powers and because Turkey had just concluded an unsuccessful war in the Balkans, in which many young Turkish and Armenian lives were sacrificed. But now it was thought that the citizens were no longer loyal and were showing signs of friendship toward foreign countries. The Turks believed that the Armenians in particular were disloyal, especially because one of the outstanding Armenians in Parliament strongly objected to further involvement at this time. I am told that he happened to be teaching law and parliamentary rules to one of the leaders of the Young Turks, Krikor Zohrob, minister of the Interior. Soon my older brother, Haroutoun (Haroutiun), was called for an interview. He was not allowed to return home but was kept in jail. My cousin and brother, both formerly close, were in jail waiting to be interrogated; one of the police officers, a neighbor, came to my brother's house to express sorrow for my brother's arrest and said he wished to speak to my father.

Deportation

Bishop Timaksian summoned the leaders of his church. My father was the only Protestant to go to that meeting. Timaksian reported that he had been ordered by the patriarch in Constantinople that "there should be absolute obedience to all governmental orders," and they were to show their loyalty to the government, and, therefore, should surrender whatever guns and ammunition they might have and submit to being searched. The patriarch left it to their good judgment to comply.

Father knew that Timaksian had no choice in the matter. He was obliged simply to deliver the message that had been forced upon him. It could very well have been that the patriarch in Constantinople had been forced to issue his orders under severe pressure from the government.

My father stood up and expressed deep regret for people who thought they could achieve anything by arming themselves. "But now," he said, "whoever is asking that we surrender our guns, watch out. Something is coming that is not pleasant. Watch and be careful, do not surrender your guns." If this statement had leaked out, my father would have been shot in public in broad daylight. But he was seventy-seven years old and unafraid.

The majority, however, decided to turn in their guns. They took ammunition as well to city hall, where their names were taken down. Even

Avadis (Avedis), the son of Haji Sarkis, and my brother, Haroutoun, sur-rendered their guns. They had to. The authorities knew that they had them. Now, as a formality, they were held in jail for clearance—or so the authorities claimed, and, of course, their friends higher up.

The police came to see Father. My brothers had a successful business manufacturing Persian shawls. Because of lack of transportation, the finished goods were stored in their offices, ready to be shipped. In case of deportation or exile, however, all belongings could be confiscated by the government. My brothers were now marked as saboteurs, undesirable subjects. In plain business language, the police suggested that my father transfer these goods to the chief of police, with the promise that "it will be beneficial to you and your family."

My father, hoping to gain favor to help his son, transferred all of the properties and the key to the store, and many hundreds of dollars' worth of ready-made shawls in accounts receivable. In exchange, my brother was not to be treated as badly as the others, nor to be chained as the oth-ers were. He was given a horse to ride to Sivas, perhaps to be tried there. We never heard from him again. Later we heard that he was shot to death before he reached Sivas.

Meanwhile a telegram came to my father, from Caesarea* in the south, saying that my other brother, Minass, was sick, and his wife wanted help from Father. The meaning was that my brother had been deported, as were others all over Turkey. Father arranged for my older brother to undertake the responsibilities in place of the exiled brother. This was dangerous busi-ness, and very dangerous times. But Father wanted his eldest son to leave town and perhaps be saved. He hired a Turkish traveling companion to act as a guard. The messenger arrived with his letter, to be paid by Father. Father often visited the city hall to see the chief of police and to arrange for our safety. By this time, very few were left free and not arrested.

By January 1915, Gurun had the look of a ghost town. Shutters on all of the shops were kept closed and locked. No one was left in the town to op-erate the businesses. Most boys of my age were drafted into the army. Most from sixteen to forty-five years old were conscripted. By some strange fate, I was not called into the army. I was registered in Sivas, where I was born, but no one seemed to care about me in Gurun. I was warned not to

*In Armenian, Gesaria or Kesaria; in Turkish, Kayseri.

go downtown anymore. This gave me time to read and study. I borrowed books from friends and neighbors.

Father seemed to want me to read more of his philosophy book, *Tesavross*, printed in Venice and translated from Latin to Kerapar, classic Armenian.[7] He urged me to read some publications translated by the American Board Missionary Organization[8] into modern Armenian. These told about a tribe of Israelis who were charged with the responsibility of carrying only temple supplies to the desert. One man was charged with carrying the stakes of the tents, where His Holiness rested, an important task. The moral of this book was that each task had its importance, no matter how small it may be.

I studied Armenian literature and grew fond of poems by Daneal Varudjian. I was excited by *The Heart of the Nation* and *The Song of Pageantry*. I found, too, a few pieces of Varudjian's writings of "Songs of Bread" in magazines. He was born not far from Father's birthplace, Mukitar. I had a sample of Rupen Zartarian's prose from Matatia Jamjamian, who was a student from the American Yeprad (Euphrates) College (in Kharput) but was prevented from continuing because it was closed for the year.[9]

The "ghost town" atmosphere extended to the homes. Women and children, helpless, kept their doors locked. Their neighbors, all of them, were afraid. No men were around in the streets. At times you could not see a soul for blocks except for helpless old men. The children were forbidden to be out at any time of the day. For the first time ever, doors were locked. These simple, generous, reliable, warm, and noble people were afraid for their lives.

In the past, nobody in Gurun went hungry; orphans and widows were cared for. Neighbors took care of neighbors, and nobody was left sick and uncared for. Somebody was always there to help with ancient remedies. You did not have to go to an inn in the city to stay overnight if you were a stranger. You could knock on anybody's door and enjoy their hospitality for a day or two. Nobody was on a diet, no pills, no modern medicines. They were a vigorous people, healthy as the wild barley in the fields and as cheerful as the brook that gurgled past their hut-like houses. They shared what they had and enjoyed it. I was happy, very happy, among these people. I was proud of these unusual, strange people, with their strange language and its musical dialect. Physically and morally, they were strong and dependable. To spare you, they wouldn't tell you of their pain and sufferings. Many times Mother would send me to a neighbor whose husband or father was gone to ask if they needed anything. They would smile sadly, thank me, and offer me some fruit.

Churches, like the shops and houses, were closed. No men went to church, followed by their proud wives and children. No more. They had no more holidays or occasions to celebrate. Children wanted to know whether their fathers would come back; all of the women and children wondered why the men had to leave, why they had been taken away from them. One tried to comfort them with some story—false, of course—arousing false hopes. Few people dared venture forth to get awful news. We learned that some had been sent from the jail with their arms tied together, and the ropes were returned stained with blood. Peasants who accidentally had come into town whispered that they had seen the nearby rivers stained with the blood of the victims.

A few boys from my school, and some from Sivas, were drafted into the army. They were poorly treated and given hard labor. These boys were students, qualified to be officers. Some had escaped from the army, traveled by night, picked up guns and ammunition, and sneaked up one of the rocky mountains at the end of the city, an area called Shougool. Many years ago, Professor Manisajian had taken pictures of these ancient rocks, next to the deep waters the natives called the sea, for his geography book.

The boys who now hid up in the rocks had to come out for food and water. Gendarmes stationed around the rocks and its entrance watched them day and night. Although short of food and water, they did not surrender. They had found an outlet to the outside for supplies. These eight sons of Gurun did not want to die like their brothers and friends, with their hands tied behind their backs, shot by the Turks for sport and pleasure. The authorities bargained: if they surrendered, they would not be punished; if they did not turn themselves in, their families would suffer the consequences.

A few escaped, but not their leader, Kanzatian, a former teacher of mine. He believed he should accept responsibility for the families, and surrendered. Like thousands of others, Kanzatian was tried, sent to Sivas, stood in front of the government building, and was shot by the Turkish army. But Vartan earlier that year was shot in view of officials and the population. They had tied him to a stake as he could not stand up, he was so weak. The only thing that could be heard from his lips was a whispered "My son." Vartan's wife was pregnant at this time—that is why he did not try to escape.

More searches followed during March and April of 1915. The authorities had ready alibis for entering our homes and checking and rechecking information they got from neighboring Turks. If a Turk envied your success in business or did not like you, he reported a concealed weapon in your basement. You would then be beaten up, imprisoned, and deported. The Armenian population was not only hushed and secluded, but it was cut off from life by fear. Of those remaining, most were women and children.

In May, we heard that the Turks in eastern cities were deporting Armenian women, children, and old men who could barely walk. From the end of town, quite far from the residential district, they received orders to ready themselves. They were allowed only enough food and clothing for a few days and were told, in fact, that they could expect pardon from the sultan. They would not need many provisions, because their destination was not far.

Many people moved without reason, like disturbed birds flying from their nests. We decided to move nearer to the center of Gurun to be near friends. One morning a Turk knocked at our door and asked if we had anything to sell for cash. We had some finished shawls, some very expensive, others not quite so. I brought out about a dozen of them, which had cost us quite a bit to make. We had to sell them to the Turk for below our cost, about one piaster, a hundredth of a gold lira. The Turk bought all of the shawls for below our labor costs. Later, two more men came to the door, and we sold them more expensive ones, again at much less than one-tenth of our cost. I was doing a good business, but someone was always there to kill the joy.

My father came home and saw me in action. He said, not softly, but peeved and disturbed, "It doesn't make any sense, son, selling these goods at less than our cost. You sure make a good businessman." I knew, too, it was illegal for Armenians to sell their goods or belongings because orders had been issued to confiscate them. Sellers were afraid to sell, and buyers to buy. I was so resentful that I thought I should burn the whole house and leave, but I knew that my father would have been held responsible. He had many other worries and responsibilities. Relatives and friends, thirty-five families or so, depended upon him for daily advice, consultation, and guidance. He managed to hold on to his contact with city hall regardless of how much the situation deteriorated. One day, he told the mayor how blessed they were who had mercy on their subjects. He left a Bible with some pages marked for the mayor to read.

Outside, he ran into Kamil, saluted him, and said sarcastically, "Soon you will be receiving a medal for arresting so many 'spies' and for serving your country so well." Kamil smiled and said, "If that had been said by somebody else, you know what would have happened." "I wondered what had happened to your friend," Father replied. "We have not heard from him yet." Truth may be a bitter pill, but it does combat the disease.

A policeman who lived next to my brother visited the family again and expressed his hope that we would not be deported. He suggested that my brother's wife deliver a message to my father: Regardless of what might happen or what we might be asked to do, we should go along with the authorities, at least until these bad times are over. He went on to say that, although we were all now living in an atmosphere of anger, it would soon pass. "It is hard on you and hard on us, too, to lose a neighbor and friend. Be sure to deliver this message to your father-in-law. I am sure he will understand."

Somebody must have reported the visit to the chief of police. The neighbor had overstepped the boundaries, infringed on the head of police's territory, and was jailed. His wife told us what had happened to her husband, so Father visited the chief of police and argued that the man had done no harm; he just wanted to find out whether the children needed anything. "God bless him," he said. "We need more neighborly people like him nowadays." With that the neighbor was released.

I counseled with my father, as our future was so complicated and uncertain. "It seems to me," I said, "that, whatever happens, I am going to be picked up—let's face it—and you will be deported soon afterward."

"We'll wait," he replied. "We'll wait and see; the tide may turn."

He was keeping his bargain with the police chief, the mayor, and Kamil, but he knew it was in their best interests to get rid of us. Eventually, they would do away with him. The only thing he was concerned about was how long it would take. In the meantime, he could be useful to the families and others who depended upon him and lived under his protection.

The police came to our house several times, but they did not find me at home. I begged my mother to let me surrender myself, for hiding was punishable by law. One afternoon we heard a knock on the door. Mother motioned for me to hide, but this time I did not. The policeman came and said, "We are going to take you to the station; get ready." I went into my room to change. He followed me. He told me to take along some food; we knew what that meant: I would not return that day, perhaps not at all.

When I left my home, I found that the whole block had been surrounded by the police. I was led to the end of the street, where a few people were waiting. More prisoners soon joined our group. I saw people I had not seen for a long time, some I did not even know were in town. A guard with a fixed bayonet ordered me to line up with a group of men who were ready to march. It took a long time for the guard to count twenty-four of us; the second count was twenty-six. We became more and more nervous. His Turkish was poor. I couldn't help wondering what made this ignoramus master over us, and what made us subject to his orders. Why had we to listen humbly and be demeaned and humiliated? As we walked the streets, we saw terrified women opening their gates at the Turks' commands to deliver to them their latest victims. Like cattle, we were herded to the nearby church, pushed inside, and the iron gates closed on us.

After the long, tedious counting and recording of names, we were grouped into bunches of fifty to be transferred to the central jail downtown, now in the *khan*.[10] On our way, I saw my father walking home with his head hanging low. He stopped and said, "Don't worry, son, we'll see. I'll come and visit you."

When I was born in March 1895, they named me after John the Baptist, also my father's only brother. Though first-born, I was regarded as the "Benjamin" of my family, above the other children. Father had always wanted a son in his own image, a Christian boy, a future minister in the service of God. He wanted a man of character and principle who would be able to serve his community and his race and bring honor to the family name.

His other sons, from his first marriage, were raised without his guidance. Three of them were married and successful in business; yet, my father was not happy with them. His son who had escaped to the New World during the 1895 massacre was over forty and not yet married, and he did not write often. My father was ashamed of him. That was one of the reasons that I could not go to America. Now my father's hopes and dreams were crumbling; it was all over. His son had to go like many others, perhaps never to return.

He had been a good father and he could not understand all this. He had hoped to see his son become a man, be educated, come home as a minister or teacher. He wanted to hear people say, "You have a fine son, useful, a good boy." He did not want me to become a wealthy man; to him all of that seemed evil. He was left with only one thing to do: pray to the God he loved so much. The *khan* was now filled to overflowing with men. The ground floor was like a corral where cattle are gathered for slaughter. There was hardly a place to move in the yard.

Most were older men, who were pulled out of their homes. On the ground floor, the shop where in happier times my father had collected coins was now closed. I wandered around and went upstairs, where travelers once had their overnight rooms. Arguments were going on among some students: What went wrong with our national policy? Whose fault was this? Had the leaders failed, or had the church misled them? A few came from privileged homes; their fathers once had been influential at city hall.

One of these students was the son of the controller of tobacco traffic. A black market for selling tobacco in order to escape paying taxes always had existed. The youth was supposed to graduate from the Kharput (Euphrates) College in 1915. Now he turned to me and said, "Someday this will end, but many people will be killed, will die and disappear. That is the Turks' plan, to put an end to all of us. But you . . ." He pointed his finger at me. "You may survive, and if you do, it will be your obligation to tell the whole world how it happened and why, and why it should not have happened. You are the witness to our tragedy. It is your duty to tell it all."

The young man looked angry, as if he were disappointed with the whole world—and with good reason. He had warned young and old alike before he was jailed: "Let us not surrender, let's get out of town." But his father and friends did not listen. Out of fear, they forced him to surrender, arguing that, because they were community leaders, there would be harsh reprisals against the remaining population.

It was late evening, and the sun was sinking over the hill. A young lady with special permission from the gate guard came in through the small door in the big gate. She was weeping. She had come from Constantinople to teach in the girls' school. The children had learned more Armenian songs since she had come, Gomidas's songs,[11] which he had revived since the 1908 revolution. She and Matatia, who also was a student in Kharput, had become engaged. Now they were helpless and hopeless. They looked at one another, saying little. When she left, Matatia wiped his tears. They would never see one another again.

Somebody called my name. My father was at the gate outside the small entry door. We exchanged a few words. My father said, "I pray, my son, you do not lose your faith in God." I felt as though God had indeed surrendered his powers to Allah and that it was too late for prayer or anything else. Suddenly the guard pushed my father aside. "Your time is up."

My father ignored him. "Since when is it a crime to talk to one's son for a few minutes?"

The guard pulled out his gun and was about to strike my father. My immediate reaction was to jump out through the gate to stop the guard from hitting my father, but somebody pulled me back and said, "Don't you know you are a prisoner? They will shoot you as soon as you are out of this gate."

A civilian Turk came up to the guard and, with a loud voice, said, "Aren't you ashamed of yourself? Don't you have any respect for an old man?" The guard released my father. Father left, humiliated.

Now it was dark. There was confusion among the prisoners in the *khan.* The chief of police came in and silenced the prisoners. He had a list of men's names; they were commanded to come forward. About sixty boys and a few men were called. My name was one of them. We were fortunate to have been separated from the rest, for those whose names were not called were sent to be butchered the next day. We were sent instead to the Central Armenian Church. Bishop Timaksian's office was locked and sealed. The classrooms on the second floor were empty and forebodingly quiet. Garbo Varjabed's chair and table were still there, and one could still hear him saying, "You are the future hope of the nation. Be a man."

The guard at the door downstairs was a dear old Armenian. Entrusted to this man, we were to stay there only for a short time, according to high orders from Constantinople. Friends and relatives sent us necessities. My brother's family sent me food and bed coverings. I was surprised to find a few of my old friends already there, including Moushegh, some distant cousins, and a few other boys I knew. Everybody was sure that I would be sent home very soon, because my father knew somebody in city hall and because he himself was still free. I thought so, too, but one couldn't go by such rules in times like these. It all depended upon the mood of the authorities. Has hatred, prejudice, or malice ever had logic or reason? In war, is there time to think of right or wrong? None of us was suspected of any real wrongdoing. Our crime was being of the new generation, the Armenians of tomorrow.

Moushegh and I carefully inspected the place for possible avenues of escape. We found one possibility but kept it as our secret. The old man at the door let us go out to fetch some water. The fountain was in the center of the town, near the mosque. In the morning I wanted to bring some water in a pail.

At the fountain, when nobody paid attention to me, I was tempted to leave my water pail and walk away. But something told me it was wrong. The gate man had trusted me and was responsible for me. Besides, where could I go, even if I had managed to escape? I would be a fugitive. What a terrible risk for one who had not even committed a crime with which to be charged. And to be an escapee in addition! It would certainly interfere with my father's plans, whatever they were, and would endanger him as well. He would be beaten until he told them of my whereabouts. So, with a pail full of water, I returned to the churchyard that had become my prison. Most of the people in the yard were old and feeble and helpless, or were very young boys. I was treated like the young boys because I looked four or five years younger than my twenty years.

The next day, my father again came to see me. He didn't look happy or hopeful about my release, but he told me that God would help us. He told me to have patience and faith and not do anything that I would regret later. He told me that many families already had been sent away, with the promise and hope that they would later return home. Therefore, he went on, "it will not be necessary to take all your belongings with you. They have said your destination is not too far."

When Father left, the boys wanted me to tell them what he had said. Was I or was I not going to be released? If I was, they felt that they, too, might have some chance. Each morning was greeted with the burning question in our minds: What would happen today?

Moushegh, a shoemaker's son, had brought a hammer with him. He taught me how to use it and suggested that we take care of our shoes, since we might be asked to leave town on foot. With his help, I resoled my new brown oxfords.

Some of the men incarcerated with me became hysterical: They did not know what was happening to their loved ones outside. They would neither eat nor talk but prayed continuously. Some went insane; some lost their speech. Others became very angry at being treated like animals. We couldn't even talk to them any longer. They were obsessed with their plight and misery. But we boys planned for the future and for our freedom.

After two weeks of isolation, the police commissioner came into the churchyard. We were ordered to come and hear his message. The place was hushed—we were like just so many frightened chickens in the presence of a hawk. We were lined up like prisoners of war. Several men were selected and told to step out of line. Each was asked his name and occupation. Each was then told to step to either one side or another.

Not knowing what was up, I stepped forward when my name was called. The commissioner asked my name. In the best Turkish I knew, I told him, very respectfully and very nervously; my voice was shaking. He looked up at me but did not ask my age. My age was in my voice.

"Step aside with that group," he ordered. I turned to my left, frightened. I knew that my destination had been decided at that moment. He suddenly stopped me and said, "Here, son, here," and he pointed to the right side.

The other men were also shaking with the fear of death. A few kneeled before the commissioner and begged for mercy; some bowed to kiss his foot. Many cried piteously. I didn't think that life was worth that much, but they did. The group sent to the left side, mostly grown men, were sent out under guard.

The police commissioner asked our group to come closer to hear him. "You are permitted to go home and are forgiven. This is the sultan's order. You should all praise the sultan." Dramatically and fanatically—and fearfully—we raised our voices in unison and cried, "Long live the sultan!" Men wept. We thought our newfound freedom deserved the payment of a lie.

Nevertheless, we were aware of the others who had not had the good fortune to be left to live.

In my excitement, I rushed out through the church gate, but stopped on my heels. I didn't know where to go! My home was on the left side of the valley, but my brother's house was just a few blocks away. I feared that I might be arrested again, by someone else, because I didn't have any identification papers, and I would have to pass through the marketplace and past city hall. I walked past city hall and reached a stone bridge. The place was haunted; not a soul was there. A guard at the city hall eyed me suspiciously. So I slowed my steps. I took a deep breath after crossing the bridge.

Nervously, I knocked on my brother's door. Nobody answered, but I knew they were there. After a long wait, somebody from upstairs called out, "It's all right, open the door. It's Hovhannes." They could not believe I had been released from the prison. My father had petitioned for me the day before but had been refused—that was why he was so sad when he came to see me. He could not understand why, when the police commissioner had refused to release me the day before, I was released the next day. He assumed that the police had thought that I was my brother's son, as my brother had a son named Hovhannes, too.

News traveled fast that I had been released, but I did not want to be seen outside. Father decided to move to the center of town, to be closer to my brother's family. It offered the protection of relative isolation, because most Armenians living there already had been deported. I made small wooden boxes for my books and notes, Varoujan's poems, and *Tesavross*, the book Father had given me. I had to bury them because the government collected all books and papers. Mother concealed the shawls in mattresses and quilts, hid some food, and took a few dishes. We locked the door and walked away, not knowing when we would return.

A few days later my father was called to city hall and held for questioning. He lost his patience and asked them what they were trying to do—he was not running away and was ready if they wanted anything from him. He was seventy-seven years old, proud, alert, and challenging. I visited him several times as he had permits for us to visit.

The friendly policeman, my brother's neighbor, was grateful to my father for having helped clear him of suspicion of favoring the Armenians. He would visit my father in jail and urged him to accept any terms city hall might offer so that he might remain at home and avoid deportation. After all, by doing so, he might save many people from deportation. Father was almost convinced that it was worth sacrificing the most valuable things in life. He asked himself whether this was worth doing for the younger generation. He was sure it was, but he hesitated, for how could he know that the Turks would keep their promises? And how about all of the noble precepts he had talked about most of his life? Could he turn his back on them now that his life was nearing its end? Or should he forget himself and sacrifice all that was most valuable in his life: his faith, his religion?

There are few things upon which one must not pass judgment. One in particular is the decision a man makes under excessive and unusual pressure and confusion. Of course my father couldn't agree with the Turks. But he was promised protection during the period of deportations if he would cooperate with the Turkish authorities.

One afternoon, while Mother was away, I was startled by what sounded like small rocks falling into our yard. I waited and listened. The sound kept coming. It would stop, then start again, and then again. I wondered where it came from, and why. So, I went out to investigate. Behind the house was a brook, bordered by heavy shrubbery and some fruit trees that ran toward the neighbors' trough. I saw a man coming out of the thicket toward me. It was my friend Sarkis. He told me how he had run away from home so he wouldn't be arrested, and how he had joined the group of young men hiding among the rocks up in the hills. They were collecting guns in the event that they were discovered. He asked me to join them. My immediate reaction was to join them right away, but Father was not home. He was in jail, and I was the eldest son, the head of the family now. I told Sarkis I would think about it and let him know. He asked if I could help them with some food. He needed flour and salt. I gave him a sack of flour and salt, and all he could carry in the way of foodstuffs. He asked if he could hide in my house that night. I didn't think it advisable under the circumstances, but he hid in the yard.

I couldn't hide the subterfuge from Mother for long; she soon noticed that I was going out more often than usual. What she didn't know then was that I was taking more food out to Sarkis and talking with him about future plans. When it got dark, we could both disappear; but I had never done anything without first consulting my parents. Strong ties bound us, and I had great respect for their wisdom, which had never failed me in the past. Mother didn't have to be told much; she sensed what was going on and would look at me sadly. She did not tell me that my place was in the home, that it was my duty to take over Father's responsibilities now that he was gone. Instead, she admonished me to protect myself above all else; but she feared that I might die of hunger if I remained underground before I had a chance to fight—she knew I felt obligated to take a stand with the boys and that I was anxious to help them. Sarkis's widowed mother came to our house the next day, begging me to tell her where her son was. I told her that I did not know, feeling it best to lie. The less she knew, the less chance the Turks had of forcing it out of her. She related how the police had mistreated her and punished her. They held her responsible for the disappearance of her son and threatened even more cruel punishment.

The following evening, Sarkis kept his rendezvous with me. This time it was the strange sound of a cat's meow that led me to him. Even in the dark, I could see the sweat pouring down his cheeks, over his smallpox-scarred face, trickling down to his chin and into his cleft chin. It struck me as odd, and fascinated me. He did not have a handkerchief with which to wipe himself, but he had a small gun on his hip, carefully concealed. He had turned desperado, like the rest, in an attempt to save his life. I told him about his mother's visit. Overcome, he convinced himself that he had to surrender in order to comfort her as best he could.

"Before you do that," I said, "get rid of that weapon." He dug a hole in the ground and marked it by placing a rock upon it, hoping to find it if he should ever need it, and left.

Upon surrendering, Sarkis was sent to the same place where my father was held prisoner. He told Father how desperately they were struggling. Although they were fighting for survival, they didn't want to do anything to endanger the other families. My father used his friendship with the jailer to get Sarkis permission to visit his mother and make final arrangements for his deportation. Instead, he met with Moushegh, who also was considering joining the radical youths. Afterward, Moushegh changed his mind, thinking that at the last minute, or during deportation, Sarkis could still escape. Sarkis returned to prison after his mission. Father was surprised.

"Why did you come back, you little fool?" "One can't suffer much more," Sarkis replied, "when one is practically dead already." Besides, Father had been responsible for securing permission for his errand, and Sarkis would not let Father suffer the consequences of his escape. He knew, too, what it could mean for the treatment of others like Father if he went back on his word. The next morning, the Turkish guards discovered that Sarkis had escaped from jail.

A group of influential people had asked that they be deported together. Because they still had a vestige of confidence in and friendly feelings toward the Turks and hoped to be fairly treated, they gave up their belongings and properties to the authorities, who promised them protection. We were to be included in the group. Then city hall arranged with the police for the deportations. In a sudden flurry, we were informed who would be with us in this special caravan. Father was released from custody, and friends and relatives told where to gather. Father had to pay a stiff price for three donkeys. Pillows, bedding, and covers were stuffed with valuable shawls. We packed little food; it was the middle of June, and we couldn't carry much food. We arranged for Father to ride the larger donkey, while our belongings were loaded on the second. My sister, Anoush, was only nine, and my brother, Vahan, was only six years old. The twins, brother and sister, were only three years old. They would ride the third donkey. Mother and I would walk.

3

Many Hills Yet to Climb

The First Day

IT WAS AN IRONICALLY BRIGHT and sunny day when our band of three hundred Armenians started to move south. Women were crying bitterly, and the elders practically had to drag along the youngsters. Many didn't know how to make a pack or load a donkey; some had hired Turks as guards. Others, tired of being harassed and searched, were happy to be leaving.

We stopped in front of the city hall. We were hopeful that we might obtain a set of guards from the mayor, who had known us so long and knew us well; we had been assured that we would have protection with us. Our group of friends and relations, mostly merchant families, had been arranged specially by city officials. A few other friends, knowing this, had joined the caravan with the hope of being with a "privileged" group and gaining more protection.

I could see close friends, relations, neighbors, church members, classmates—all good people who had worked hard and always helped others and their church and schools whenever asked. Many of them did not know how to read or write, but they had a keen sense of right and wrong. These fine people were now being made refugees only because they had clung to their ancient beliefs and the faith of their ancestors. They marched proudly under a yoke of hatred, prejudice, and bigotry, their morale high, their spirit as yet unbroken. They knew that their only "crime" was being Armenian. They had deep convictions about this, held for centuries, never broken by the ups and downs of history. They were robbed of their belongings, their homes, and their security. Who was entitled to their homes, their properties? They were built by their fathers, and their fathers' fathers before them, and so on way back. Were they now to belong to the barbarians who came to ruin them, to burn, destroy, and kill? By what right? These are questions that must taunt our civilization: Who are the rightful owners of the nests and homes of these victims?

From city hall, we traveled south. We passed by our own house, looking at it perhaps for the last time. Our hearts were heavy, strained by the frustrations of the past. I tried hard to get my father's attention and involve him in conversation, but he could answer only in monosyllables: "Yes." "No." I felt shut out; I couldn't reach him. The children walked, holding either my hand or Mother's. We started climbing the hills as we left Gurun. I asked Father if it might not be better for him to ride because the hill was getting steeper and harder to climb. He said wistfully, "There are many hills yet to climb."

The Turkish population opened their doors to watch us go, gleefully cursing us for wasting the things we took along for just a "short trip." They begrudged us even the little we took. Like scavenging ravens, they would rather we had left it to them.

Late in the afternoon, we entered the small Turkish town of Albistan,* about thirty-five miles over the hills and due south of Gurun. The people there were shabbily dressed and poor. As we entered the center of town, these Turks greeted us by pelting us with rocks and spitting on us. Even children and teenagers called us bad names, while their elders showed their anger by cursing us.

We trudged a few more miles past Albistan, then stopped when it became dark, not sure where we were. I released the donkeys of their burdens and gave them some feed, hanging a bag over each donkey's head. We sat to eat and spread our covers. Father blessed our simple fare and thanked God, begging Him for mercy.

The children were now worn out. I wandered in search of water, which I found and brought to Mother. Our band comprised more than fifty Armenian families and was broken into five groups. Through the night I

---

*Also Elbistan, in the northern sector of Marash County in southeastern Turkey.

visited other family camps to learn who they were. I talked with my two brothers' families and an elderly grandmother who fondly had told us stories when we were young and who always gave us fruit. Now she was in her late eighties.

I located Moushagh and Sarkis. Because we were young men, we had to be prepared for anything that might happen. We discussed emergency plans for the group and even the possibility of our abandoning the group and running away to the hills, to be free and out of the grasp of the Turks.

Second Day

The next morning, the Turkish guards told us to pack up quickly. I made sure that the donkey Father was going to ride was secured well with harness and belt. I learned to do this from Hagop-agha on our journey home. Mother gave some food first to Father, then to the children, then to me, and last to herself. This way we would have something to nibble on en route. After a while, my three-year-old sister wanted to be picked up, so I carried her. Her twin brother also wanted to be lifted. I put down sister and picked him up. My sister, Anoush, and brother, Vahan, were doing well. Father, weakening, would raise his head once in a while and repeat, "Many hills yet to climb."

In the afternoon, as I walked by Father's side, I saw a woman beside the road. I concealed it from my father. She was motionless, exposed under the hot sun, the old eighty-year-old grandmother we had known so well.

We trudged on. Mother never complained, nor did Father, but he was losing faith in the Turks' promised destination. He concluded that this was a road leading nowhere, but he was kind and encouraging nevertheless. He felt responsible for all of us in this unpredictable world.

Late that afternoon we came upon a small village and stopped nearby. The Turkish guards never allowed us to stop where there was a river, a brook, or water. We were all tired, thirsty, and hungry. I told Mother I wanted to go to the village to try to get some food. We were eating cheese and bread, some boiled eggs, and dried food. But I was not sure if the group would leave while I was gone, or if I would ever find them again.

I went down to the village, found a cottage, and begged a woman to make some pilaf. She understood my Turkish and asked me how many were in the family. I told her we were seven, four children, my parents, and myself. She boiled the water on a quick out-of-doors fire, melted some butter, mixed it with bulgur. She charged me one piaster worth, only forty para; I had to buy the wooden container in which to take the pilaf back to camp.

I returned to our camp. The children were happy to see the pilaf. We ate, and I left to make my rounds for getting information: Did anybody know where we were, where we were going the next day, or our final destination?

We slept as a horde of sheep in pasture. Families were very close to one another. Elders surrounded the young, especially young girls, inside their circle. Twice I walked around and found Mother awake. She motioned me not to talk, pointing at Father who was asleep.

Third Day—The Hill

As we left Gurun, Mother arranged that Father should carry no money with him. I would have some, in case I was separated from the family. She sewed two precious Hungarian gold pieces on my shirt, close to my armpit, and gave me a few coins for daily spending money. But all of the remaining valuables and the coins Father had collected she sewed in a belt for my sister, Anoush. She tied it securely around her and instructed Anoush not to lose it and not to be separated from us.

We were climbing hills up and down and turning endlessly, ever higher. We came out between two peaks in the Taurus Mountains and stared into the Jihar River, eight thousand feet below.* We had to hug the precarious side of narrow cliffs, so close to the edge that even the sure-footed donkeys had a hard time securing a foothold. We moved carefully, one by one, in single file. A donkey with a heavy load brushed against the side of the hill and teetered, but his feet held steady. Father, still on foot, walked behind me. Here was a road you could not turn back on and you could walk no faster than the people in front. We had to keep the same pace as the others.

I smelled something strange. It seemed to be gunpowder, but we heard no gunshots. By this time, I had become separated from my family—I

---

*The Taurus Mountains are a range in Turkey, separating the Mediterranean coast and Mesopotamia from southern Turkey and the Armenian highland. The river the author is referring to here is likely the Tigris River, which flows from its source, Lake Hazar.

often walked ahead of them so that I could warn them of danger and so that I could look for water. Slowly, carefully, we reached the summit, where the road widened and exposed to view the hill and valley below us. People were running helter-skelter, grabbing whatever animals they could, shooting and killing with whatever weapons were at hand—knives, hatchets, and guns. Some rolled burdened donkeys downhill. I left my donkey and proceeded slowly. The acrid odor of burning flesh and the cries of a woman filled the air. I stopped a moment to decide what to do but saw that it was already too late.

One of our guards with a raised gun stood behind us. The villagers, Kurds, were scurrying up the hill in a hurry. Alone and separated from my family, I hollered as loudly as I could to all around to throw or roll rocks down at the advancing Kurds. We stopped the horde for a moment, but we could not hold them back any longer. They swarmed around us from both sides, each man armed with long-bladed knives and guns. Few were shooting: They did not want to waste their bullets on Armenians.

Standing in this confusion, I saw a Kurd face-to-face in front of me. He could say only "Para!" I tried to explain to him that all I had were a few copper pieces inside a handkerchief, which I volunteered to hand to him. My clothes were shabby and dirty—no better than those of these Kurds. This man searched me all over, as they do the prisoners of war, repeatedly asking me for more money and threatening: "I will kill you if you don't give me more money!" I told him that it was all I had. He left, cursing his bad luck. Others had been stripped and wounded, and were unable to walk.

I unbuttoned myself, leaving my chest bare, picked up a piece of wood to lean on as if I were wounded, and walked, limping, toward my companions, now gathered like cattle. They were all frozen and frightened, or shaking and desperate. There were the sharp cries of women and men. A Kurd was dragging a girl by her hair. I saw a man tied to a tree, burning alive—he was the barber, Phillip.

While the shooting and killing continued, the guards surrounded us but without the slightest attempt to stop the carnage. These so-called security guards, appointed by the Gurun authorities, had taken most of our money as the price for "protecting" us. A group of women were bowing their heads and weeping. I signaled to Sarkis's sister, asking where her brother was. She motioned back that he was gone. Suddenly, somebody pulled me down by my clothes and said, "You fool, sit down!" and covered me with her dress. From my hiding place beneath this stranger's clothing, I could see the field before us. The corpses of our people were scattered all over. The animals had been taken from them and their loads—pots and pans, shoes, clothing, bedding, food—still lay on the ground.

Nearby was a small book with one of its pages marked. A breeze blew the pages back and forth, but the book stayed open at the same spot. As the wind pushed the little book toward us, I could read: "The Lord is my shepherd, I shall not . . ." The breeze blew the pages again, but then came back to the same pages: "Yea, though I walk through the Valley of the Shadow and Death, I will fear no evil, for Thou art with me." A gust rose and closed the chapter.

The group was silent now, literally frozen. We could hardly breathe. Finally, one of the guards fired a gun, and the murdering Kurds scattered down the hill, leaving many of our band wounded or dead, strewn over the mountainside. As the wild slaying and shooting stopped, an oppressive silence descended. It was the end of the day—for many, the end of life.

I found Anoush with relatives, but she did not know where Mother was. I walked about and found my mother and the children huddled together. Father was still missing. Finally, someone told me that Father had been seen not long ago. He had been slapped, abused, and spat upon but not injured. Our belongings—food, bedding, donkeys—were all gone. We were frightfully hungry, tired, and thirsty. We had no covering for my brothers and sisters, or for my old suffering father. Mother gathered the children in her lap to comfort and lull them to sleep without food or drink.

Only a few days before we had what had seemed to be everything we needed. Now I had to stay away from my family in fear that the authorities might pick me up. I walked away regretting that I had not joined Sarkis and Moushegh in their escape to freedom.

Not far away, in the dark, I spotted a hut. I could hide myself against the wall, where nobody would be likely to see me till morning's light, and I could watch my family. Short of the hut, a dog stopped me, but I was not afraid of him; I was only afraid of man. I stood alone and forlorn, and the dog went away. On my knees, I crawled on toward the hut and leaned against a wall of large coarse sacks made of goat hair. Their contents appeared to be charcoal. With my fingers I tried to pull out a piece and smell it. It tasted like dried wheat mixed with yogurt, used for the winter soup. I had a hard time chewing it, but I let it soak in my mouth and ate enough to assuage my hunger.

In the dark, I saw shadows moving toward the captain of the guards. Slowly, they surrounded our camp; they were Kurds from the village below who had come to finish the job. In our caravan were merchants, some wealthy, some old. Until now they had been able to buy security with bribes. Somehow these local people had learned well-to-do people were in our camp. We were in their territory, so they were told they could do with us as they pleased.

So the merchants went to meet with the captain of the guards, who had been changed the day before, together with our original guards, who had been assigned by the authorities to escort and protect us. The captain asked these merchants if they could produce enough money to cool off the Kurds, pretending that he didn't have enough manpower to protect us. The deportees told the captain that they had been robbed, stripped of all of their belongings, and that their cash was gone. However, a few men got together and consulted with others in an effort to raise enough money to avoid being butchered. But who had any money left? They managed to collect some jewelry, small coins, and gold pieces to pacify the barbaric villagers. For the time being, they left our destitute group of helpless and hopeless people.

Leaning against the wall, I couldn't help falling asleep, I was so weary and laden with the horrors I had witnessed that day. I napped fitfully until the morning chill awakened me. Remembering my good fortune that night, I filled my pockets with the precious dried wheat and yogurt and went to find Mother. Father was miserable. I gave him the cheering news that we had a good captain, that he had gotten rid of the Kurds the night before and told them not to come back. "I wonder," asked Father, "what makes the captain so kind."

I told Mother about my treasure store. She asked me what it was. I said it was edible, and showed it to her. She looked at me and the food I held out in my hand, and shook her head. "You did not pay for it?" she asked.

"No." We had no pot to warm it in, or water with which to make the soup. I saw a fire someone had made and went over to borrow a banged-up, dirty pot. At least the children were getting some food.

By now the sun was up. Whatever had been concealed in the dark came gradually into view. Phillip, the barber (and village doctor and dentist), had been burned alive. The man who was moaning all night finally had died of hatchet wounds. My very close friend Mugerdich, the handsome boy in our class who had just returned from college in his new suit, had been shot. All of the animals were gone: The men who had been paid to carry the family's belongings had disappeared, taking with them the horses that belonged to the women. The earth was soaked with blood. We had to keep chasing the dogs from the villages below that had come to get their share of their masters' butchery. The little windblown Bible was crushed and torn to shreds. Nobody paid any attention to it; it seemed that most of our people had forgotten their God, the Almighty One who had abandoned them to this horrible carnage.

Like the rest, I was as shabby, dusty, and dirty as a beggar boy. I had asked my mother the day before to let me wear my corduroy pants; I was ashamed to go around the way I looked and felt. She replied, "We are not going to a wedding party. That is why you are alive today—they don't care about poor people. They are after the rich."

I asked Father how he was feeling. He said that he was all right, but I noticed blood on his cheek. I refrained from telling him about it and didn't attempt to clean it, for my handkerchief had gone with the few coins I had.

Unconsciously, I reached for the gold pieces Mother had sewn under my shirt. I had forgotten them in my fear. I asked Mother if Anoush was all right. She said, "Yes," which meant that the belt was secure.

We were ordered by the guards to move on. A woman bending over her son's dead body paid no attention to the orders. She continued weeping as she had done all night long, oblivious to what was going on around her. Friends urged her to join the group, but she refused to budge and remained with the body of her beloved son—choosing to die that way rather than leave him.

In a way it was a relief not to have anything to carry, but I worried about my father. How long could he walk without water or food? I heard him say, "Let's go." He picked himself up, stood erect, and as usual we let him lead us.

Gurun people have a vitality that no other city people I know have. They are built strong, sturdy, and energetic. They had to work hard, and only if it was necessary would they fight. It must be the water they drank, the clean air they breathed, or the apples they ate.

Or it could have been the hard struggles, for centuries, by which Armenians were steeled as they fought their wars with the Persians to the Mesopotamians. They built cities such as Kharput and Dikranagerd. Under the reign of Dikran (Tigran the Great),[1] they organized a small but strong kingdom. Fighting, surviving, they built more cities. They were the first nation to accept Christianity as a national religion. They fought less, as the Holy Book commanded them. Between the barbaric Romans and the pagan Greeks, the Armenians lost their empire but formed a small capital at Cilicia.[2] Then the barbaric hordes of Osmanly Turks came from the east, burning and killing; since then, the Armenians never have had peace.[3] Thereafter, angry mobs would march on the population, pillaging, looting, burning, and killing. Occasionally, the Armenians would resist.

But in 1915, things were different. These new German barbarians from the west extended their hands to the barbarians of the east to complete a perfect crime. And the Armenians were in the middle, alone, helpless, defenseless—a wandering, hopeless people, left hungry and desperate. Now we did not know where we were going, or what had happened to our leaders—just a horde of hungry deported people in the wilderness.[4]

Our people began walking stooped and with bowed heads. Many could hardly walk any longer. They had left behind too many memories.

I kept close to my father. The twins, so young and helpless, each held on to Mother's hand. Anoush and Vahan were sent ahead to stay with friends, for we were moving slowly because of Father. I picked up one of the twins but kept my eye on Father. He had not had food or water for a long time. His steps were short and weakening; sometimes he would tremble. I asked Mother to go ahead and let Father and me alone for a while. It was safer for her to be among the group.

The sun was getting hotter, and the dust the group stirred up made us thirstier. I asked Father if he wanted to stop for a moment. We rested. Others passed us but turned their backs to follow the track of the groups that kept walking. We became separated from those we knew and trusted. Everybody just dragged along, holding on to the hands of their little ones, who unluckily survived.

At the end of the caravan, a guard on horseback came alongside and ordered us to keep moving. "Keep going! You'd better leave that old man, or else I'm going to shoot the both of you."

"Soldier," I replied (I didn't choose to say "Sir"), "the old man is my father. I can't leave him alone." He put his gun back on his shoulder and left us.

Father was loved and respected by all, but out here in the wilderness he was a nobody. When justice and order disappear, injustice and barbarism prevail.

Father begged me to join Mother and the children. He felt they needed me more than he did, but I believed that I belonged here beside him.

As the evening shadows began to fall, we rose and proceeded, step by step, following the tracks of the groups ahead of us. We reached the groups where they were resting. The children shared our misery in silence. They seemed to have aged overnight. They never complained about the lack of food or water—they knew that if there were food, we would share it with them. I lifted up my youngest brother, Dikran, the twin, and hugged him tight. He smiled wanly. He and I had a strange and special attachment to one another. I can't say why, but we always remained that way.

I asked for a few coins from Mother. She secretly put them in my palm. I was looking for a village for food, but none was in sight. I asked if others knew where we were. We were away from the highways and away from the cities, in some nightmarish land, and no one had any idea where we were.

I had become the head of the family, and it was my responsibility to look for food. When the guards were not watching, I left the group and followed a horse track down a heavy, dusty road. There was a hut there, with smoke rising from the chimney. A donkey was having its evening meal in front of the hut. I dared not enter, but in a loud voice I yelled, "I'm lost and do not know where to go. Can someone help me?"

An old woman came out and wanted to know what I wanted. I said I was lost and was very hungry and could she give me a drink of water. Water in the desert is a God-given gift and should be shared even with infidels and beggars. It is a custom in the Middle East never to turn away a beggar empty-handed. I told the old woman that I had a few coins with which to pay her, if she would give me some food. I told her that I had a very old father and mother, and children for whom I wanted to get some food. She brought out some dark bread. She asked me why I was not eating the bread, and I said that I had best keep it for my younger brothers and sisters.

"Are you Armenian?" she asked me, "Are you a refugee?" She did not wait for my answer, but went on: "Poor, stubborn, foolish people. Why do you not accept our holy faith, become Muslims, save yourselves all this trouble? Boy, your people deserve what is coming to you." She packed a few thin pieces of bread and told me I had better leave before her men came back and found me. "Flee for your life from this place, you fool. You should not have come here."

My father and mother were worried about my delay. When I returned with the food, we all prayed the Lord's Prayer without putting any meaning for it—there was no meaning left. We chewed our dry crusts, and someone loaned us a tin cup. It was the most valuable utensil I ever knew. Some people supplied us with water. They thought we were more unfortunate than they as we had four children and an old man to care for. They spoke with Mother, wishing that God would save me from all evil— that was all there was left: a wish! We slept comparatively safe and sound, with nothing much to lose anymore. We had nothing to worry about; we had seen and experienced the worst. Under these circumstances, life didn't mean much to us anymore.

When the guards roused us in the morning to start our journey, the remaining members of yesterday's generation were deeply involved in prayer. It was Sunday, the first Sunday away from home without a church. They had once been assured that wherever they might be, they could pray, and the Lord would answer them sooner or later. But now they had lost communication with their God and felt guilty. They felt punished, although not knowing why, and begged for forgiveness. But the Jehovah of Israel was angry. Or was there a God after all? It made one wonder. It seemed as though all the candles they had burned in church in front of Mother Mary, with the infant child in her lap, were in vain—hopelessly in vain—that all the Commandments were in vain, Heaven was in vain. Or was it a fraud? How could it be? Their fathers and their fathers' fathers had held the faith for generations. The church had been built on this faith. Was this all that it led to? They needed help and guidance, but even God seemed to have deserted them completely.

The guards, watching the women kneeling in prayer and crossing themselves, were at a loss to understand. The entire group moved about automatically, unaware that they were walking because they still lived in the dream of yesterday.

Back in Gurun, when all were dressed up, the fathers would hold the children's hands, and the mothers would proudly follow their husbands. He was the pillar of the family, the king of the household. Families didn't go to church to show off their attire; that was sinful. They went because they were told that the seventh day belonged to the Lord God, our Father. And then, perhaps, to show off their graceful, growing children. "My," one would say to another, "how nicely your children have grown up. God bless you." "God bless you, too," the other would reply. In church, the priest would bless them all and end by telling them that now it was their turn to forgive one another, even as God had forgiven them. He would suggest the kiss of Holy Brotherhood, and the people would bow to each other in gestures of kisses and peace.

But now we were walking like winds on the desert, the waves in the sea, aimless and ignorant of our destination. We held yesterday's dream, which gave no vigor or happiness, but simply added to our sadness.

It was noon and hot. The groups slowly dragged along on their tired, aching feet. That whole morning, I had worried about food and water. We had neither, and there seemed little chance of getting any. My only hope was to leave the group and go in search of a village where I might find some food and then join them later. I might get lost or be shot by the guards, but I had to do something.

No smoking chimneys were in sight, nor other signs of life that would lead to a village or a hut, so I returned to the caravan. The sun sank over the horizon, and evening shadows fell and enveloped us. Some couldn't budge a step further and tried to rest by the side of the road, but the guards forced them to move on. I began looking ahead to the next turn in the road, hoping against hope for signs of a village, but the guards stopped us.

Somebody whispered that a village was nearby. If only I could make it . . . I darted out and disappeared into the brush. Although I looked repulsive, one couldn't help but pity me. There is an irony in that: When you are at the bottom of life's ladder, you have a degree of safety from harassment. You can't fall any lower; there is nothing you have that people want to take from you, and there is little about you to attract or call attention.

Soon I heard the gurgling of a stream, which was like music to my ears. I ran toward it to quench my parched throat. It was the Milky River, so named by the natives because it ran so forcefully from the mountaintop that its white foam looked like milk. A woman was making bread on an outdoor fire. She was using a round tin on the fire. She must have thought I was a beggar coming from strange lands; she motioned me to go away. I wasn't used to the idea that I appeared to be a beggar. I showed her some coins, and her eyes gleamed. We bargained quickly: I got some food and left the village as fast as my feet would carry me.

Nobody knew that I had gone off. Mother was looking for me desperately, wondering what had happened to me. She had lost Father on the way. I had to find my father, and nobody seemed to know where he was. I was just about off in search of him, but Mother stopped me, insisting it wasn't safe. Instead she went to the captain of the guards and begged him for help. The captain was an army physician who promised to send a man to find him.

Hours—agonizing hours later—the guard finally brought Father to our camp. I thanked the guard and was about to help Father down from the donkey when he said, "Easy, son, you're hurting me." Blood was gushing from his left hip. He had been shot because he could not keep pace with the group, and the guards said it was the best way of getting rid of him. Father begged for water, and more water. I ran to the nearby village and got a goatskin full of yogurt mixed with water. All night he bled, without any help or medicine. There wasn't even a rag with which to wrap his wounds.

By night the captain had gone; the command would be changed in the morning. I went to the new captain's tent and asked if it was possible to get an animal on which my father, who was so old and wounded, could ride.

"What's wrong with him?" the captain asked angrily.

"He was shot during the day," I replied. I guess it was the wrong thing to have said, for he became angrier and shouted at me.

"How can anybody get shot with the protection of so many guards?" He commanded the guards: "Get rid of that lying dog!" They hit me with the butts of their guns until I could run away into the woods. Some guards were cutting long sticks from great pines, fashioning spears. They saw me running and tried their new weapon upon me. I got back to our group, and mingled with the waiting crowd.

A man was waiting with his donkey. "The captain has assigned this donkey to my father," I said. He handed me the rein that he was holding; he was afraid of punishment if ever the captain questioned him. With Mother's help, I put Father on the donkey's back, but the donkey wouldn't move. In the distance a very young donkey seemed to be lost. Apparently, it was the offspring of the donkey I was trying to lead, and neither would move without the other. We persuaded mother and child to walk with us. My mother led the young one so that its mother followed. When the young donkey stopped, the mother donkey would, too, so we made little progress.

We told the twins to go ahead and join friends, not to wait for us. Soon the group was gone, and we were left with this unwilling beast and a sick father who could neither sit up nor lie down on the donkey's back. I tried to hold him up but couldn't. I thought that I should tie him to the back of the animal, as we had no saddle. All of this handling, of course, hurt Father. I could not tie him too tightly, for it would hurt even more; and if I tied him too loosely, he would fall. Mother and I held him as best we could from both sides of the donkey, trying to provide him some support and comfort, but the little donkey was roaming from one side of the road to the other, making the mother donkey stop. We lost track of the disappearing caravan because of the dust cloud in their wake. I did not realize it was late afternoon.

The yogurt drink in the goatskin was gone now. Father had drunk it all. With a small shake, Father fell to the ground, crushed, hurt, and desperate. He begged us to leave him alone and join the group ahead before it was too late. He worried about the children getting lost. We argued against it, but he insisted upon staying. I motioned Mother to help me lift him up, this crushed, weak, exhausted body of a saint, forcing him to stay on the donkey so we would all be together, but he fell again. We couldn't hold him up. This was our worst tragedy.

We couldn't convince him to travel with us, and we couldn't see an end to his torture. Besides, we had obligations to the children. I thought that perhaps it was best to return later with a hired man and bring Father back with less further injury. We decided to leave him there and go for help. I promised to be back as soon as possible. We placed him in the shade of an old oak tree and left without looking back.

Mother was frighteningly depressed. It was difficult to convince her that as soon as we reached the group, we could go back and pick up Father. We walked down the road where we thought the group would be. The road entered into the woods, where the road divided at a fork with a left road and a right road. No traces of the caravan were in either direction. As the group marched, the heavy dust settled on and covered all traces of footprints. I asked Mother to let me stop for a rest. I was tired, weary, weak, and very sleepy. I couldn't go on; I had to sit down and rest. I fell asleep. I dreamed of a river with cool flowing waters. A sharp cry awakened me. My mother was calling. I jumped to my feet, afraid she had been assaulted, and rushed toward her. "What was it?" I asked her. "Son," she said with her pitiful look, "let's not get lost, the children are waiting for us."

For the first time, I wanted to die. I was worn out and couldn't take another step. I had been beaten up that morning, had walked all day long, and was grief-stricken because I could not help my father. I was terribly thirsty and parched from the dust. For a moment we thought we had lost our way and were wondering which fork in the road to take. We decided upon the right, which would lead us out of the woods. Still, we were without a trace to follow. My unwilling legs refused to respond to my wish to keep going. The children were all waiting for their big brother to come and give them something to eat and drink.

We searched for a trace, some clue, on this endless, pain-laden road. I was sure we were lost and didn't know whether to go back or continue. We could make a decision, but there was no way of telling which road was the right one and which the wrong. With some animal instinct and human sense we continued our journey; we could not stop as long as an ounce of energy was left in us.

Soon we saw faint traces of footprints, which became more and more distinct as we walked along. Was it wishful thinking? A mirage? What delight to see that they were actually footprints! Oh, yes, they were, for I saw the imprint of an ox cart's grooves in the dusty road, and, looking ahead, a dust cloud far away. It buoyed our spirits and gave us the energy we so sorely needed to catch up with our little ones. We walked faster and faster. We saw half-dead bodies along the way. Some were resting, soon perhaps forever.

When we finally reached the caravan, some children were piled up on a cart, like so many wilted vegetables, more dead than alive under the intense broiling sun. A woman was carrying a dirty container. I approached her, but hesitated; I was afraid it would be too much to ask. I held the side of the cart for support. The woman, whose children were on the cart, gave me a suspicious look, as if I were going to grab the water container from under her arm. I motioned Mother to go ahead to look for the children. I wanted to climb onto the barely moving cart. An old woman was walking beside me. How could I show her how weak I really was?

I shouted to my nephew, Manoug, my brother's older son, only a year younger than I, walking ahead of me. He asked about his grandfather.

I told him that I was very thirsty and tired, and he said that nobody had any more water, but pulled out two grapes from his pocket and handed them to me. "I have a few more left, but I am keeping them for my younger brothers," he said, putting the fruit cautiously in my palm, like the precious jewels they were. I put one of the luscious fruits in my mouth and sucked avidly; it was gone before I knew it. The second one put a little more moisture in my mouth, enough to make me feel alive again, but far from normal. I asked Manoug if he had seen any of my brothers or sisters. He said no.

When we stopped for the evening, we were close to a village by a river. A woman ahead of us already had gone into the village. The villagers resented us before they knew who we were. It was dangerous for anyone to venture forth into this village. As a rule, and by tradition, Middle Eastern people are charitable to the poor and destitute. With the hope of acquiring a few more copper coins, they could be induced to be more sympathetic and tolerant. I drank all of the water I could from the running river. I managed to obtain some food from the villagers and returned to my family with their first food since morning.

Mother had found the children. They gathered around us in a semicircle, ready to get their morsel of bread, but Mother stopped us. "I wonder what has become of your father?" she asked.

I didn't know what to say. The children were very hungry, and the talk of their missing father only added to their misery. As soon as we had eaten, I would go after Father with renewed vigor and confidence. So, mother bit into a piece of bread, and the children followed her example. I didn't waste any time praying—it was a sure waste. While still munching the precious dry bread, I jumped up and said that I would go see if I could find somebody to help me find Father. All I wanted was someone to accompany me. Everyone thought it dangerous and foolish of me to search for Father in the dark and in such a strange, hostile place. But emotions have no time to measure danger. I decided that I must find Father, come what may, regardless of the danger. He needed me desperately.

But I could not find transportation or a donkey to carry him back. I thought of approaching a guard—after all, he was human, too—and promise him some money. But that perhaps wasn't safe either: He could easily take the money, shoot me in the back, and nobody would ask him what had happened to me. Besides, possession of money in itself was dangerous.

I went toward the road that led back to Father, not yet knowing what to do. Shortly after leaving the group, I saw a shadow creeping toward me. Fear gripped me, for it was very dark and lonely. Gradually the shadow took form, and a one-legged man on crutches came forward. He was one of our group; against all odds, he managed to stay up with the caravan. He recognized me and stopped, asking me where I was going. I told him how we had been separated from Father and that I was on my way back to fetch him.

"Son," he said, "I saw him. You have no need to go back. He has left this sad vale of tears and sorrow." In a way, it was a relief. I felt a strange kind of happiness for Father: Death had been sweeter than life. It was the end of his unbearable humiliation and suffering.

Slowly I returned to my family with the tragic news. Mother did not sleep that night. Each time I would awaken from my own fretful sleep, I could hear her weeping, softly, in her own private way. She did not want to inflict her personal loss and sorrow upon anyone else, especially not on the children. She wouldn't even confide in me or seek my sympathy. This was the first time we had ever been separated from Father. He was not only a husband and father; he was her partner, her beloved king, her leader, her pride, and her crown. Without him, nothing could be complete. He had been her choosing. He was many years older, mature and wise. None of the other young, strong men could measure up to him. She had chosen him and had never regretted her choice, even though she was twenty years younger than he. On the contrary, she was proud of him, and said, "A gentle and noble man like your father should be spared the sorrow of disappointment."

God Is Great

Day after day, the group dwindled. One or more members of each family would be missing or left behind. The tender and refined noble women gradually shed their sweet manners. One would see a woman who had never allowed her ankles to show, who never went bare legged, now walking in tatters, in rags that barely covered her body. They became mean, selfish, possessive, and indifferent toward others, interested mostly in obtaining food and water for their desperate little ones. They would stoop to anything for a bite of bread and a drink of water. These proud creatures, once the queens of their households, were reduced to begging, dirty, rejected, and repulsive, their hair matted and in disarray. Their bright smiles were replaced by dark, hollowed chins and protruding cheekbones. Suffering and misery had aged them rapidly, devouring their beauty.

The group ate whatever it could get—vegetables, grass, or bark—with seldom enough water to sustain life. Life no longer had meaning. If they hung on at all, it was for the children.

Days followed days, weeks followed weeks, after the day of our first steep climb uphill out of Gurun. From then on, we were cruelly deprived of the essentials of life. Indeed, death seemed the only possible happy solution to our misery. We often thought how lucky were those dear ones who no longer suffered the humiliation, degradation, and pain we the living continued to endure. It had become more a moral struggle than a physical one. People who had hope, a goal to aim at, survived, not because they were physically strong, but because of their strong moral stamina. They had a dream—a dream of tomorrow. Be things as they may, there *was* a tomorrow, and tomorrow was still alive. What did it matter that we suffered so much—just one more day—just another day, and still another, but soon we'd see a new horizon. A better life.

After the big hill, we had marched south. In the fourth week, we came upon green trees and grass, and before long we saw houses in the distant hills. We had almost reached the city of Antep (Aintab/Ayntap),* but we were not allowed to enter it. Instead, on the outskirts of the town, near a stone bridge, we were ordered to stop. We were now in a different Turkish state. The Turkish government had not yet forced these Armenians out of their city. The order had been first to remove them from the original Armenian states in Turkey, such as Van, Moush, Arzeroum, Sivas, Kharput, Diarbakir. The Armenians in Antep, who had heard of our arrival, dared to visit us. Many groups before us had taken the same painful road. These Armenians knew what we had been through and how hard it was to survive. So, they came to us with food and clothing. They went from family to family, back and forth, with more food and clothing. They understood how we had suffered, and just for being Armenian.

We were allowed to camp outside the town. Among our new friends from Antep was a lady who was desperately looking for our family. She was Nishan Baliozian, from a family from Sivas. Her husband was teaching

---

*Now Gaziantep in south-central Turkey.

in the American college in Antep. Not many years before, she and Mother had been friends. She asked Mother if she could help us with money or clothes or anything. Mother refused aid. "If you would please bring me some thread and a needle," she said, "we'd be most grateful."

The lady left hurriedly. No one knew how long we'd be staying here in Antep. She had already used her wit and mastery of Turkish to get permission from the authorities to contact our group.

Meanwhile, a peddler was selling grapes to the hungry. They had but a few copper coins in their palms. The peddler, a Turk, had a handmade scale: two metal trays hung from a rod. In one of the trays was a small rock, which was supposed to be a weight. The hungry victims crowded around him, and he did a bustling trade. A Turkish policeman approached to see what was going on and stopped the man. He pulled the man's white turban from his head and said loudly, "Shame on you, you don't deserve this turban of white. Aren't you ashamed of robbing these poor creatures? Aren't they punished enough? Have you no fear of Allah in you?" Seeing me next in line, he turned to me and, noticing my dirty, shabby cloches, said with pity, "God is great, my son; His grace be with you." Then he threw away the peddler's rock and the fake scale and left.

Mrs. Baliozian returned from the city, having made a very fast dinner for us, with extra bread and cheese, a pan we could use for water, a cup, and a few pieces of clothing. She told Mother that we might need it for the children. Mother thanked her graciously; they called one another sister. Mother asked her if the schools were open and if I could continue my education, thinking I might be protected that way. She told her that the schools were closed, and these Antep Armenians also expected to be deported soon but didn't know when. She asked, whispering in my mother's ear, if we had had a revolt against the government in Gurun.

Mother said, "No, why?"

"We were told that Gurun had revolted," she said, "and that the government, in order to protect itself, was compelled to deport and murder all they could."

All wars have excuses, and all crimes have alibis. They build a story to promote an issue for war so that the people with tender hearts would not weaken. We were also told that Mr. Partridge and his family were still in Sivas. Mother asked what day it was, and she told us that it was the second week of July 1915. It was Sunday.

After a few days we were moved to the small city of Killis, a town with many orchards and groves of oranges and lemons. Again, we were not allowed to enter the city, but we had a good chance of getting food by going back and forth into the city.

It took us several more days to arrive at Ghatma (Katma), a railroad center that connected Constantinople and Baghdad. German engineers were in a hurry to connect the northern railroad line southeast into Baghdad. It was in Ghatma that we discovered why we were deliberately delayed in our journey: The slaughterhouse was not yet ready for us, and the Germans and Turks did not want to crowd any place with desperate mobs that might get out of control.

A train came after our arrival. The guards, without asking questions, shoved everyone into open wagons, like cattle, to be sent inland to the deserts of Hama, Homs, and Der el-Zor. Mother and I made a fast decision. I told Anoush to get lost in the crowd and, if anybody asked her anything, tell them that she was looking for her mother. We watched her. The younger children were told to keep away from the train and hide among others. Guards hurriedly packed the crowd into the train, and in a very short time loaded up the women and children, especially the newcomers from Gurun. The train started slowly. Anoush started back slowly toward us, and once more we were together.

A woman tried to get some water from a faucet in the railroad station, but a guard cursed her and pushed her away, thinking he deserved the water more than she did. Evening came, and we considered ourselves lucky not to have been shoved onto the train. I learned that close by this station was the city of Aleppo. I began going around investigating the possibilities of getting to that city. I saw my nephew Manoug arranging transportation to Aleppo. Nearby, my niece, Arshalous, was holding her two-year-old child's hand. I learned that the only safe way was to sneak out, and at an appointed place, arrange for transportation to Aleppo. The price was very high. We were six persons, Mother and I, Anoush, Vahan, and the twins—and we had to pay two liras in gold. I bargained for six mejidie in silver, which was not much for saving our lives. In the meantime, we provided more passengers to the carriage man for a full load.

We met late that night at the appointed place. We sneaked away, crawling to the coach, and proceeded from one unknown place to another. It was a dark and moonless night, and it was hard to tell what was going on outside. The coachman would cautiously slow down at times, and at others he would goad the horses faster.

We soon found ourselves among other travelers on the road who had come from Marash; they were under the protection of army soldiers who were leading the coaches on the road toward Aleppo. These were families of Armenian officials whose husbands or fathers held important army jobs. They were moved out of Marash before other families had been deported. The guards were provided for their protection. They were traveling faster than our coaches. Our driver drove at full speed and soon caught up with them, getting mixed in with the other coaches and giving friendly salutes to the guards as he continued on his way. He passed two checkpoints. The official families gave the impression that we belonged to the same group. Then we became separated from them. Our coachman saluted a guard near a street corner, turned left, and entered a large gate. In Aleppo at last, he dumped us off and disappeared into the dark.

4

The Reverend of Aleppo

The Deportees

THE PLACE WHERE WE HAD BEEN delivered had been the former residence of the British consul, now standing empty. It was well protected, with a large gate and a guard at the entrance. This is where our driver dumped us.

When we woke with the sunrise the next morning, a swarm of flies descended upon us. The place stank like a garbage dump. Indeed, it *was* a dumping ground for the Armenian deportees who had been there since the night before. Observing the fields around us, while surrounded by these desperate and strange people, I wondered whether we had made any progress at all. I told Mother I would go into Aleppo and see if I could find somewhere better.

I managed to get out through the gate and found myself in a large bustling city, where it would be very easy for our family to get lost. Mourning doves in the trees were cooing their sad refrain. To my surprise, I could not communicate with the people on the street. In Turkish I inquired about an Armenian church, but they answered in Arabic. The first words I learned in Arabic were "I do not know."

Soon I was in the center of the town with crowds all around me, and I wondered which way to proceed. I noticed two people who appeared to be

Armenians crossing the street. We conversed in Turkish for several minutes, during which they told me of a man in Aleppo called "The Reverend."
If I wanted help, I should see him. I followed their instructions—six streets
to the left, four to the right—and got lost!

I saw more Armenians on the street. Fortunately, they knew The Reverend, and at last I was directed to his house. I pushed open the heavy door
and entered a courtyard. A man who must have been The Reverend was
talking to two women in rags. Misery had left its mark upon them; they
had that tortured look and appeared sick. I wondered if they didn't need
him more than I did.

At last, he turned to me and introduced himself as Reverend Eskijian*
(see figure 4.1) and asked my name and what I wanted. He said that they
had filled up with deportees a small place outside the church, but that the
church could hardly take care of them; there were too many, and the funds
were quickly being exhausted. I said that I was looking for protection more
than anything else. When I told him my name was Minassian, he asked if
Mugerdich was related to me.

FIGURE 4.1
Portrait of Reverend Eskijian

---

*Hovhannes Eskijian, native of Urfa.

"Yes, he is my oldest brother," I said. He had come from Caesarea with the family of Minass. Reverend Eskijian told me that Mugerdich's family had arrived the night before with Manoug and his mother and younger brothers and sister. Then Reverend Eskijian suggested that I seek help from my brother.

As I was leaving, a woman who seemed to be in her late thirties came out of The Reverend's house. Seeing me in my rags, covered with dust, she asked me if I was hungry. Considering the social class in which I had been brought up, this was a most humiliating experience. She asked if my mother was with me and whether any other children were in the family.

She was The Reverend's wife,* and she then whispered a few words to The Reverend, while I glanced inside the clean house at the beautiful furniture. It had been a long time since I had seen anything like it, and I relished the sight. My attention fell upon a frame on the wall with Armenian letters saying in Turkish, "Emanuel, God is with us."

The Reverend's wife returned and said that she was sorry, but she could not do anything for us. There was a place where refugees were being sent, but it was now overcrowded. "However," she added, "if you are still in the city, won't you come again later?"

That whole afternoon I was busy asking people if they knew where the Hotel Autry (*Khan Autry*) was. Of the several dozen people I stopped and asked, no one seemed to understand Turkish, and I didn't know a word of Arabic. Luckily, someone understood Armenian and knew the *Khan Autry.*

When I found my brother Mugerdich, I asked him for advice. It was a relief to have someone to turn to whom one could trust and find respect. He had learned through his family of Father's death. However, he was now loaded down with the responsibility for three families and couldn't do anything for us. He took me back to The Reverend's house and tried to explain our situation to The Reverend.

At last, I was taken to a place where some twenty deportee families had been crowded into a courtyard; all were in tatters and slowly were dying of hunger and from lack of care. Barely alive, they had little protection here, but they did have a friend in The Reverend; they didn't even know his last name. They called him simply The Reverend, as though he were the only one in town. Indeed, he was the only one they knew. Mugerdich advised

---

*Gulenia (Danielian) Eskijian, native of Aintab.

me that I had best bring Mother and the children here, at least overnight, and that we could see what happened tomorrow. This was the place that Mrs. Eskijian had told me about, where there was no room, but I had no choice. We were six more desperate and miserable people to add to this already overcrowded place.

With a boy to lead me, we managed to get my mother and the four children out of the gate and the British consul's residence and returned in a hurry to the shelter, our new refuge. We joined the other people with their strange stories of weird and horrible happenings on the road. These people had arrived by even harder and more tortuous roads. Of the hundreds of families that had been deported, only a few made it, and they arrived in rags, tortured bare bodies blistered in the broiling sun, swollen legs wrapped in more dirty rags. They had no shoes; their heels were cracked and sore. They were sick and hungry and desperately needed clothing and shelter. They thanked God, still, that they were lucky enough to find The Reverend.

At a nearby bakery, I got some bread, and a few streets further on I found a well and managed to bring water to the children. Then they slept peacefully, for the first time in weeks. Mother met a few other women, and they exchanged news and stories of their deportation.

Aleppo was awash with human misery. They had come from all over, this debris of human wreckage—driven here by the storm of hatred and genocide. They had not seen the greater horrors at Der el-Zor,* a wilderness place of slaughter, hunger, sickness, kidnapping, and enslavement by the Arabs who profited from this human travesty, which their God had devised for their enjoyment. Once man reverts to the primitive instincts, he loses all human dignity, and there is nothing to keep him from resorting to barbarism and its unbridled looting, ravaging, and killing.

Thousands had arrived at Aleppo, and the police would pick them up as soon as they arrived. The Reverend, however, broke their traditional rules of behavior, as well as a minister's rules of good behavior. Reverend Eskijian had the support of a few natives and some Armenians in his church. He demanded that his parishioners work for the salvation of these victims who had come to them from the far corners of the Turkish

---

*Also Deir ez-Zor; Dayr az-Zur; open-air concentration camps in the Syrian desert.

Empire. He dared the police to prevent him from doing his divine work to help his fellow Armenians.

It was, indeed, a challenge, for a thirty-five-year-old man who had been a preacher for only a few years. The local and federal governments were against the movement to save the Armenians, yet Eskijian heroically tried his best for his people. Many, probably most, were captured by the police and shipped out again, or one by one they fell like autumn leaves, faded, dry, and lifeless. Once they had been like nature's gift to humanity, but now the sanitation department simply picked them up and carted them off to the garbage dump, covering them with lye to make certain they were dead. The Reverend tried to absorb as much of the misery as he could, to counteract the unspeakable crime organized by the Turkish government.

We were among the luckier ones, but how much longer could we survive? We had no protection from harassment or capture. Around noon one day, a man with a strange Armenian dialect came to the shelter with a sack of flatbread. He gave one to each family but ran out by the time he got to our group. He looked at my family and asked when we had arrived. "Yesterday," I said. He was sorry that he didn't have any bread left for us.

Later in the afternoon The Reverend came and visited his people, asking each how they were doing and promising that he was trying to do a little better for them, giving hope and encouragement. "This will all pass someday," he said. "It will pass if we have the patience and the will. Someday we will be back in our homes, building, repairing, and beginning a new life."

His soft reassuring voice intrigued me. These words did not come just from his lips, but from deep in his heart. He turned to me and asked how I had found this place and why I was here when I had been warned against it. He sounded resentful but not angry. I felt guilty for not having obeyed such a man as he. I explained to him as softly as I could and in the best Armenian I could that after many weeks of traveling on foot under unbearable conditions, my family needed a rest. I heard about this place as a shelter and came. He was saddened, not because of my situation, but because he couldn't do anything for me.

The next morning a man by the name of Setrak Sevajian came and spoke to me in fine Armenian. He told me that this place was not safe for us. He took me a few blocks away, to a shoe repairman, Shamlian, who had come here a long time ago from Marash. Shamlian had a small shop, and

Setrak asked if it were possible for me to come here and hide if I should need to, and possibly use one of his aprons, so no one would suspect me of being a refugee. Shamlian was in his fifties and very kind. He agreed and asked where I was from, and told me that I was welcome any time I felt I was in danger. "Just come here and hang an apron on yourself," he said, "and we'll take care of you."

Setrak told me that he would see to it that we had our daily bread as a ration from the shelter. I told him that we did not need bread. What we wanted was shelter and protection from the police. He shook his head, smiling.

Later, as we became friends, I asked Setrak Sevajian where I could exchange some gold coins into cash. He took me to a store, spoke Arabic to the shopkeeper, and asked me to show the man the gold piece. The man offered me only half the value of the coin in exchange. I refused. Then Setrak took me to an Armenian yardage shop and explained that I needed the cash for some clothing and food. The shopkeeper paid me the full exchange rate. When I returned and told my mother how many wonderful friends I had made and the good luck I had had in exchanging the gold piece, she was delighted.

As the days passed, I wondered if we had any chance of our renting a place in which to live. I learned quickly that landlords would inform the police if we did not bribe them; and once started, there was no end to it. But I had great faith in The Reverend and hoped he would be able to do something for us. One day The Reverend told me that he wanted me to be in charge of medicine and food at the shelter. A few days later I was engaged to distribute these to each family.

One afternoon The Reverend came in upset and distraught. He talked to each family. Upon seeing me, he said, "I want you to go to my house, right now and stay there until I come. There will be a police check in here soon. Go now!"

Mrs. Eskijian, with her motherly smile, gave me some food, asked about my mother, and said she would like to meet her. She herself had two sons, one five years old and the other two. She did the clerical work for The Reverend—not at the church, but for the deported orphans and widows, helping the sick, sometimes finding work for the older ones, placing them in Armenian families or with sympathetic Aleppans as domestic help. Sometimes she would find a place for a child to be adopted. Aleppo had several Armenian physicians. They gave all of the help that they could and did their best to soothe the sore, heal the sick, and supply free medicine. A Dr. Altoonian (Asadour Altounian) ran a hospital at which he refused service to no one; he had room to take them in and shelter them.

I stayed at The Reverend's overnight. The next day was Sunday, but I could not go to church in my shabby clothes. I would look like a beggar and didn't want to sit next to anybody for fear I might offend them. So, I went to the shelter instead, and to my surprise found it empty; only a few people remained, and they had been out when the police raided the place. I found that the police had picked up the refugees and taken them back to the railroad station to be shipped out.

I asked a coachman if he could understand Turkish. "A little bit," he said. I asked him to raise the top of the coach, take me to the railroad station, drive inside the gate and tell the guard that I was visiting one of the refugee families. When I came out, he was to pass the gate quickly.

He saluted the guard, passed inside the gate, and waited there for me. Mother was there, still with the children, but the night before she had been robbed by the woman who had lain next to her like a friend. We all jumped into the coach, which was meant only for travelers of means and wealth. We returned to Aleppo—not to the same place, but to another shelter the police didn't know of.

It is understood by most that the Germans were the engineers and architects of the destruction of Armenians; but it is also a fact that a group of influential Christians in the German government had invoked the Turks to be more tolerant, at least with members of the Armenian Protestant Church. The Reverend took advantage of this directive and sent a man to the railroad station to pick up the Protestants who had been taken there.

Hovhannes Juskalian was the man who promoted this. "He spoke perfect Turkish, some Armenian, and good Arabic. He would bring back people who wanted to be called Protestants, even if they were not actually Protestants. The Reverend knew of the ruse but asked no questions. He wanted to save lives before he saved souls."[1] They all needed help, whether or not they were Protestants. But he was terribly short of space and money, and not enough help was forthcoming. He tapped all of the sources he could, especially members of his church, but it was not enough. The demands were just too great, and the immigrants continued to pour in daily.

The Reverend's friends were wonderful coworkers, but they worked in vain to save most of the deportees or orphan children. They had become an underground organization for the gospel of love and service, but against the Turkish government's wishes.

Reverend Eskijian visited his friend, the American consul, Mr. Jackson, and pleaded for help. Jackson, in turn, reported to the American ambassador in Constantinople, Henry Morgenthau. We needed relief now. We couldn't wait for tomorrow to bring the help we needed today.

I was told to keep away from the shelter but to stay in contact with The Reverend. He kept me busy with small errands. I was sheltered in his churchyard and often saw him at work. Across the street from his church lived Nazaret-efendi. He had been a resident of Aleppo for a long time. His clothes and language gave no hint, however, that he was an Armenian. Born in Antep, he spoke excellent Turkish. His manners suggested that he was a prosperous Turkish merchant. Nazaret often would come to the churchyard and talk to the church beadle; in turn, this man would tell us whether Nazaret said it was safe for us to be out.

It had been quite a few days since I last had seen Mother. When Nazaret-efendi one day told us the weather was going to be good and it would be safe to venture out, I went to see her where she and the children were sheltered. The place was vacant—not a single soul in sight. I thought I was in the wrong place, but a man nearby, dressed in a dark robe and white turban, asked if I had any relatives in the group. "Yes," I said. Though he was not a Turk, he understood Turkish. I asked him if he knew where they had taken them, and he mentioned a square where the water well was. I asked him if he would be kind enough to show me where and if he could wait a moment first. I ran to Shamlian, the shoe repairman. When I asked to borrow his apron, he said of course. I put on the apron, ran back to the white-turbaned man, and asked him again to take me to the square. I explained that my employer had relatives in that group and I had some money to take to them, a widow and her children. "Sir," I asked, "would you be willing to help fulfill this man's wish, for charity's sake?"

He led me to the square where a guard stood around the group. I asked my newfound friend if he would explain the situation to the guard because I couldn't speak Arabic and, furthermore, I did not want to reveal my or my employer's identity. He did well at explaining the situation and asked me if I could recognize my friends' relatives. "Yes," I said, thanked him, and mingled with the group.

I found Mother and told her not to show any emotion and made a fast plan. I didn't want the guard to suspect any relationship between us other than that of an employer's agent. I tried to convince Mother that I should join them wherever it was they were going so that we could stay together. She argued that it was dangerous for me to travel with them and that I had better protection from The Reverend; if I remained in the city, I might have a better chance of bringing them all back to Aleppo.

I reminded her that it would be hard for her to take care of the four children alone. She replied that I couldn't really protect them either. We finally agreed that I not stay with her, but that we should divide the burden of the children between us. The four-year-old twin, Dikran, my special love, looked at me sadly, and I asked him if he wanted to come with me. He hid his face and cried. Mother said that he had had a headache that morning and did not want to be separated from his mother, but he didn't want me to be away either. Mother went through her shabby clothes and pulled out a few gold pieces, saying, "You need some money. How are you going to keep the children?" She kissed Anoush and Vahan good-bye and told them to follow me.

Without being able to touch her, with neither kiss nor hug, we separated in the square around the well. I told Anoush to lead Vahan around the corner, and I would join them shortly. The man with the dark robe and white turban was still waiting for me. He asked me if my mission had been successful. I told him that the poor woman had needed some money and my employer wanted to help her. "I hope it will help her, "he said, and added, "The dogs!" I thanked him and called him friend.

I joined Anoush and Vahan around the corner, where they were waiting for me. They sensed danger in the air—children always do. They followed me until we arrived at the Eskijian churchyard.

Each evening after that, a man would come and give us a slice of bread each and a small piece of cheese. This was not enough food, but we learned to survive on little. When he saw Vahan and Anoush, he asked what I intended to do with them. I turned to Haygaz and said, "You have a job to do, and I am sure you can perform it nicely."

Aharon Sheriazian, a minister, maintained a small orphanage, supported and protected by the German consul of Aleppo. Consequently, the local government did not interfere with him. The government was now only barely tolerant of the Protestant Church. Reverend Sheriazian was the

Protestant minister in Marash. Using his administrative ability, and with the help of German missionaries, Sheriazian organized his missionary duties with those of the orphanage.

Reverend Eskijian had neither the connections nor the facilities to do what Sheriazian was doing. And, for some reason, Sheriazian and Eskijian were not on good terms. I knew that my association with Eskijian would be reason enough for Anoush and Vahan to be rejected by Sheriazian's orphanage. Although it was crowded, I felt sure that they would have hot soup each day and shelter and protection at Sheriazian's place.

So Haygaz took Anoush and Vahan by the hand to the orphanage. When Mother Takouhy, who ran the place, opened the door, Haygaz recited his part: he had found these two lost children on the street roaming around without parents. Would she be kind enough to take them in? She refused, of course, it was too crowded already, and shut the door. Haygaz knocked again on the handle of the big door and again Mother Takouhy opened the door.

"I'm sorry, but I can't take them in. We're filled up," Takouhy said, slamming the great gate shut.

"Well," Haygaz yelled at the gate, "I have done my job. I'm sorry, but I'm leaving them here." He left the children at the door, said a loud good-bye to the children, and hid himself around the corner to watch the gate. The big door opened slowly. Mother Takouhy saw the frightened children waiting for somebody to come and take them in. She reached out her hand and pulled them inside the gate.

I was always doing errands for The Reverend. One morning, before I started my day, he held my arm and begged me not to blame him for the separation of my family. "You must know that there are too little funds to go around. This is a gigantic task, saving so many people from destruction. The war is going to last a long time yet, and we are trying to choose whom to save, because we can't possibly save all. Our plan is for the future, and the future is for the young men of your age. Regardless of what effort we may exert, young children will die. But by protecting groups of your age we are confident that you will survive and that you will build a new generation, the future of Armenia."

I admired Eskijian for his simple way of telling the truth. He was giving me other duties now, and in order to perform them better, he ordered me some native clothes. A woman sewed a gown of plain printed cotton, buttoned up to the neck and divided in the front, which overlapped on one side. I put on a wide cloth belt, a "coin belt," for money was metal coins then. Now I looked like a native, dressed with long stockings coming up to my knees, and a jacket. I had a haircut, went to the bathhouse, and came out like a real native boy—without knowing a word of Arabic.

My clothes were good camouflage, enough to fool the most experienced police in town. I became a messenger from the railroad station back to The Reverend's house, a dangerous job. I took the sick to the physician and, worse yet, visited daily almost all of the underground hideouts in Aleppo. College professors, ministers, and young graduates in hiding were all subject to arrest. The Reverend would give me money to hand out to these people; in return, they would ask me to buy food for them, or a little charcoal to warm their cold, dark rooms. They were in constant fear that the government's arm would reach them and re-deport them.

I got to know most of the important people in town who enjoyed the protection of The Reverend's one-man army. I began delivering messages in folded envelopes to Mr. Jackson, the American consul, who, when evening fell, would send his first secretary to visit Reverend Eskijian to leave him a small canvas bag. The Reverend, in turn, would give the secretary a heavy typewritten envelope prepared by his secretaries, hidden in the basement, who seldom came up for fresh air.

In the meantime, the number of young men staying across the street from The Reverend's church multiplied at alarming proportions. This "vacant" house mysteriously filled up during the night and was emptied by morning, for all scattered according to the instructions of Nazaret-efendi.

One day Reverend Eskijian suggested that I go see Mr. Jackson and tell him who I was. The American consul received me with a warm smile and asked what he could do for me. I asked him if it were possible to let Mr. Partridge at the American college in Sivas know that I was alive and in Aleppo.

Jackson learned from Partridge that I had been a student in Sivas and would be glad to hear more about me and help me financially if possible. I told Jackson that other students from Sivas and I would be most grateful for any help and that Mr. Partridge probably would assume the responsibility of the expenses.

The deportees from Sivas told me that most Armenians had taken their valuables—gold coins, diamond rings—to Mr. Partridge for safekeeping before they left the city. They asked that, in case they did not return, he please give the proceeds from the sale of these valuables to deserving ones. There was no greater security and protection than Mr. Partridge, the principal of the American college, sent to us from an unknown part of the world. They trusted him implicitly and believed in him.

Haygaz visited my sister and brother in the orphanage, but I could not visit them, and missed them; they always asked for me. One day I knocked at the door of the orphanage, and a young boy opened the gate. I told him I wished to see Mother Takouhy. She was dressed in black and had a sweet smile. I told her that I was the brother of Anoush and Vahan, but that I had been unable to come any sooner. I did not tell her why, but she knew of my connection with Eskijian.

"You shouldn't worry about your sister and brother. In fact," she added, "we like your sister very much. Vahan, too, but he is always sad. He is not playing with the other children. I will send them to see you soon."

They were happy to see me, but they were two desperate orphans. Vahan looked like a skeleton, missed Mother's love and her soothing touch and comforting ways. I could give them nothing. I was their big brother, but I could not relieve them of their misery. Nobody could, except their mother, and where she was, or what had happened to her, we didn't know.

The Orphanage

The deportees were still pouring into the city, a most depressing sight. Every day people in rags, hardly able to walk, wandered around Aleppo's streets in search of help. Sick, starved, desperate, and separated from their loved ones—separated, indeed, from the world.

The American consul* called Reverend Eskijian to a meeting and told him of some funds he had received for the orphans. In Mr. Jackson's office at the American consulate, the two formed a plan. According to this plan, more refugees would arrive in the already overcrowded churchyard. They were from Sivas, Kharput, and Malatia, and even more desperate than the refugees before them. They were tortured both mentally and physically. The Reverend, in an inspiring appeal, gathered some of his people to help feed and shelter these new deportees.

---

*Jesse B. Jackson. See endnote 1 for biographical information.

This was when Juskalian, called Hovhannes-efendi, was first engaged. He dressed as an Arab, with turban and flowing robe. If he wanted to, he could sometimes look like a Kurd. He had the shrewdness of a fox, yet could be as simple and sweet as a dove. His amazing mastery of Arabic and Turkish, with some Armenian, enabled him to adjust to all circumstances. He had an extraordinary natural intelligence. With equal aplomb, he could face a general of the army or an Arab chieftain. He could beg if necessary, and rob if need be, or bargain if he must. He had a unique way of flattering to suit his purpose, and to challenge boldly. Often one couldn't tell who or what he was.

There was no doubt that Hovhannes Juskalian was an amazing man. He would act as a civilian official and untiringly play the game of fooling an official and grabbing a few more orphans from their nefarious grasp at the railroad station, detouring them from the butchery in the desert. He would venture into the railroad station, tell the guard who he was, and, with the gesture of an important official and a loud voice, call attention to the new deportees, telling them who he was, saying, "I have come to take you away, but only members of the Protestant Church, so will those of the Protestant Church please come forward."

This he would say loudly in Turkish, but in a low Armenian voice he would tell them, "You are Protestants, aren't you?"

No? "Yes, of course." And if they still faltered or hesitated, he would grab a young boy, for instance, and say, "Son, you look like a Protestant," then he would push the child into the crowd and bring them all into The Reverend's fold.

The Reverend was incredulous at the number of members of his denomination, but Hovhannes-efendi would calmly, and with his usual aplomb, tell The Reverend that he, too, was surprised. Sometimes he would say jokingly, "They are new members," and would whisper in The Reverend's ear, "I baptized them myself."

Hovhannes-efendi would sometimes ride his horse to isolated tribes in search of wheat, which was not sold anymore in the open market. He would salute an Arab as an Arab would; they would return the salute and say, "Salaam Alaikum."* Then he would approach the chief's tent and explain that he had plenty of gold to exchange for wheat. He would have

---

*Translated from Arabic: "May peace be upon you."

made a wonderful politician, for he knew well the art of camouflaging the truth and substituting polished, meaningless words. At a time when it was impossible to buy bread or even flour (the army confiscated all such supplies), Hovhannes-efendi would convince the Arabs to load their camels with hay straw to hide the wheat and dump the wheat at designated places.

The bakery shops were operated by Armenians who had settled in Aleppo years before. They were called *Sasounies*. The natives did not know their origins, for they looked like anything but Armenians from Sasoun. Hovhannes-efendi made a few friends among the bakers, and bread soon started coming to the refugees. The churchyard was not big enough for these ever-growing activities. So, The Reverend rented a large house and sent a few orphans there with elders who volunteered to take care of them. A few good women from local families answered The Reverend's call for assistance for these less-privileged people.

At this time, I went to visit my brother Haroutoun's family at a hotel and ask them to help with the orphanage and suggested they seek protection from The Reverend. Haroutoun's wife, who had several children with her, refused my request. She, who once had servants of her own, claimed it was too hard for her to be a cook. I replied that I wished that I could have made this offer to my mother while she had been here. Still my sister-in-law refused. A few weeks later, when I visited them again, the hotel owner informed me that they were gone. Somehow, I knew where. I never saw them again. My brother and the three families for whom he was responsible had been shipped to the desert of Der el-Zor, where, like thousands of others, they perished.

After months of long waiting, I received a postcard from Mother. It had been censored and was written in Turkish and addressed to me care of Reverend Eskijian. It read:

> Dear Son—I want you to know we are here and Mr. N is taking care of us. I am sure you're taking good care of Anoush and Vahan. Please write care of Mr. N. Hamah.
>
> Love, Mother

Nobody knew how The Reverend, without funds, could organize such a staff of volunteers as his workers. Nazaret-efendi had rented a large home with an enclosed courtyard that extended along several rooms. Hovhannes

Juskalian administered the orphanage, provided the food, bribing, bluffing, begging, and supplying food to these children.

Local merchants would donate goods, and local women would sew for the children. By this time, there were forty orphans from all of the Turkish states. Most came from nearby towns, because people from distant cities couldn't survive the trip. Soon the number rose to sixty, then eighty, adding some young girls and women. The Reverend obtained a permit to have an orphanage for a limited number of orphans within a limited age group, but the number of orphans grew rapidly beyond the limit originally decided upon by the authorities. How could anyone decide who was deserving and who was not? It required a heart of stone to reject any of these children. The police didn't sit by idly, however. They made a daily check on the orphanage to make sure that the limit and age group were strictly adhered to. They were especially interested in how many young girls were there above sixteen years of age.

My secret mission was now enlarged. More people were being hidden away close to the center of Aleppo, and that was The Reverend's compound. He had moved to a house with several rooms and a small yard. The kitchen had a secret door leading to the basement, where, among other things, charcoal was stored. This secret basement sheltered The Reverend's staff. Mrs. Eskijian fed these people and washed their clothes. When evening came, they came up for a meeting with The Reverend. There were former ministers in the group, professors, graduate students, and teachers from Antep and Tarsus, making reports of the tragedies and crimes of war, and the desperate need for help. These reports would find their way to the United States, and Henry Morgenthau would see a great response from the New World, but alas, all too late.[2]

Then the typhoid epidemic started. Those who, by some miracle, had been saved from earlier torture and death now died for want of care and medicine. Hundreds of thousands perished. These weak bodies had no resistance to the onslaught of typhus. In our shelter, the strongest and healthiest boy from Gurun developed a fever. With deep red cheeks and brightly burning dark eyes, he would curl next to me for warmth, for the nights were chilly and the covers were light. A few days later I, too, was sweating uncontrollably and wanted just to sleep. I heard strange noises that irritated me as never before. I grew weaker and weaker. My cheeks became hollow and my skin yellow. I could hardly move. At times, I could hardly recognize people or things. Next to me was another boy, and other boys were around the room. Upstairs, six more boys of my age were sick in their dark room, left alone without food or medicine. Setrak-efendi did not show up anymore, nor did he visit us. Nevertheless, he protected us. He made his regular trips to the police station, had coffee with the chief, and obtained information about what raids were planned at which places.

Sometimes I would sleep and dream without end. It could have been Christmas or Easter; I had no idea. I dreamed of my friends from the Gurun orphanage coming for the holidays to stay with us. We would play and eat each year that Mother had invited an orphan to spend the holidays with us and share the festivities.

While I was in a coma, a woman would wake me by calling my name. She would give me a spoon, which I was to dip into a tin container to get some soup. My eyes were half closed, and unconsciously I managed to finish the soup. Then I would sleep more. I do not know for how long I slept, or for how many days I was in the coma, but the woman visited me daily. I never knew her, never saw her before or after.

One morning the boy next to me asked how I felt. I told him I didn't feel any better than before. He was looking outside the wind into the yard. He whispered, "I saw a policeman going upstairs."

As he held my hand, I jumped from the bed and together we sneaked out the gate. A garbage wagon was waiting at the door; a few bodies, half dead and buried in lye, had been thrown there. We turned to the left, where the coppersmiths were, and we disappeared into the crowd. I felt very dizzy as a cold sweat oozed down my back. I leaned against a nearby wall and fell to the ground. I couldn't stand the noise of the hammering from the coppersmiths' shops. It felt as if each hammer blow was over my head, and it jingled in my ears. I knew I wouldn't make it. I did not have the strength or the will to take another step. I thought of Anoush and Vahan. I didn't know how long it had been since I had seen them. And there was my mother's note. I thought of the wagon—the lye covering the half-dead bodies, and the police—yes, those frightening, relentless police—not far away from this corner where I found myself helpless on the ground. I held on to the wall, pulled myself up, and tried with every bit of energy I could muster to take a step, but I couldn't make it.

This, I thought, must be how you die. Then I wondered: *If I don't die, where would I go? Would anybody look for me or wonder where I was? Must I die on an unknown corner of the world, beside a stray dog, in an unfriendly, alien place? Must I die so early, before the spring? Must I?* Indeed, this was a strange way to die. I wondered if they would find my body and report it to The Reverend. I didn't even have a chance to express my gratitude to the man. He didn't know how much I respected and loved him; not so much for what he had done for me, but because of what he was doing for the others. Would he inform Mother of my death and take care of Anoush and Vahan?

The sweat down my back had dried. I could see clearer, but I still couldn't stand the constant hammering of the coppersmiths. Slowly, painfully, I dragged my unwilling body, hugging the wall until I was able to take a few steps. I turned the corner slowly until I could see the end of the street where the church and shelter were. The wagon was gone! I rubbed my eyes, scarcely believing, but I couldn't see the wagon or any movement on the street. I took a chance going into the churchyard. I knocked at the door, but it did not open; they were probably afraid of the police. I went across the street to the building where I had been staying. The place was vacant. I couldn't see a soul. They had apparently raided the upstairs and thrown them in the wagon to be doused with lye to make sure they were dead.

The next day, Nazaret-efendi came by our shelter. He was surprised to see my friend and me. We were the only ones still alive. My friend Setrak had disappeared, but Haygaz, who was away at the time of the raid, came back as I had. The Reverend came the same day and looked at Haygaz and me and said, "Tomorrow you must both come to my house; I have a plan for you."

The next day, The Reverend found a home with a family for us where we would be more secure and where we were given a hot meal once a day—a piece of bread with soup in the morning, enough to keep body and soul together. He paid our board for us. The head of the family was a preacher from Marash. We were not told, but we had the feeling that Mr. Partridge was sending funds for the two of us. This family was secure for us; the woman was the sister of an Armenian physician and of Hagop-Monoushagian, whom The Reverend had put in contact with the army general in charge of supplying clothes for the army.

Haygaz left the table without touching his food, went out into the street, and did not return until dark. When he returned, I whispered to him, "Are you hungry?"

"Hell, no! I visited my favorite grocery stores and sampled everything they had, as I asked the price of each item. The grocery man got suspicious of me, so I ran away, loaded with butter and raisins!"

The head of the family asked me if I approved of what Haygaz had done and what had been bothering him.

I replied as mildly as I could that he was always hungry and never had enough to eat. Perhaps I should talk to The Reverend and see if he could pay more for our board. The family tried to improve our food, but could not. They had two young girls to feed on the same budget. The Reverend called me one day and asked what the trouble had been. I said simply that we were not comfortable in this family.

We were then moved to a neighboring family. The woman was congenial, the husband friendly and talkative. She had been raised in Aleppo and spoke excellent Arabic. The neighbors didn't know she was Armenian. We were now more secure and more comfortable. We became friendly with the family and spent many evenings telling of our pasts in Gurun and Marash.

I became a confidential coworker with The Reverend. I learned the operations of The Reverend's secret mission. One day, when we were out on a mission, we walked into a corner marketplace off Bab el-Nassar. We stopped in a secondhand clothing place and asked a man to fit me for a jacket. We selected a black-and-white tweed, which almost fit me, and a fez* (see figure 4.2) for my head. I looked like a Syrian or an Arab merchant's son. I had acquired a few Arabic words by now and was doing the shopping for The Reverend, so I learned names of a few foods, fruits, and vegetables. I became bolder and dared to go to more places, feeling more secure and free in my new native attire.

Orders from the authorities in Constantinople would come to Aleppo complaining that the local government was allowing too many Armenians to roam the streets. At the same time, I had prearranged channels of communication by which I could quickly reach The Reverend in case I was arrested. He was my security and protection.

We were always notified ahead of time of police raids, and we would get out of the house, or stay in, according to the order, so that we would not be arrested on the street. We were playing cat-and-mouse games with

---

*A red felt hat, usually with a tassel attached to the top.

FIGURE 4.2
Minassian in Turkish fez, 1917

the police, just missing each other. The family with whom we were staying kept two other boys from Marash who were related to them, and who, because of their father's reputation and the bribes that were paid for them, were kept from deportation.

One day we were told to stay home. That afternoon, a neighbor notified the lady of the house that the police were in the neighborhood searching for Armenian deportees. She told the neighbor nonchalantly, "Thank God, we have no Armenians among us." She came in and rushed the four of us down to the basement, the older boy, his brother, Haygaz, and me. We could just barely see one another in the dark. We fell on a pile of charcoal, which made a lot of noise. Gradually, our eyes became accustomed to the dark and we started breathing through the small aperture.

The sound of hammering on the door reached us. The lady of the house went to the door and received the police, welcoming them cordially in sweet Arabic: "Welcome to my house. It is indeed an honor you bestow upon me. My house is open to all; now what can I do for you?"

The police were fooled by her fluent Arabic. They told her that they were looking for Armenian deportees. "Please, come in and look for yourself," she said coolly.

We could see the policemen's boots through the opening. The older boy almost fainted. He whispered, "They have us this time." He was shaking like a skittish horse, muttering curses upon them. The police entered the house and were standing over our heads. I wondered what they would do to us if they found the four of us in hiding. We were only a few houses away from The Reverend's house. The lady above cheerfully led the police wherever they wanted to go. Apparently, she had won their confidence. Finally, to our great relief, they left. We took a deep breath. We were told to come up.

The oldest boy was still shaking, pale and yellow. Once again, we had been given a new lease on life. Although the police had been told not to bother searching this section, they did so on their own initiative, hoping for bribes.

I made it a habit to go only on chosen streets. I would go to Akaba, a section of town where my sister and brother were, crossing Bab el-Farage Square, with its big fountain next to the police station. I didn't go through byways or back alleys. It was safer to walk in front of the police station and on to the next street. I felt sure of myself and believed they wouldn't ask that cursed question, "Do you have a pass?"

Only once, when I was walking in front of a grocery store, where there was a display of dried fruits and grain, did I hear the measured steps of heavy military boots following me. It was a policeman. A gun hung from his shoulder, and he had both right and power to ask for my papers. Closer and closer he came, until he was a few feet behind me.

I spoke loudly to the grocery man in perfect Arabic. "How much are the raisins today?" The policeman, hearing my Arabic, passed by and walked on. My Arabic was magic that saved me.

Once, when I was supposed to deliver a message to Mr. Jackson at the American consulate, I saw a guard following me as I neared the building. (We had gotten word that they were checking visitors to the American consul.) So I passed the consulate and continued on to the bazaar.

Once again, when I was in Eskijian's house, there was a knock at the door. I opened the door to face a gendarme who wanted to know whether any deportees were in the house. I said in perfect Arabic, "No."

"What about you?" the man asked. I couldn't answer him without revealing my identity. Mrs. Eskijian hurried toward him and in an angry voice told him that this was The Reverend's residence and he had no business coming in. She ordered him to go.

He left, and she slammed the door behind him. I was amazed by this woman. Her force carried weight, and her action was decisive. The gendarme had left looking rather sheepish, having made a stupid mistake.

The Winter of 1915

The winter of 1915 was very tragic for the deportees. They were scattered all over the desert up to Mesopotamia, gradually decimated in number. Some of the women found shelter among the tribesmen. If they were young and able bodied, they were adopted for marriage to their sons. Other young ones would survive as added members of their harems. But the government also ordered the deportation of families in the several cities where they had had the privilege of remaining at home. In the middle of storms or blizzards, they were forced to leave their homes and take to the road on foot. They were scattered over snow-covered hills and exposed to the severe winter.

One day I was told to pick up a family from a certain section of the city and bring them to a safer place among the natives. The woman who answered the door pretended she could not understand Turkish, and in Arabic she told me that I was mistaken. I answered in Armenian that I had been sent by The Reverend, and a voice from the yard told her to let me in. I entered, and a woman welcomed me with a smile while the man stayed inside. It was Nishan Baliozian, professor of Turkish from Antep College. We were all surprised. They relaxed as soon as they saw me.

After a short review of my family, I led them and their two teenage daughters to the designated place. The professor told me that he couldn't believe all of the things that had happened. Once his friend from Sivas had led him to safety and security; now his son did the same. They insisted that I should visit them often.

Haygaz, who was staying with me in the same house, was told not to roam around unless it was necessary. At night, when everybody was asleep, we made plans for the future. He was born in Shabinkarahisar, where my mother was born, and we were classmates in Sivas. Deported

---

from Sivas, he had not been able to join his family and didn't know what had happened to them. We often talked about other students and our teachers. We would say that after the war, we would continue our education, graduate, and become full-fledged teachers. But when was the war going to end? Never, it seemed. We wondered what the big nations were doing, such as England, Russia, France, and the United States, the country we admired the most.

Each day we waited for a miracle to happen. The English army would march, and we would be freed. Then Haygaz would say, "Someday . . . if we last that long." He told me that he had learned that The Reverend was under investigation. If that happened, what would happen to us? When The Reverend was questioned about his activities, Miss Rohner, a German missionary from Marash,* talked to the German consul, but he refused to interfere in government affairs. With her influence, however, she did succeed in having the investigation stopped.

I asked The Reverend one day if he could help me enter a local school, where I would be more secure as a student; besides, I was eager to continue my education. He agreed, wrote a warm recommendation to the German consul, and asked him to use his influence on my behalf. He sent me to the consul with it. When I knocked at the gate, a secretary came to the door, and I gave him the envelope. He opened and read it while I waited outside the gate. He went inside, without asking me to enter. He came back shortly, saying, "Sorry, all the school's rooms and facilities are filled." He then closed the gate, without knowing who I was nor where I came from.

On my return home, I passed the center of the military police. Next to their headquarters was a small shop where I overheard Turkish being spoken freely; I asked the shopkeeper if he could direct me to a certain address. He answered me very warmly and asked if I were Armenian. How could I deny it? In fact, I was delighted to see another Armenian. But suddenly I wondered what he was doing next to the M.P.'s office. I shook, thinking of the possibilities. Now I wasn't happy that I had come for information. I said, "Yes," and waited.

"Where are you hiding, young man?" When I told him that The Reverend was protecting me, he grimaced, which seemed to imply: "How low

---

*Beatrice Rohner was Swiss but served in Marash as a member of the German missionary society Hilfsbund für christliches Liebeswerk im Orient. During the war, she was allowed to operate an orphanage in Aleppo and saved many Armenian children.

can one stoop for protection!" He was not a member of the Protestant Church. He asked my last name, and when I told him, he asked, "Are you from Gurun?" I relaxed. He asked me if I knew Onnig from Gurun, and I said, "Yes." He told me that he was Onnig's uncle and added that Onnig helped him in his shop, and that I should come in and meet him some time. The place was hardly five by eight feet, very little room for two people behind the showcase. A few days later, I met Onnig, and he told me that Haroutoun was also in town from Antep College and hiding. Haroutoun was the cousin of Vartan, whom they had tortured in Gurun and killed in Sivas.

The orphanage that Mr. Eskijian had organized took shape. Workers daily devoted themselves to healing, clothing, washing, and substituting as mothers and teachers, each in her or his own language, either Armenian or Turkish. Once when I was visiting the administrator, I heard the very weak voice of a child crying for its mother. One of the women said, "I am your mother; here I am." Food was very scarce, and Juskulian was having a difficult time smuggling it in.[3]

Each day a few died, and each day more orphans came, as if this were the lighthouse in a seaport of desperation. At least they were not outside, subjected to harassment. This was especially true for the teenage girls and young widows. Mrs. Eskijian took many of these girls with her, because the police investigators would take them away for their leaders or would pick one for themselves. When new girls came to the orphanage, Mrs. Eskijian would send a woman, who would choose a girl and take her to her house. Each girl had to have a family secured for her. The Reverend would tell these families that one more mouth was not too much to feed. "How fortunate you are that you can do this for these little ones." Some would reject The Reverend; others divided everything they had, even risking their own security; they did this because these people of Aleppo had the right leader. On Sunday, The Reverend would stand in his pulpit and open the Bible. You could hardly see his solemn, peaceful, smiling face or hear his voice. He would read a passage from a chapter . . . "Because you fed me when I was hungry and sheltered me when I needed shelter . . ." And he would close the book. That was the day's sermon.

The winter was severe for the people who had no clothes and no shelter and no food. Many died because of the lack of medical care. Mr. Manoushagian, through his organization and his contacts in the army, was able to convince Faik Bay and secure a few jobs for women. This enabled many to come out of hiding and earn a loaf of bread a day. They became free and independent of charity. This was God's way of helping the desperate and scattered people. Although they were in rags, they were willing to do any work to survive. Onnig told me about Kurken, a boy who dressed as an Arab and did errands for the mistress of an Arab harem.

Many elderly women were placed in an Army hospital . . . in jobs that were not safe for the younger girls. The population of deportees was estimated at twenty thousand, but more were concealed and could not be counted. Meanwhile, the police were still picking up whomever they chose and deporting them—without questioning—to the desert, where they would starve to death.

Genocide was very successful with the help of the winter and the Turks. The Reverend's secret mission was not secret anymore, for the job demanded more each day. His door stood open, and he never got any rest. Women who had heard his name would come to him for help. I often was at the door to receive them. I tried to screen them to lighten his burden because these desperate people became more selfish and demanding. His jobs multiplied: Couldn't he contact somebody from out of town? Couldn't he get a job for someone? Couldn't he spare a few coins, or some shelter for a sick child? Or save a kidnapped widow from a Turkish harem? He would help when he could.

When they thanked him, he would say, "There will be a time when you may be able to do something in your turn." These people never forgot him; they could not. He served them with a smile, as if he were enjoying his turn. He spent many days without proper food or rest. His wife worried when he wouldn't come home for lunch, or came late in the evening—sometimes at midnight. Where was he? What was he doing? We feared that he may have been caught, jailed, or deported. Anything could happen in the darkness of the night in the darkest days of our lives.

One day he was informed that there would be a raid on the house of a local merchant who had stored goods for the orphans. The Reverend could not afford to lose this merchandise to the army, so he led me to the house, and we carted away many bolts of yardage. He asked me if my load was too heavy, while he, himself, carried a big load on his shoulders. We made several trips from this man's house to The Reverend's. When we settled down, he said with great satisfaction that now we had some clothes for the children.

In Aleppo, you don't see snow, but the wind is cold and penetrating. Houses are built mostly of stone, thick and heavy, and hard to heat. Children's clothes were shabby and filthy. The Reverend did all he could. He certainly did not want to deprive the children of their daily bread, but couldn't help it.

These people were half starved, cold, and pale. They had once been teachers, professors, and ministers. They were depressed and wondered what would happen to them. I was the only contact that these people had with the outside world. They often would ask me about The Reverend, the orphans, the police, and if it was still as bad as before. They read the Bible every day, and at night they turned to certain passages for comfort. Several valuable professors were separated from their families and cut off from the world. Once they were the upper intelligentsia, the cream of the nation's culture, useful and important. Some of them even taught Turkish to Turkish children. But now, even though they were not involved in political activities, they had to hide away like criminals.

Many of their kind already had perished—in prison, in the desert, or shot by gendarmes. These people were not revolutionaries. They did not have firearms or ammunition, but their knowledge made them a danger to the Turks. It is said, "The dark is afraid of the light." But a young Armenian poet told us many years ago, "The sunshine will never be buried." The cold, long nights compelled these people to live like cavemen of the wilderness, without light and without heat. Survival was the main issue of the day. Tomorrow, the war would end, the nation would gather. They pinned their hopes on the future, planning for the next generation, for direction and rebirth. But very few of these people survived.

Mr. Eskijian, disregarding the danger of the 1916 typhus epidemic, visited the sick, the widows, and the orphans. He would hold their hands to console them, ignoring the dirt and disease. But he neglected himself most of all, skipping meals and missing sleep. He caught a minor cold at first. His fever went up, and Doctor Altunian diagnosed his condition as fair, but the fever continued to climb; when the doctor came the second time, he ordered The Reverend to Altunian Hospital. Mrs. Eskijian wanted somebody to accompany him, but because what he had was contagious and dangerous, his closest friends turned down her request. Mr. M., a close associate and his assistant in the church, was too busy that afternoon and couldn't go with him to the hospital. I offered my help, but Mrs. Eskijian refused me. I insisted and ordered a coach. We covered him with warm blankets and slowly drove to the hospital. We found that they did not have help to carry him up the many stairs. We secured a cot, and the coachman ahead of me helped me place The Reverend, with his head almost touching my chest, upon it. We lifted the cot and slowly climbed the stairs. I tried my best not to let his body touch the steps. The load was on me now. He noticed it and said softly, "Why did you have to come?"

Mr. Juskalian was already in the hospital with typhus, too; and his condition was very bad (similar to The Reverend, who contracted typhus). That night I remained with Mrs. Eskijian quite late. I did not want to leave her alone, and she was the person I was closest to in the world. The following morning, Juskalian's horse was available for me, and I rode to the hospital. I was denied permission to see him. Mrs. K., whom I knew from Sivas, told me about him.

Mrs. Eskijian visited the hospital that afternoon, and she was sad and depressed. Friends got together in her house and prayed with her for The Reverend. Hundreds of children and women joined our prayers when they heard the sad news. The Reverend was the only friend they had left, and he was dangerously ill. Only a miracle could save his life—but that miracle didn't come.

A few days later when I rushed to the hospital, the nurse saw me and started to weep. She looked at me hopelessly. All I asked was, "May I see him?" I followed her along the dark corridor, then she led me to the basement, where the bodies were kept overnight. It was a strange and wonderful sight. I had seen many dead people, but never such a peaceful, contented smile as I saw on The Reverend's face. It seemed to be saying, "The mission that you assigned me is accomplished, my God."

I returned home and found Mrs. Eskijian, getting ready to go visit her husband. I ordered a coach to take us to the hospital. On the way I told her about her husband's death.

When we came back, I rushed to the orphanage to tell them. Five minutes after my arrival, all of the orphans and the widows were on their feet for a silent moment of prayer for their beloved departed father, brother, minister, and God-sent angel. His life had been molded after his master, the son of a carpenter from Nazareth, who had given hope to the world with his devotion. Reverend Eskijian gave new meaning to the Christian faith with his dedication, love, and service. His life, like a morning sun, outshone all of the other stars, subduing all God's men in his time, creating new standards to follow, new horizons. This man, the son of a cobbler, was born in 1882 and had died in the spring of 1916, but he had lived a full hundred years.

Next morning was Sunday, and we held a memorial service, although it was dangerous to expose hundreds of people at the cemetery. There were no newspapers, telephones, or anything like that, yet it seemed as though the whole population of the city had heard the news.

One of the greatest privileges I have ever enjoyed was to be up among the hundreds who were in the church and outside to pay him homage. When my name was called, I crossed through the crowd, and stepped up to the platform. Quickly, I buttoned and straightened the jacket he had bought for me (it was always too big). Few would enjoy my chosen words in Armenian, because only a few could understand them, but they were all silent and waiting. I began my eulogy of a man who had captured our hearts forever. Many were weeping, not necessarily for my words, but because of the sad reality that no one could take his place.

As always in war, children are the first to suffer. Mr. Eskijian's death affected the whole community of Armenians, but the orphanage suffered the most. Funds dwindled, and the food supply became shorter because of Juskalian's death. Women did what they could to relieve the sorrow and the need of the children who had lost their mentor. Life had induced others to volunteer for the suffering, but now there was indifference about what each person should do for the betterment of all. A lack of discipline and irregularities followed. Juskalian's office holders lost the power of dedication. Mother Takouhi, who had come here to assume responsibility, was ignored. The burden shifted to a widow in her late thirties, who had two small children of her own. She made a visit to the orphanage. Forgetting her own personal sorrows, she helped others who were more desperate than she.

I was told to direct a group of Juskalian disciples to turn over their responsibilities to Mother Takouhi and to move out. In the group was a family of four: two children, a husband and wife. They were hidden and protected under the guardianship of Juskalian. I delivered the message as softly as I could. The task hurt me, but it was a must in order to preserve law and order and the program that Eskijian had started and created. I arranged to move them to a vacant house with a few of their belongings—a nearby place where they could hide. I often visited them to show them my goodwill.

Mrs. Eskijian arranged for an elderly man to supervise the orphanage. The police picked him up and exiled him. She sent a young undergraduate from Antep College. After two weeks, they took him away, too. She decided that I was the only one who could do the job because the police probably would not pay attention to a young boy. I didn't realize what a big challenge I had, until I became the only boy to supervise, consult, direct, and work with an all-women group, including teachers. Mrs. Eskijian expressed faith in me as the right person to take the place of her late husband. She added, "God must have a plan; this must be your call." I had neither the experience nor the ability to meet all of the responsibilities, yet she insisted.

Mother Takouhy told me that they needed someone to impart strong discipline, and she felt sure they would listen to me. Each morning she would give me suggestions to deliver to the children after their watery breakfast of flour soup. The children and the elders were attentive. I would give them their daily tasks, reminding them of their jobs and how important it was and how fortunate they were to be able to be doing their share. I often visited the classrooms where they were singing or reciting in Turkish. I would encourage the mothers and teachers, who were girls of about my age or older. I was very much aware of my age among this group, but I was also prepared and decided that regardless of what happened I would not show attention or partiality to anyone. But soon I noticed that they were paying too much attention to me, and that worried me. Although I used to smile generously before, I stopped doing that now. My plea turned to the tone of solemn orders; I spoke like an army captain. This was not being myself, but I had to do it in order to prevent misunderstandings among the old and the young. I also noticed that I was being observed by the older women. If I lingered in conversation with a teacher or smiled at one, that was it.

My room was in the middle of the building beside the main office, and faced the gate, and the courtyard was exposed to all. An elderly woman was assigned to take care of my room—bedding, cleaning, and laundering—for it was not considered good taste to allow men to do these things when so many women were around, but I saw a young woman coming out of my room. A few days later, I noticed a soft-spoken teacher blushing as she answered my questions, and I could not help blushing in return. She politely ended each sentence with, "Yes, sir," and this annoyed me, but my position made such a response normal.

One morning before our assembly, I was preparing a speech. I noticed that she watched and followed me, and she noticed that I knew she was watching me. She bowed her head and disappeared. During prayer meeting, Loosin, with a broad smile, enjoyed each word I spoke. During the day I avoided her; and if I did see her, I did not even smile. But that same night, I could not sleep.

Puritanism among Armenians

When the American missionaries came to Turkey in the early 1800s, they ignored the fact that the Armenians had a very old culture; they did not see the high steeples of the Armenian churches and the crosses on top of them. In fact, Armenians had adopted Christianity long before the discovery of America. For centuries, our ministers had studied and taught the Bible, which they translated from the Greek to Armenian to ensure a faithful translation of the spirit of the original.

After accepting Christianity, the Armenians became less aggressive than the Persians, Romans, and Greeks and showed greater endurance of injustice imposed on them by these armies. But the arrival of missionaries made them humbler and more inclined to leave their destiny to God's will. Members of the Protestant Church were unfairly and unnecessarily taught the fear of God. We children suffered the consequences. It was a sin for us to play on Sundays; it was a sin to play marbles, a sin to play cards, and a sin to dance. Wine also was taboo because it would make us drunk. It was a sin to run fast, and a sin not to, and a sin to sit down. We had to listen to the prayers on Sundays with the adults, attend Sunday classes, recite biblical verses and quotations, and read biblical stories. As I grew older, I became almost a theologian by right. Yet I could not understand a word of the theory of the Holy Trinity.

This religious teaching made Protestants a strange people among their native Armenians; we did not celebrate the glorious day of Vartevar or Saint Vartan or even Saint Gregory the Illuminator, who had introduced

Christianity to his nation. The copying of Puritanism among Armenians was so perfect that the facsimile became clearer than the original.

Members of the Protestant Church didn't know their national heroes or their ancient history. They knew nothing of the Renaissance, when young men had translated Greek and Roman classics that combined their Eastern culture with Western civilization and their arts. We were deprived of these glories of the past. We didn't even know the names of Sahag and Mesrob, who were called saints of Armenia for discovering our alphabet. Our parents gave us instead all that was delivered to them—rules and regulations based on the fear of God and life hereafter. We children were prepared for heaven rather than for life on earth. We did not have the joy and happiness of singing peasant love songs; it was forbidden. We did not know any national anthems. We sang only the songs that were chosen from old Mr. (Elias) Riggs's translation of hymns from English into Armenian, mostly old, stale, meaningless words.

Indeed, we were strangers among our people and were justly considered stepsons of the Armenian Church and were rejected as such by the whole nation. If it had not been for my father's wise decision to send me to an Armenian National Church school, I, too, would have missed the history and literature of my own nation and its language enriched by Persian and Greek words. The music of the Armenian Church expressed the Armenian heart and spiritual desires.

But the glorious days of ancient Armenia were gone. Pageantry was gone, and their heroes were dead, replaced by Jehovah. Now we were a semi-Western culture, preparing for heaven. With this background, I was entrusted with the supervision of an establishment cut off from the world and from life itself. I was chosen to be the head of the orphanage, a substitute for The Reverend. That was a big order, indeed; bigger than I had realized.

One day Mrs. Eskijian sent a messenger to me to come see her. Upon my arrival at her house, she did not search for words. "I have motherly responsibility for you," she said.

I listened to her as a son should. She spoke to me without fear of misunderstanding her, so she was justified in taking me to task. She said, "I think I have made a mistake in sending you to the orphanage among so many young girls. You also are young. I have decided to call you back to save you from troubles and temptations and unnecessary hardships." I looked her straight in the face, which I had never done before, and vehemently told her that she had no right to recall me before she had evidence that her fears were just. I was indignant that she challenged my trust. My short speech shook her. She replied, as all mothers would, "I just wanted to remind you not to blame me." Then we exchanged friendly words, and I left for the orphanage. On my return, Loosin gave me a broad smile. I pretended to ignore her but told myself, *You big mouth, go ahead and suffer.*

I had to change the boy who guarded the gate because he was openly making love to one of the girls. He complained when I assigned him to the next building where only a few elderly women and boys were sheltered. I told him that if he did not watch the gate with care, we would not be able to hide as many women as we did now. He promised that he would not fail again and begged for the chance to prove it. He said he felt isolated at the other building. But I could not give in; I was the administrator and had assumed all responsibility for discipline.

The police made several visits to the orphanage in order to make a list of the grown-up girls. Each time they came, we had to hide the girls in the office attic. They would turn pale at the thought of the terrible things they had heard about why the police picked them up. Mother Takouhy, Mrs. Eskijian, and I decided to place them in different houses. But how could we safely place them as maids and housekeepers? These people, already heavily burdened with volunteer work, did their utmost to help—even though they were subjected to the authorities' harassment and punishment.

We interviewed several girls and a few widows, explaining the dangers in a place like this, and informed them of our plans. We let them decide for themselves, in case they had contacts outside. There was one especially young and beautiful girl, Asdig. A Syrian family took her in as a servant and tried hard to communicate with her in their Arabic. It was difficult for her, but because of their patient effort, she finally learned their language. And thus, one by one, we placed them.

Loosin, of course, was disappointed. She looked at me with her doe-like eyes as if to say, "Are you also deciding this for me?" Without hesitation, I said in front of Mother Takouhy, "We are doing this for your security and welfare." This was the truth, but the truth hurt me. Our friendship had deepened, without a touch or a compliment on my part. Love has a strange way of expressing itself: a soft smile, a warm "good morning," and long, lingering looks. It has a language of its own, thoroughly understood between two individuals. All of the noble things I had learned flashed through my mind. I was called upon to protect those in need and in danger, but here I was, practically helpless. I recalled the massacre on the hill and how a young girl had cried out for help that I couldn't give. And here now, Loosin. She, too, was ready to cry but was too proud to show any weakness. Yes, one by one, we placed them in different homes.

We instructed these girls to keep in touch with us, and we told them we would contact them as often as possible. This was a big order. It was hard to travel and not be noticed; it was even dangerous to walk a few blocks. I was assigned to visit each of them, as a "brother" or "cousin." I would knock at the door, and someone would answer then shout to the girl, "Your brother is here!" I acted like a big brother to assure them that I was overseeing them and to let the households know that these girls had a protector.

The second week of Loosin's departure from the orphanage, I visited her. She was living now in Azizia, a better section of Aleppo, an especially rich neighborhood. When I knocked at the door, an aged woman opened it. I told her that I was calling on my sister. She gave me a strange look and accepted me. Then, for the first time, Loosin and I were left alone. I spoke formally to conceal my thoughts, using my words as a shield against the danger of revealing myself. I talked of many subjects. Without protest she listened. She agreed almost automatically with whatever I said. I knew she was disappointed in me, but she didn't realize how much I wanted to be responsible for her. She didn't know how she charmed me, how often I dreamed of her, how in the wee hours of the morning I would open my eyes only to sleep and dream some more about her. The truth hurt me. Our friendship had deepened, without a touch, doing this for her security and welfare.

Azneev

One afternoon, when I was returning from my routine calls to the orphanage, I heard a woman's soft voice calling my name. I knew no one in this section, yet slowed my steps. A door opened. I hesitated before climbing the stone steps, when the door opened wider, and the same soft voice asked me to come in. The room was shuttered and dark. When my eyes became accustomed to the darkness, I realized who she was.

She was hardly twenty-five years old when I knew her. We had hidden in the same courthouse. She had been living then with her mother and two young sisters. Their wealth had saved them, and they arrived at Aleppo after paying many bribes. We were told that she had married to avoid evil eyes and the police, but somehow they had arrested her husband and exiled him for taking her in as a maid. She had no chance of running away; and if she did, her mother and sisters would be in danger, and she, too, would be deported. Her body was as white as milk; she had charm, beauty, and her movements were full of grace. She was one of the most desirable women I had yet seen. Her large, dreamy, dark eyes had a magnetic power. She had on a dress almost to her ankles, but it was transparent, outlining her body against the black silk. Her white arms promised her hidden beauty. The dress was cut low, almost to her bosom, revealing, as no Eastern woman would dare to in the presence of a man. She smiled at my glance and said, "You didn't recognize my voice."

Without raising my head, I whispered rather coolly, "I didn't know that you were in the city." Then I asked if her mother knew that she was here. "No," she said. She was not embarrassed by my presence, nor did she even try to cover her carelessly exposed bosom, but stood, challenging my innocence and the noble things I had been taught and thought that I was proud of. She ordered coffee for both of us from the maid, and we talked. She told me how secure and protected she now was, and that her life was comfortable. She also mentioned that the master of the house was out of town, to make me feel more comfortable.

Finally, I asked her if she would like to get out of here, to hide away, or go to her mother. "It is very hard for a woman to be as decent and noble as one wants to be," she answered. "I'm going to stay until . . . I am quite protected here; and if I leave, another man will get me soon."[4]

I suggested that the war would not last forever. Soon all of us would return home, rebuild our families, and that someday someone would marry her, and she would become a proud mother. "Someday," I had said, but I was not so sure when.

"Nobody will marry me if they know my story, and I do not want to be a disgrace to my family by joining them now or later. Please," she begged, "understand me . . ." She wept and said, "I wish I were dead or that I had a few scars on my face so I wouldn't attract the 'dogs.'"

But here she was, her bosom so exposed that I couldn't look her squarely in the face. She moved her arms freely, as though unaware of the situation. Once she had been a noble woman; now she was shameful and shameless. Yet I wanted to get closer to her, to comfort her and take her out of here. I was caught in a dilemma. I could not suggest to her what l was thinking. She was right when she said she was living in hell, but hell was outside, too. Once she would not show as much as her ankles; and now she sat exposed, staring at me as if I were a stone or a piece of furniture in the room. The coffee she had ordered was already cold, and I couldn't finish it. I put my cup on an inlaid Damascus table, made of walnut. I also noticed a Persian rug and the rich Oriental atmosphere. Indeed, this was a palace built in hell. She could see through me, I noticed, and I had to struggle not to reveal myself and to control my anger, because I could not do anything to help her situation. She must have sensed that I was disappointed in her as well as in myself.

But as I left, I felt a certain sympathy, even love, for her; for if it had not been for the war, she would have been God's gift to humanity. We degraded her kind to suit ourselves, using the war as an excuse for our bestial behavior. And now I was no longer thinking with a boy's simplemindedness; war left no woman safe or unspoiled. All over the world, sisters and wives, or children, were robbed, killed, raped, because war made it "legal" and made the soldier's job more attractive.

These are the beautiful flowers, yet we throw them into the gutter; perhaps sometimes we save them to curse them and call them names without daring to look at ourselves in the mirror—just enjoying the fruits of war like pigs in our "civilization."

I had asked the boy who did errands for us to stop by and see Loosin. In great excitement he came back and told me that she was sick and had begged him to ask me to visit her. The following day when I knocked at her door and entered, she covered herself. She was very pale and tired, very nervous and on the verge of crying. It looked as if she had not slept for days. I asked her how she felt and what was the cause of her illness, and unconsciously I held her hand in my palm. Tenderly I whispered to her that she would be all right, but she shook her head, holding on to my hand nervously. "Please," she implored, "do something for me. Take me away from here!" She said that she was not safe here, or in the orphanage; that she was not safe anywhere. "I want to get out of here," she repeated, "and as soon as I feel better, I'm going to look for my mother."

Men are humiliated when a woman asks for help and they are powerless to do anything to better their situation; they hate themselves for not being able to justify being "a man." I wanted to take her out of there, but there was no security anywhere else. It was a responsibility I could not well undertake, if at all. I could be arrested any time. Nobody was sure. Seeing my helplessness, she cried. "I do not care where you take me, just take me away," and she continued weeping. I tried to comfort her as best I could with words, but they sounded hollow and meaningless, and I left her with the promise of planning some way to take her out of there, although not knowing how nor when.

I consulted Mother Takouhy, and blushingly Mrs. Eskijian also, about how to save this tortured girl, to save her from the shameful situations she was subjected to. She was trying to hold herself aloof from them all—with all of the effort she could muster. She struggled all alone against a hostile world, and she considered me to be the only one she could depend on and trust. The following day the boy gave me a note, folded in such a way that only the receiver could open it up without destroying it. It read, "Dear, I decided to leave this place as I had to . . . I made contact with Mother in Hama. I am on my way to see her, Loosin."

Mother

Mother, I received the news, that until the last moment, you were communicating with your God, asking pity for your children who are dying from hunger and want. You wanted to be near me, yet you stopped me from continuing the journey with you. In a dark corner of a cold and filthy room without a cover or food, you tried to warm the children with your body. But God could not hear you, and man could not help you. It is a shame, a tragic shame, that we human beings are allowed only a few things in life to enjoy and yet we are deprived of the love of a mother, or the love of a son.

You said that God put us on this earth to suffer. I think it is cruel—I am confused; I do not understand. I'll confess, Mother, I also lost my God. I am happy that nobody in the universe, even God himself, can hurt you anymore. I miss you. I miss your comforting tender hands on my head. I need you because only you could tell me there still can be beauty in every one of us, and I'd believe you. That we all may be good, that love is best to have, and that an extended hand is always blessed—that nobility of man is inside of him and that the greatness of a man lies within his heart; that regardless of what things may appear to be, the future is for one who has love and kindness; that the world will continue its difficult course toward betterment, slowly, painfully slowly, but surely, that love is greater than hate as the sun is stronger than darkness, even in our darkest days of our dark ages; and eventually love must triumph over hate.

You taught me that compassion for mankind is more fundamental than the misleading cult of hatred. That wherever there is culture and ethics and a higher degree of civilization, religion is distasteful and degrading to the noble heart. This I learned for myself from life. And no God in heaven is the answer to the evils in this world. Man, himself, is the solution to his miseries.

There is nothing Man cannot do, or undo, if he sets his mind to it; even abolish war from the face of the earth and establish peace. I miss you, Mother, and will love you forever.

(December)

Perseverance of Nation and Holy War

Cut off as we were from the whole world, we knew nothing of what was going on outside. We didn't know where the battlefront was or what country was winning the war. But we heard that the British Army was attacking on the Baghdad front. The Germans in Turkey were trying to complete the railroad to Baghdad while General Townshend's* army near Baghdad was desperately trying to break the Turkish line.

Kut-el-Amara†

By this time, the Turkish government had a plan for joining other Islamic nations to create a greater Turkey. It was their aim to destroy all of the Armenian males from five years and up. Orders came from Constantinople's Interior Department, issued by Talaat Bey, to make sure that the deportees had reached their destination—DEATH! The sultan declared a

---

*Sir Charles Vere Ferrers Townshend (1861–1924), the British Imperial general whose Anglo-Indians were besieged at Kut al-Amara in Mesopotamia and finally surrendered in humiliation on April 29, 1916. He was held captive by the Turks until October 1918, as the Ottoman Empire prepared to surrender to the Allies. See Townshend's own account, *My Campaign in Mesopotamia* (London: T. Butterworth, 1920).

†On the siege of Kut al-Amara (December 1915–April 1916) by the Turkish Sixth Army commanded by German Field Marshal Colmar von der Goltz, see Nikolas Gardner, *The Siege of Kut al-Amara* (Bloomington: Indiana University Press, 2014; A. J. Barker, *The Bastard War: The Mesopotamian Campaign of 1914–1918* (New York: Dial Press, 1967).

holy war against all Christians, demanding that they all be killed wherever they were. If these young Turks would have believed that the world would hold them responsible for their deeds, that eventually they would punish them, they probably would have been reluctant to commit such barbaric acts and atrocities against their defenseless subjects.*

Our orphanage was raided time and again; all of the older and teenage girls were taken until we were not able to continue. I was advised to leave my job for safety. Miss Rohner assigned me to work as a teacher in her orphanage and thus enjoy her protection and security. My friend Haroutoun asked me to join other boys who were also teaching classes at the orphanage and live with them. Then we heard that the police had picked up about thirty-five young boys from the orphanage, all under fifteen years of age, and sent them to Turkish schools to be raised as Turks. Kegham was one of them. When they tried to circumcise the boys, a few ran away, for this was the worst insult for an Armenian boy. Some children came to Miss Rohner's orphanage for safety, because her position as a German missionary offered privilege and protection.

My Garden of Flowers

Sister Anna, who was an assistant to Miss Rohner, was also a German missionary. One day she was making a record of the newcomers from other orphanages and was questioning a boy of about eight years of age:

"Are you a Baptist?"

"No."

"Are you an Evangelist?"

"No."

"Are you a Seventh-Day Adventist?"

---

*Talaat Bey, later Talaat Pasha (1874–1921), was a chief perpetrator of the Armenian genocide. He was one of the Young Turk triumvirate who ruled the Ottoman Empire during the First World War. With minimal education, he was able to secure a job as a postal worker and eventually rose in the ranks of the Turkish nationalist party, the Committee of Union and Progress (Ittihad ve Terakki), where he befriended Enver and Jemal, the other members of the triumvirate who seized power in 1913 in a coup against the elected Ottoman government. Talaat served as minister of the interior and of finance and then in 1917 also as grand vizier or prime minister. He initiated the state-sponsored anti-Armenian measures in April 1915 by ordering the arrest and exile of Armenian intellectuals and community leaders in Constantinople and then mass deportations of the Armenian population throughout the empire beginning in May 1915. Soghomon Tehlirian, a member of the Armenian Revolutionary Federation, assassinated Talaat in Berlin in 1921.

"No."

"Are you Catholic, or Protestant?"

"No."

"Then, Congregationalist?"

"No."

"Then what are you?"

The boy raised his chest as he had been told to do long ago and said proudly, "I am an Armenian—Armenian!"

Four of us would teach in the orphanage, and in the afternoon, we would go to the Army Labor center to supervise workers who were making uniforms for the army. This was a great help. The job was created by Mr. Monusahagian. Many women survived because of this job—they earned a loaf of bread and had a piece of paper to identify themselves. Now they had the right to breathe and possibly to suffer more. The four of us now had our security papers as army employees, and we were free from police harassment. Our red bands on our left arms proved it. Each day, with a loaf of bread under our arms, we would come home to rest, happy with our privilege of knowing Miss Rohner and enjoying her protection.

One day, the police called to tell her that they were coming to inspect the orphanage. She invited the officials in and showed them the children in their classrooms, saying, "Come in and see 'my garden of flowers.'" Their skeleton-like little bodies, sheathed in their shabby clothes, were living proof of hunger nearing the starvation point.

We had a hard time disciplining the unruly boys of the class, who came mostly from homes of slavery. They were starved, weak, and sick looking, about to drop dead any time the first wind blew.

I was notified that my brother, Vahan, was very sick. I went where he was in isolation; he was skin and bones. He could not recognize me. His disease was "starvation," cruel, brutal starvation.

My sister told me that he had wanted to eat lamb chops. Four days later I was called to the orphanage. This time the administrator, Reverend Shirazian, asked me to visit him in his office. He told me that they had done all they could, but that it was common to see a young boy die of starvation. This was a victory for the Turkish army. My little brother died of hunger.

We four boys were considerate of each other and cooperative. One of the boys, who was to have graduated from Tarsoos (Tarsus), an American college, was now our chef. He would go to the market and shop in search of cheap food, spend a few coppers for vegetables to make stew, sometimes with a few pieces of lamb ribs, sparingly chopped in equal sizes of an inch. Sometimes he would make a soup of lentils with onions, no meat.

For breakfast? A piece of bread, slightly dipped in olive oil, flavored with oregano, which the natives called *zartar*. Some evenings for supper we would have a piece of cheese, which wouldn't have been enough even for a mouse. If we had any bread left over, we would eat it with our piece of cheese, a cup of tea without sugar. Army officers and prominent civilian officials of the state had everything they wanted. We, who had been robbed and cheated, could hardly get a few raisins to sweeten our tea; at times when I looked at the tasteless soup that orphans had and watched them hungrily lick their spoons, I felt guilty for what we boys enjoyed.

One evening our chef asked us to pay our coppers toward the evening meal, and, while I was washing dishes, he told us the rumor that the army was going to cancel our passes as civilian workers. We would have no protection as teachers. Miss Rohner tried to see the authorities, even the governor of the state, to plead for our protection and safety. She told him that she needed us for the education of the little children. Soon we were called to her office one by one. She told us that she had failed. The governor turned her down because he said that he had orders from party headquarters of Ethehad, directly from Talaat Pasha.

Miss Rohner told me to leave the city before it was too late, for it was too dangerous at my age to stay. All of my dreams for the future were thus denied. I had only two reasons to live: for the safety of my sister and to help The Reverend's cause. I had promised this to my mother—you never break your promise to the dead. I volunteered for The Reverend. I couldn't invest my life for any better cause.

I made an attempt to see Mr. Jackson, the American consul, for a recommendation to the German consul for entry into a school protected by them. He obliged me congenially for the second time. I was at the door of the German consul. The new secretary opened the door, looked at me like the city's well-dressed man would look at a pig, and closed the door, keeping me waiting outside. Soon it opened again, and I was rejected in my appeal for security. I wondered if I could do better with the Turks.

A young lady teaching in Gurun was a friend of the family because she was involved in a love affair with my nephew, Manoog—a love that died in the bud, like early flowers when a harsh wind blows. We had been in close contact since her arrival in Aleppo. Now she was taking care of the family's children. I had asked her to leave the orphanage months ago. In spite of that, our relationship remained friendly and congenial, for I was instrumental in finding their hiding place.

The German railroad company was in a rush to extend the line to Baghdad. I contacted Mr. Dedeian, who supervised the food supply depot at the end of the line to Baghdad, a small station called Darbasia, near Mardin. I asked him for a job. The army controlled and scheduled this railroad, but the personnel were managed by the Germans. Mr. Dedeian said I could get a job if I could get to that section. He told me, too, that I could not ride on this line without the army's approval, but that he would instruct his men to help me when they arrived in Aleppo to get supplies for Darbasia. Shortly after, his wife told me to meet a man by the name of Rajah. He instructed me to get some cash in case I needed it and suggested that I meet him at the railroad station Sunday at 8 a.m. "Pass the gate guard, do not talk to anybody, but wait for me inside the gate. If you do that, I have a plan for you. It may not work, and it may fail; but you will know the result; if everything goes well, we will have done it." I agreed, but I did not know how I was supposed to pass the guard at the gate. If anybody asked me where I was going, I would be caught. My Arabic was not good enough for an argument.

I told my plan to my very close friend Haroutoun. He opened his eyes wide in surprise. "What a chance you are taking," he said. "But if you make it, you sure will be secure." He envied me. Today was the issue of the day, and in a few more days, who knows? The will to survive makes one less afraid of danger, and the dream of tomorrow makes one stronger and more ready to accept a challenge. I could not afford to miss this opportunity.

5

Escape

Before leaving Aleppo, I went one last time to see my friend Haygaz, who had been my classmate in Sivas and my companion in Aleppo. He had been helping an innkeeper in exchange for his room and board, but I learned that he had been sick for several weeks and had died from lack of food and medicine. I recalled his red cheeks, his bright, large, dark eyes. He had only a few years to graduate from Sivas Teachers College. He had planned to join others in his city to improve the education in Shabinkara-hisar. I was depressed; I felt as though part of me was gone.

I made a great effort to see another friend of mine, one of the best young gentlemen I had ever known. He was nineteen years of age, strong as a bull, and soft as a dove. He would never bow, never beg favors, and tried his utmost to be self-sufficient and help anyone he could. He had escaped from the city to get a job as a stable boy for an Arab who raised horses outside of Aleppo. He ran away because they mistreated him. Dejected and shamed, he hid himself from the world and got lost. He had been a valuable friend. He was a true son of Gurun.

I visited Miss Rohner to say goodbye and tell her of my plans. She wished me good luck. Then I stopped by Mrs. Eskijian, sharing my schemes for traveling and consulting with her. She asked me if I had money, and I told her that if I could make the trip, I would not need money. Actually, my future was doubtful and quite vague. She wished me good luck and insisted that I try to keep in touch with her. I went to Mr. Dedeian's home to see Esther. She slipped several majidias* into my pocket, telling me that I would need them, for one never knew what may happen. Although I thought it degrading and felt ashamed of myself, I was obliged to accept. This was the first time I had received help from a woman. I thought it justified if it helped me survive, and I was sure that I would pay it back as soon as possible.

I went home, excited and eager for the next day's adventure. Haroutoun made me promise to write to him as soon as I was settled. I promised that I would send for him if I found any opportunity to help. We went to bed with the hope of tomorrow—a better tomorrow.

The next morning, he walked me to the railroad station. His job was to watch me and see how far I would be able to go; if anything went wrong, he would report to Miss Rohner. I said goodbye to him at the gate, and we parted.

I was told not to carry anything with me. I saluted the guard and passed a few steps toward the railroad tracks. Nobody saw me. Several more steps and still no one stopped me. I was all ears and eyes, waiting for someone to stop me. I found the spot where I was supposed to wait. The night mechanics were leaving, and the day workers were coming in. How long was I supposed to stand there? The minutes seemed like hours.

It was getting dangerous. I was the only civilian on the railroad track, standing by the switch. A line of boxcars started rolling toward me on my right, closer and closer. The first wagon passed me, then the second and a third. The switchman came to open the switch without paying any attention to me; then the cars started rolling back and forth from left to right. It felt as though a year had passed. I was scared. All I needed was for somebody to ask me who I was, and I would be arrested for sabotage of an army train. Then somebody started walking toward me with a calfskin hat like the railroad company employees wore. It was Rajah. He motioned me to stay where I was and disappeared. A mechanic came by, cut open the wires of the sliding doors on the boxcar, and told me to jump in. The door slid back, the man replaced the seal, and the car started rolling. I was inside, on the supply wagon, concealed and put away with sacks of flour, beans,

---

*Silver coins.

bulgur, chickpeas, and lentils. I didn't know which way we were going or where—I was just happy that we were going.

The train, with its wood-burning engine, moved slowly, barely thirty miles an hour. There were no windows or ventilation. A small beam of light came through a knothole in the boxcar paneling. It became my watchtower. I could see Aleppo's fruit orchards, mostly apricots, and the gardens full of lettuce passing by. The train rolled downhill, but when it started climbing again, the engine could not pull. The Turkish army didn't have coal to run the trains on this line, which transported supplies, ammunition, and troops to the fighting front.

For a moment I had a chilling feeling. This would be my very last chance. If this plan didn't work, it would be the end of all of my struggles. Yet, I clung to my vision and hope. Our progress was slow, and I was tired of lying on my belly. It was hard to sit up, let alone stand. Near noon, Rajah tapped on the wagon and whispered, "Are you hungry? After the next stop we will let you come out."

Rajah, an Armenian from Antep, concealed his identify by taking a Turkish name. His companion was Isaac, a thirty-year-old Jew. Both worked for the railroad company under Mr. Dedeian's jurisdiction. These two served as messengers and guards for the goods brought to the supply depot at Darbasia.

The train stopped. This was Ras ul-Ayn, a Turkish army headquarters and one of the most vicious centers of butchery against Armenians. The captain at the railroad depot had to screen all passengers for possible saboteurs heading for the battlefront. The guards checked each wagon, calling out that everything was okay. They passed my car—it was sealed and had a sign that read INSPECTED.

With the approval of the station captain, our train was off again, picking up speed as we rolled into the desert. Rajah rolled open the door at the end of the car and asked me to follow him to his compartment, where Isaac waited for us. He was an unattractive, skinny fellow with a sloppy mustache and dark skin. He smiled with the satisfaction of one who had outsmarted the rest and enjoyed seeing the young man whose safety was his business. They opened some food and a bottle of arrack.* Isaac,

*An alcoholic spirit made from the distilled juice of grapes, mulberries, or other fruits and often anise flavored.

celebrating his victory, turned to Rajah and, pointing at me, said, "He would make a good clerk, wouldn't he?" He saw that I was nervous and, in order to calm me down, he told me not to worry, that we had passed the worst checkpoint. "The commander of that station is a dog!" This gave me some hope and confidence and courage. At last, I could eat. A man, going from wagon to wagon, came to our compartment while we were eating. He greeted Isaac and Rajah, then asked who I was. Without hesitation, Rajah replied that I was an employee assigned to him for the Darbasia office.

"Does he have his papers?" the man asked.

"Oh, no," Isaac chimed in with a positive tone. "They did not have his papers ready yet. That is why they told *us* to take him along."

"This story is very interesting," said the inspector, "but I am the one who is responsible for this line. Being your friend, I will stop this train so that you can get rid of him, and I'll be free of my troubles. Let him off as soon as I stop the train." And he left us.

Shortly after, the train stopped. Rajah's face was ashen, and I shook. We were in the middle of the desert, miles from anywhere, but surrounded by robbing and murderous barbarians. These Arabs would shoot me for the fun of it. Isaac and Rajah looked at each other and pretended that they were still eating. The train started again, the engine huffing and coughing, and the investigator came back and angrily demanded an explanation. Isaac, softly, and with a friendly gesture, told him that he, too, was working for the railroad company and that his job was for the security and the safety of this boy. "He is my responsibility, you know, Inspector," he said.

The inspector said that if I were discovered without my papers, I would be shot. Isaac replied that he didn't want anything like that to happen to me. "Let us look for a solution."

He invited the inspector to join them in their meal and offered him a small container of the milky booze. The man hesitated; he did not want to come in and drink with us, yet he did not want to turn Isaac down either. He took the drink. Rajah nodded to me to come inside and asked me for the silver majidias. I had six concealed in my pocket, and I carefully placed them in his palm. He turned to the inspector, who left our compartment shortly afterward.

The three of us took a deep breath. Isaac gave me a broad, victorious smile. Now I had a friend, and I relaxed. We started talking about the railroad company because I wanted to know more about where we were headed. I could imagine how isolated it would be in the Mesopotamian desert. A strange thought came to me: Why was I always running away?

Centuries ago, man ran from the wilderness and the beasts to the cities, which gave shelter and protection. Now I was running away from civilization. Society puts a tag on you, calls you a refugee, an undesirable, and sets you apart. You are chased, hunted; your survival is a gamble. Yet you have done no wrong. You were taught to be a good citizen, you had a good family, which helped build and maintain your community. You were on your way to becoming educated in order to better that society. You fully understood your obligations and responsibilities to your countrymen. Why then are you rejected?

Things were turned upside down. Wrong became right, and good turned to bad. Such change is brought about by the warmongers. Crime is justified under the shadow of darkness, prejudice and hatred reign, and the devil will take care of the rest. All hell is let loose, and the cry of children becomes "music" to the ears of the warlords; running blood becomes the "sweet wine" of intoxication.

These thoughts kept me awake and restless during the night. I thought of Isaac, who didn't leave me in the middle of the desert, and his soft smile. I would be dead if it were not for him. I have wondered whether survival is worth that much. But my young heart told me that it was fun just to be alive, and to my surprise nobody bothered me anymore, and each time I looked at Isaac, he gave me that soft smile—the satisfaction of having had the wits to outsmart the inspector and save at least one young life. We shared the deep understanding that in helping me he did his share in righting the wrong.

Morning came, and the sun was up; the desert air was cool and fresh. Rajah and Isaac prepared for the next stop—Darbasia. They told me to stay inside the wagon until my friend from the office contacted me. Before the train stopped, Rajah jumped off and ran to the depot office. I was shaking like a kidnapped child in a strange land. I stretched my neck to look out and saw the commander of the station giving orders to search everyone who got off the train.

I saw Mr. Dedeian with a group of people coming toward my wagon. He saluted me as a man of importance and welcomed me. He was talking very loudly, ordering his helpers to carry my belongings, even though I had none. Acting as the head of the welcoming committee, he shook my hand

and asked me if I had a comfortable trip, apologizing in case the journey had not been comfortable. Speaking loud enough for the commander a few cars away to hear, he continued, "I am glad that you have arrived. We have been waiting for you." Then he held my arm and led me to his office and locked the doors. He whispered, "Your name is Habib Georgi. You were born in Aleppo in the Akaba District. If the commander ever visits you, you are employed by the railroad company. I will see if the chief engineer will be kind enough to listen to me."

The chief engineer, Dr. Hoffman, listened to the story that his brother-in-law had come unexpectedly, and he needed me very badly as trusted help. While he was gone, the station commander came to welcome me. When asked my name, I replied, "My name, sir, is Habib Georgi." Although Mr. Dedeian was an Armenian himself, he was an important man employed by the railroad company. The commander of the station could not offend such a man, so he politely explained that this was a matter of a friendly visit to welcome me and compliment me for my good Turkish, which was unusual for a Syrian boy.

"Of course," I replied, "I went to school just to learn Turkish." This would explain why I was employed by this office.

He left me, very friendly, but I do not think he was satisfied with my answers. Yet, for reasons of his own, he continued to salute me politely every time we met.

Prisoners of War

I was instructed to socialize with no one, not even at work, and especially not outside the office. The next day the workers put up a white canvas tent for me between the office and a bakery next door. I was proud of my new assignment in the bakery. This shop produced the daily bread for workers, prisoners of war, laborers on the railroad, and officials. There were prisoners from Russia, England, and many from India. It seemed that most of them still wore the clothes they were captured in. Some were Kurd refugees from the Russian border.[1]

My job was to give each worker his weekly ration and a daily loaf of bread. Sometimes we would supply the German officials with steak; the leftover meat went to the workers and prisoners of war. The Hindus got a live goat for each group. The Hindus insisted on baking their own bread with flour that we supplied them.

At noon, I would take a horse-drawn wagon loaded with sacks of bread to the workers on the railroad line, call their names from my list, mark their daily work, and hand them their loaf of bread. A young man in his midtwenties helped me pass around the bread to these hungry people. He looked like either a Kurd or an army escapee. His red beard made him look older and uglier, which is why they called him Sakally (bearded). Without him, I would have been mobbed by these people, which is why I never left the wagon. He was very nice and friendly and wanted to talk with me, but Mr. Dedeian and his right-hand man had warned me never to engage in a conversation with strangers.

A few days after my arrival, Dr. Hoffman, the chief engineer, came to see me. He spoke in hesitant Turkish, although he knew that I spoke English, too. He wanted to put me in charge of about twenty English prisoners of war who would supply wood for the train crews day and night. Mr. Dedeian told me that I had impressed the chief engineer.

The most unusual person I ever met was Haji. He was forty-five years old when he took the job with the German railroad company. Born in Diarbakir, he had always lived in Aleppo. They called him Haji,* as they did all who had visited Jerusalem. He had the tender heart of a child, but could be mean and tricky. He would warn me against all contacts. In this desert haven were secret army agents who spied all over the territory.

"You're lucky that you are not an Armenian," he said, winking at me. "I am also a Syrian from Aleppo!" But at night, when we were alone in the storeroom and the doors were locked, we would speak Armenian, very soft and low. And when we heard the steps of the night watchman, we would start giving orders in Turkish. Mr. Dedeian spoke Armenian well, although his mother tongue was Turkish, because Turkish is spoken all over his state of Marash, just northwest of Aleppo. Haji spoke Armenian well and enjoyed it, often teasing Mr. Dedeian that "your Armenian sounds Turkish." Mr. Dedeian spoke English fluently, as well as French, because he had gone to an American college. Soon he started conversing in German to please Dr. Hoffman and other German officials.

---

*Term of honor given to anyone who makes a religious pilgrimage—Mecca for Muslims and Jerusalem for Christians.

Two workers were in the storeroom, husky laborers. They were friendly and called me Habib-effendi. I thought they were doing this to please the boss, Mr. Dedeian, whose brother-in-law I was supposed to be. One of these workers was in his late forties and was called Mahmad. The other, Ali, was about the same age. I thought they might be Kurds.

What thrilled me most was Haji's dog, red-haired and of no special breed, but a thoughtful and studious listener of his master's voice. Each morning he would come to the storeroom with Haji, who would talk to him loudly as if he were talking to anyone who was nearby. The dog would listen carefully until Haji's voice changed, and then he would bark. Often, he would place his chin between his two paws, his ears hanging down. At a signal from Haji, he would growl. I didn't understand this at first, until one day I heard him lecture.

"Listen, you are a spoiled dog; you think you own everything. One day the war will be over, and I may have to abandon you and leave you forever to the Arabs. You would be a nobody! They will shoot you because you are a nobody and do not count anymore. They do not know Haji and couldn't care less for a dog."

I saw the army commander passing by and listening to Haji talking to his dog. Haji smiled at the officer as if his words were meant for him.

Haji had many characteristics of a real Middle Easterner. He was short and energetic; bright, witty, and fast in speech and work. He was polite, but arrogant; full of smiles, yet very melancholy; easy to communicate with and cautious with his answers. He was in full control of his emotions, but, above all, he had a tender heart—that was his weakness. He told me not to worry about the boss's anger because he had many duties to perform. The head office had put more responsibilities on one man than a man could handle—especially the rationing and flow of supplies—and he was an intense man. Haji, Mr. Dedeian's right-hand man, supervised the warehouse and the workers there. They respected him, and loved him, and were afraid of him, for he was sweet, friendly, and dangerous. Everybody needed a friend like him.

One night, Sakally, my red-bearded assistant, and Haji disappeared but reappeared at work the next morning. I heard Haji whisper to Mr. Dedeian, "We had a close escape." I learned that at night they went into Mardin, the small city about ten miles away. They came back on horseback, dressed like Arab sheiks.

By now I had made a few friends among the English prisoners. They were half-starved and wore their summer uniforms in the cold winter.

We swept the floor each morning after we gave rations to the workers the previous night. I would sweep up chickpeas, lentils, and a few grains of peas or beans, for which the children of Kurdish deportees would wait outside. They would jump at the grains and pick them up, carefully putting them in their ragged pockets to take home. At first, I would get angry, but I began to like the game so much that the children soon discovered their crop was especially bountiful if I did the sweeping. Everyone was half-starved. The young children who received only half a loaf of bread a day suffered the most. But Haji's friends were well fed. He would order the butcher to provide part of a lamb, and somehow, from out of a clear blue sky, he would manage to find fresh vegetables and, proudly and artistically, he would make the best stew one could imagine and order the bakery boys to take care of the food.

One late afternoon, Sakally and I were on our way to feed the workers. Women and children were piling rocks on the roadbed so that the Indian prisoners of war could carry tracks to be laid along the bed. Sakally, without stopping the wagon, spoke to me in Armenian. I pretended not to understand him because I thought he might be tricking me.

He turned to me. "Habib, let's get acquainted. My name is Armen and I'm from Zeytun. What is your name? I am sure that you are as good an Armenian as I am."

"What do you want to know?" I replied. He said, "I'm a friend and I want you to be one too." And he shook my hand. "I suspected that you were an Armenian. You know something else? Mahmad is not a Kurd but a runaway from Van, and so is Ahmad—didn't you notice how they enjoyed having you here?"

Then he told me his own story of how he had run away during deportation, escaped on the way from Der el-Zor, grew a beard, became "a Kurd," and now was a coworker at night to spy and locate Armenian children in harems and elsewhere in Turkish homes. That is why he and Haji often disappeared during the night. They were kidnapping deported Armenian women and children and bringing them back to camp. Sakally acted as a servant. They were quite successful, tracing information, bribing officials, and snatching girls and women but seldom boys. The next day there would be newcomers in the camp, but nobody knew about them except for Haji, who would secretly take them to the nearby army hospital supervised by Dr. Herashdagian.

One day Sakally told me that he had been to Mardin again, where he learned that one of his neighbor's daughters from Zeytun had run away to the city. He brought her to his own tent and, for security, told everybody that he had found his wife. But he told me how hard it was to have this attractive nineteen-year-old under his protection and not be able to marry her. To be sure, he would not take advantage of her. Yet she had to sleep in the same tent next to him. "I have a tough problem," he told me. "I cannot marry her, yet I have to protect her. She is not protected unless she is my wife."

I have seldom met a person with such a high moral code, and he was only twenty-three years old. He would consult with me and talk with me about his anguish; finally, he and the girl agreed to call each other husband and wife. Later, he told his story to Dr. Hoffman, and the girl was taken into the hospital as a nurse. Often, he would tell me with a smile that he was going to visit his "wife." When we were on our noon trip one afternoon, checking the laborers and giving them their daily bread, Sakally asked me if I had seen a man in the captain's tent by the name of Mousa. "Yes," I told him. "I was wondering how the captain was allowed to have a personal tailor at company expense." Mousa's real name was Armenag. Every time I entered into the tent, he would stand up, salute me respectfully, and call me "Sir." This unusual formality bothered me. The men were all older than I, but because I was from headquarters, I was supposed to be a person of power and decision.

On our way to camp, Sakally explained to me that Mousa, one of the active members of Tashnag (party),* had been deported from Constantinople but had somehow survived. As a discharged army man, he got a job as the captain's personal tailor. A week after, I had a uniform made for me from a surplus German uniform. He made me an old gray coat and a hat from dark brown calf; I was a regularly uniformed railroad man.

One day, I stepped from the wagon to make sure that I had the right names in my book. I asked the foreman, a Kurd, to let them give me their own names, while Sakally handed them a loaf of bread. At the end of the line was a girl in rags, about sixteen, who approached me blushingly and

---

*See chapter 2, note 6.

gave me her name. When she reached for the bread, her olive skin was exposed. So young, yet she had to carry a basket of rocks to continue her survival. Her foreman noticed my attention and asked me smilingly, "Anything that I can do for you, I will do, Habib-effendi." He woke me up. Whose fault was it that this little girl suffered such punishment? Some blamed the Russians. Most were told that the Armenians had brought this trouble upon themselves, and so on. Crime has no father; it is always someone else's responsibility.

Nilson, a prisoner working for the chief engineer's office, would speak to me each time he came for his ration. One day I asked him to visit my tent. When he came that evening, we had tea, and he told me about the mishaps near Baghdad under General Townshend's command. The food never reached the British military while they were surrounded by the Turkish army. Finally, they surrendered—about forty-five thousand of them—mostly Indians.[2] After that evening, Nilson would cautiously slip into my tent, and we would exchange the strange stories of our lives. I grew fond of him, and we promised to correspond when the war ended. I was cut off from all papers and books, and I practiced my English with him—he was my dictionary and instructor. One night, however, I heard the slow footsteps of the night guard close by my tent. I cautioned Nilson to stop his visits.

One day I visited the tents of the English boys. They had a small fireplace outside, and I saw black, burned grains dumped nearby. I asked what it was, and one of the boys said with a smile, "That stuff you gave us to cook, we burned it and made coffee." That was wheat bulgur for pilaf. Now I knew that they were hungry, but what could I do? They were prisoners of war, and I couldn't be too friendly. Yet we Armenians respected and loved the British and considered them our next-best allies. Now I realized why Haji had warned me, "Make no friends; you will get in trouble if you do." These people were hungry and cold, some were only skin and bones, and they were all hardly twenty years old. The British army had picked these schoolboys and sent them to the front lines to starve, sicken, and die.

One day, some British prisoners under my jurisdiction and supervision approached me with a complaint that their rations were insufficient and asked if I could do something for them. Later, they discovered that I had upped their daily ration for twenty-four people to twenty-six or more loaves of bread. This continued until one day Haji asked me if my counting was wrong. He came and dumped the bag on the floor and then, after counting out twenty-four loaves, left several lonesome loaves of bread on the floor. I was called upon to explain things to Mr. Dedeian. He said he was sure that I was not doing it for personal gain, but only out of sympathy; nevertheless, he reminded me that he was responsible for any shortages. He asked me to please stop.

Our camp did not have a food store. You could not buy extra bread unless you were employed by the railroad, and then your ration was only one loaf of bread a day, and the one loaf or any extra was charged against your earnings, five piasters a day, survive or not. I never forgave Haji for what he had done to the starving British prisoners, but I knew, too, that he was doing his job. The boys did not get any extra bread from me after that. Nevertheless, many half-loaves and quarter-loaves were unaccounted for.

Nilson asked me if it were possible to talk to me some evening, alone. I told him to come late, to make sure it was safe. I would wait outside the tent; he should not come in unless he saw me there. Sakally stood guard for me when Nilson entered my tent. He told me that a few of the English boys had made a secret contact in Mardin who promised safe delivery of each English boy back to the front. They guaranteed their contact through Arabs, assuming that the English army would reward them behind the lines. I tried to explain the dangers of traveling—the possibility of capture, the duplicity of the underground agents. It would be wonderful if they could reach their destination, I told him, but I reminded him, too, that we had no idea how far we were from the fighting zone, and this increased the danger of double spies. If it were so easy, I said, I would be the first to run away. "Please tell them not even to try." He promised to deliver my message to the boys. I knew them, and they knew where the message came from.

Winter came, and many POWs got sick. The clothing promised by the American Red Cross by way of Aleppo never reached them; the wagon had caught fire on the way, and soon Turkish officers wore British army shoes.

"Please, Look Up!"

At noon the boys from the bakery would bring us our dinner, prepared by Haji. He loved to fuss and take his time to prepare it. We loved him for assuming such responsibilities and carrying them out so well. If the boys failed to follow his instructions, he would raise hell; they wanted to please him more than the top boss, Mr. Dedeian.

One day, as usual, we closed the shop to have our dinner. The dinner came from the bakery, hot and sizzling, a lamb rib and part of the neck, broiled, with fresh tomatoes and onions on the side. We were ready to start and asked the help to call in Haji. He and Mr. Dedeian had a habit of gulping down a milky drink before dinner—I never tasted it, for I had learned about the evils of drink from Proverbs. Mr. Dedeian shouted loudly, "We are waiting for you, Haji. Come to the table!" Slowly, he came to the room, guilty that he was late, but he refused to touch the food, and he begged Mr. Dedeian to excuse him. Haji was always a good eater and loved eating. And it was our luck that he did.

"What's the matter, now?" Mr. Dedeian asked angrily. Haji, who had traveled and learned much from the world, pulled out a handkerchief from his pocket and wiped his eyes like a child.

"A year ago, I was employed by the railroad company to lead a German engineer to investigate proper locations for planning railroad lines. I was asked to lead him on the Euphrates by rowboat. A man was assigned to us to row the boat while I directed him. The German engineer would mark on his book the names of places and destinations from the river side or any village nearby.

"It was late August [1916] when we started our trip, and we were isolated for many months.[3] I did not know what was going on outside, but the river brought clues—dead bodies interfered with our progress. I noticed that the German officer was not annoyed by all this; something made me uncomfortable. I asked the man to row the boat to the center of the river so that we would stop hitting the corpses with the oars, which made me sick. Finally, I could not look at the bodies floating by anymore.

"Suddenly, a woman's sharp voice rent the silence and echoed back to the river. A woman in tatters, holding a child tightly to her bosom, was running toward the river. She saw us, and encouraged by uniformed Germans, cried out for help. I asked the man to stop rowing when the woman came closer to us. I noticed that two Arabs were running after her. Then the woman called once more, 'Alaman!' ('Help, please help!')*

---

*"Alaman" probably means "German" here and refers to the officer wearing a German uniform.

I told the officer what the woman was running from and that she was asking for our help, and I asked him if we could stop, adding also that she must be an Armenian refugee.

"He ignored my plea and turned his face so that he could not see her, and ordered the man to proceed rowing. The Arabs noticed that we were not interested in the woman with the child. The woman rushed to the riverside crying out, 'Alaman! Alaman!' and crying again: 'Look up, look up!' Pointing to the sky, asking us to look up to God. While we were following her motion to look up, she jumped into the river with her child grasped tightly to her bosom. The water got muddy and slowly swallowed mother and child. The officer gave orders for us to proceed on our way, as if nothing had happened."

Haji said that he could not forget that day. This was the anniversary of the event. "Excuse me, please," he said, "I must go now," and he retired to his tent to be alone with his memory of the tragedy he could not erase from his mind. We could hear him sobbing for a long time.

The winter months came and with them Mr. Dedeian's family—Esther and the two girls—because they were not comfortable in the large city. Our way of life changed. Haji and I used to be together, but now he served the family. Mrs. Dedeian would send us our dinner, still prepared by Haji. Cold evenings and nights were long and slow because we didn't have anything to read or do. I used to go to the station telegraph office to learn the codes and tried to read some messages because the man in the office was also Armenian. By now, it was an open secret that I was an Armenian. Nilson stopped visiting me altogether because he suspected that the guards were watching both of us at night. In the middle of the night, Sakally would bring fire from the bakery to warm my tent on his way home from work. Because I was young and delicate, I became a favorite. They all wanted to help make life a little easier for the boy who was deprived of his home and family.

One night, about midnight, I went to the telegraph office to see why the train was delayed, or if they knew when it was due. The man couldn't tell me, so I went back and fell asleep. Then I heard someone scratching at my tent. The night guard was calling my name and telling me the big boss was angry and was looking for me. "The train has come. . . ." I rushed to the nearby tent to wake the English prisoners and get them to help me load the wood, and then rushed back to the station to face the enraged officer.

The British do not respond well in emergencies, particularly when they are prisoners of war. But I thought I could sway them; that they would help me pacify Dr. Hoffman, who was pouring out mad German words. I rushed the poor boys, who were half asleep, hungry, and cold, to the station. The train was waiting for us. Dr. Hoffman accused me of neglecting my duties by German army standards. Next morning, he called me to his office and gave me more abuse. I was humiliated, degraded, and insulted. I went to the British prisoners, explaining to them that if they had been a little faster the evening before, the officers would not have humiliated me so. They responded with anger and disappointment, and said they didn't give a damn if the whole train was loaded with Germans and went straight to hell!

At work I played the part of the disciplined soldier. The prisoners didn't know that my heart bled for them. They didn't realize that my sympathy for them made me unpopular in the office.

Shortly after the episode of the late train, on my way to the bakery one morning, Esther stopped me. She said that she wanted to talk to me soon. She came back to me in a hurry and told me things that made no sense to me. Finally, she said that I had better leave, that was the advice of Mrs. Dedeian, who had secured this job for me. I told Mr. Dedeian I wanted to leave and asked him if there were any jobs farther up the line. He replied coldly, as all big bosses do, "I will take care of that. When are you leaving?" The train did not arrive that morning, so I talked to Sakally about my plans. He did not want me to leave. We shook hands and bid each other goodbye. I managed to see Nilson, too. He gave me his London address, and we promised to write to each other in better times. Haji pretended to be sorry for my leaving, but I am sure that he was not. I saw Mr. Dedeian in the store, and he said sarcastically, "I thought that you were leaving." I told him that I was waiting for the train. He said, "Make sure that it is the only reason you are waiting."

I went to my tent, put on my company uniform, collected my notes in a hurry, putting them under my shirt, and took the road that followed the track and the telephone poles toward the east. I was told that the distance between Darbasia and the next station was only thirty or so miles. I thought that I could make that easily, and besides, if the train passed by me, I could easily jump on. But I was wrong on both counts. Noon came, and I still had a lot of energy because I was still angry. But I had forgotten to bring anything to eat with me; and in the desert, you do not easily find things to eat or drink.

I wondered what had happened to this land. Once it had been the cradle of civilization, the food basket for many nations. Not a soul remained except a few barbarians who burned the land, killed the population, ruined the temples, and enslaved those left behind. The Ottoman Turks took over and victimized the populace until the land became empty; even the animals left. The Turks continued to do so because nobody ever asked them not to or tried to stop them. Now they call this land a desert.

Two Indian prisoners of war and a German officer on a handcar passed by me on the railroad track in a two-man hand-pump car. The officer seemed to be enjoying the ride. They did not seem to expect a train that day. A dull, uncomfortable feeling plagued me. If some Arabs happened to pass by before I could say "Salam," a bullet could easily stop me. No one would ever know what had happened to me; there would be no trace. *Is that all?* I asked myself. The past twenty years I had been struggling for a better life. Now I would be lucky if they shot me, for death was more painful when they saved their bullets.

Yet the sun was still shining, and the sky was a heavenly blue. The will to live coursed through my veins. One could be happy just being alive. I could not see how or why, but it felt good to be alive, just to be alive.

I was nearing a village that I had never heard of. A few peasant women were pulling water from a well. I acted as if I were checking the railroad line and making marks in my book, paying no attention to anyone. My uniform identified me as a company man, which saved me. I could have stopped for a drink of water, but I decided against it. I kept walking along the line, pretending to be checking the defects of the railroad tracks.

I found myself asking, *What is the purpose of life? Who put us on this earth? Where is He now?* All of a sudden, I thought of my father. He had so many good reasons to be alive in this world. Poor Father, if he only knew that, most likely, within a few hours his son would not be alive either. What a waste! You should have taught me to be aggressive, Father, so that I might get what I wanted and not look so pitiful, so helpless, so hopeless. My steps quickened. I saw that the sun was now behind me.

I bent down to listen to the railroad track. There was no vibration. A German army airplane passed overhead, toward Darbasia. I felt my hat getting heavier on my head. Then I remembered Mousa, who carefully had made it for me. Was he really an active revolutionary Tashnag? How had he escaped? Would he be able to survive? Many thought that the revolutionaries had caused the deportation. They did not know that the revolutionary parties were only being used as an alibi. The fact is that the Turks had sold us to the German government, and they decided our destiny. Young Turks were desperate for power. They jumped in to join the Central Powers and, before they knew it, they were involved in World War I. The Germans, sure of their success, wanted weak allies for their expansion, and they wanted the country without the Armenians. Why? Only politicians and the generals could give the answers.[4]

My mind drifted to Sakally. Who was he, this man so strong in body and in character that he would sacrifice anything to uphold his principles? Was he being honest when he said that he loved the girl but wouldn't marry her because it seemed to him that he would have been marrying her under duress? I wondered if I would ever see him again. I was sure that I would never meet anyone like him again.

The desert is a wonderful place in which to think. Nothing interferes with your thoughts, and when you hear your own voice, it is because of loneliness. You start thinking and talking and walking, always following the telegraph poles or the railroad tracks, the only thread that links you with humanity. Evening came, a welcome relief from the broad daylight. The thirty-five miles stretched far; it seemed as though I had traveled forty miles already. Track points gave me no clue to the next station. Then I remembered why I happened to be there. Wasn't it foolish of me to have left comfort, freedom, and protection? But I had been forced into it. Mrs. Dedeian had asked me to leave, and that was like a command, because she was a friend. So was her husband, who did not object to my leaving and made not the slightest effort to keep me from going. What had happened? I did not know. I am sure it was not jealousy, for they seemed to have a lot of confidence in me and respected me. They were happy to know me. Had the times changed so much? Do people change with the times? We had always been good friends, and destiny had made me her brother. I remembered how once she had unwittingly remarked how very proud she was of her newfound brother, Habib. No? How can it be?

I was sure that Nilson had done nothing against me. Then I began thinking of my sister, Anoush. What would happen to her? She hadn't had much out of life, an orphan, and now she would be without a brother. I recalled the vows I had made to my mother. And I thought of my friends and my principal. "I am sure that someday we shall be proud of you when the evil times are passed," he had said. The Reverend had said, "I have invested in you my hopes for the future, that someday you will be a useful member of the new Armenia. I'm sure you will be, my son."

No trip in my life has been as educational as this one was in the strange land of a desert, walking, talking to myself, debating. I still could not see any sign of a station along the lonely road. To kill the monotony and the loneliness, I began singing, with all of the voice I could muster and all of the strength I had; I sang the Armenian national anthem. I could hear the band play and the steps of marching soldiers as in a parade; brave soldiers, marching for their country. But the band soon died away, and I was brought back to reality and the railroad track. I was tired and hungry and needed rest. I felt very thirsty and weak. I thought I had to be close to my destination. I sang, or rather whispered, "Nearer to Thee, my God, nearer to Thee." It gave me a boost, and I poured my heart out with the desire of being nearer to God. I stopped, exhausted. Is it possible that I was singing at my own funeral?

It got darker and darker, and my hopes faded, too. I forced myself to walk faster, but the power was gone. I tried to calm myself, but I became frightened of the dark, and the pervading loneliness enhanced the fright. I could do nothing but keep on walking, walking, walking, without apparent end. Then I heard a sound on the track. It didn't sound like a train, and when it came close, I saw two men pumping a handcar. I thought of motioning them to stop, but they could not see me in the dark. Miraculously, they slowed down, and before they reached me, as if a miracle, I heard a voice calling my name. Two Indian prisoners of war were returning from their trip. They stopped. I did not remember knowing them, but to my astonishment they recognized me. They placed me in the officer's seat and within half an hour we were at a railroad station.

The storeroom manager, who had worked for Mr. Dedeian in Darbasia, gave me shelter for the night. They told me that the train for Nissibin would arrive the following morning, and that there would be work farther up the line where they were extending the railroad tracks toward Baghdad. After dinner, my host took me into his office and gave me a few suggestions and some information in general, which he had collected through channels of his own, without revealing the sources. Once the army gave up hope of winning the war, they were determined at least to cover up their crimes. My host added, "If the war does not end very soon, we are all in danger of annihilation from the retreating Turkish army, and the Germans could not protect us as their employees. Once in a while, on an isolated hill, you could hear gunshots; a man would fall and be dumped in a ditch by the road. Thus, the Armenian nation would lose great poets, cultural leaders, journalists, teachers, preachers, physicians, great parliamentarians—the heart and soul of a nation, sons of Armenia." Indeed, this was not only a crime against one nation, but against humanity itself. "Don't worry," my host went on, "they know who we are."

Nissibin*

Isolated as we were, we were dependent on the grapevine for news. Most of it would be exaggerated or based on wishful thinking. "They are just looking for a chance to get rid of us. They still need us to operate the railroads. That's why you and I are still alive." The next morning when the train arrived, I had a valuable envelope in my pocket, addressed to the chief engineer of Nissibin, Mr. Pfalz. This served me as a pass on this new line of the railroad thinking, but the gossip always had some basis in reality, or at least some reasons behind it.

For example, we heard that the British Army was very close to the Dardanelles, the straits that connect the Aegean Sea to the Sea of Marmara and on to the Black Sea, and was about to enter Constantinople. This kept all Kurdish-looking Armenians happy. Prisoners of war were pleased. In fact, many of the Turkish soldiers who had defected were happy, too. Even those Turks still in the army hoped that the war would end soon. The country was weakened and exhausted, hospitals were full of the wounded, and many died from the epidemics.

The hills and mountains were full of desperadoes and deserters. Some would live day-to-day by robbing and killing. Others would join the Arab bands to destroy the railroads, but the Arabs and the Kurds did not really trust the soldiers unless they joined them with their army guns. Meanwhile,

---

*Also known as Nisibis, now Nusaybin, a town in southeastern Turkey, known as a major center of trade in antiquity from its strategic position on the upper trade routes from Mosul.

the legendary Lawrence of Arabia* was organizing the Arabs to revolt against the Turks.[5] The Turkish government, fearing defeat, instructed its governors to get rid of all Armenians, regardless of their status. Thus, they would do away with the last vestige of evidence against them.

Rasul ul-Ayn once more became a center of massacre, for the last Armenians from the nearby northern states were gathered there. The news indicated that about twenty thousand had been butchered.[6] The train was slow and monotonous, and time hung heavy because I was anxious to meet my friend Haroutoun, who was supposed to meet me there. Along the railroad track, I saw many groups of workers, mostly women and children, filling up small wagons with crushed rocks to be carted away. Men, mostly Indian prisoners of war, were crushing the rocks. The train had to stop in order to make way for the workers.

We arrived in Nissibin, just southeast of Mardin, in the late evening. I found that the headquarters were a mile away. By the time I walked there, the office had closed. I saw a young man leaving the building and asked him in Turkish if he knew Haroutoun; but instead of answering in Turkish, he asked in Armenian, "Are you Armenian?" I said that my name was Habib Georgi. He told me to follow him and led me to the tent of one of my most faithful friends.

Haroutoun was surprised and received me as Armenians do. He hugged me and kissed me on the cheek. He asked me to sit, offered me some food left over from lunch, and introduced me to the friend who shared his tent. We talked all night, as he had much news to give me. He was not sure whether I would get a job right away, but he said that I should try. He told me that his office manager was also an Armenian and promised to talk to him about me and try to get me a job.

He asked me to stay with him until I could see a way out. He told me not to worry, because he had enough food for the two of us. "I want you to be with me. We shouldn't be separated anymore, and whenever we see our way clear, we'll be together." Of course, we were planning to escape over the border to the British forces, but that opportunity never came. We stayed together, however, sharing our sorrows and problems, day by day. Life seemed a little easier now that I had a friend. He fixed a bed for me in

---

*Thomas Edward Lawrence (1888–1935), an English dramatic writer and legendary spy-diplomat who played a key role in Arab uprising against the Turks during the First World War.

his one-man tent, in which I was now a third man. He had not asked his friend's permission but reminded him that I was a close friend and added that I would stay for a while.

"How do you do, Mr. Habib?" I had said that my name was Habib Georgi to be sure that he would remember it.

The following morning, I went to see the head engineer but talked instead to his secretary, Mr. Melik. He told me that there were no openings just then, but that there might be later on. By the time I returned to the tent, Haroutoun already had gone to work. I was safe only if I stayed indoors because the Turkish army controlled the labor camp and knew all who were engaged with the railroad. Everyone had a verification card and papers to identify himself in his job, his status, and the office he worked for. Thus, the army easily would spot a newcomer. I had no papers to identify me with the office.

When Haroutoun returned, I told him what the secretary had said. "You can't do better than that," he told me. "I'm sure he will help you if he can; he's a native of Aleppo and an Armenian."

In the meantime, he had talked to Mihran, the head of the supply department, regarding a job. Mihran apologized for not having an opening and said he hoped that a job would become available soon. But Haroutoun and I feared that the army officers would spot me and that I would be called into the commander's office to explain what I was doing in the army-controlled barracks without an identification card.

The commanding officer's name was Shoukry Bay, and his coordinating officer was Sulaimine. At first glance, you could see that Shoukry liked trouble. He would insult you if he did not like you, and he liked no one. He was polite only to German officials.

Sulaimine, a middle-aged man, was milder and very polite but not congenial. In fact, his politeness seemed to demand something from you. For example, the supply depot official was Armenian, and Sulaimine was polite to him, for he knew that he could use him and his workers.

Haroutoun and I agreed on the advantages of going southeast toward Mousul (Mosul),* where new labor forces were assembling. A contractor was looking for all kinds of help—both labor and clerical—to organize the

---

*Mosul, the modern capital of Nineveh province in northwestern Iraq. From 1534 to 1918, the Ottomans ruled the region as a trade center and political subdivision.

force. A man was leaving the next day with an oxcart of tools for the work-men, midway between Nissibin* and Mousul. I agreed to go, for this would give me an identification card and free me from harassment by the gen-darmes and MPs. More important, I could lose myself in the city of Mousul, and I would be closer to the Persian border. I welcomed the adventure.

The next morning, I met the contractor, who explained to me that this was a new project, and it might provide me with a better job than the one I had been promised. The oxcart led the caravan down a dusty road. The village of Nissibin disappeared from sight. Once again, we were isolated in the desert, following the sun and dust. We saw a few people work-ing to ready the tracks for the railroad tracks. Our caravan leader was a rude, coarse man with a dark, wrinkled face. His Turkish was common. He told me how foolish it was for me to make this trip, because I was not built for the place, not meant to work in the weary desert, rife with disease and malaria.

"You can't help it; it goes with the land. The swamps are very close to where the mosquitoes nest, and they attack you like an army; then you have to watch out for yourself. By the way, who are you?"

When I told him who I was and why I needed a job, he said that he almost thought I was an Armenian. So, we became more communicative. We stopped for lunch on the roadside. He let me join him and shared his water from a goatskin bag. Food is essential for your body, but water in the desert is an absolute; you cannot do without it. It is the main source of vitality because the dust makes your throat dry in no time, and the clumsy steps of the oxen made the steps more unbearable. You quickly tire of the slow progress. At long last evening came, and we stopped. The man with the rough voice and the coarse accent gave me some rags with which to cover myself. "During the night you might need them," he said, and he let me shelter myself near his wagon.

I tried to close my eyes, very much in need of sleep. But as soon as I shut my eyes, the mosquitoes started buzzing like a swarm of wasps. They swooped in and around from their nests near the oily swamps. Thousands of them. The sound was strong and annoying, and their sting so constant

---

*Now Nusaybin, a town in southeastern Turkey, known as a major center of trade in antiquity from its strategic position on the upper trade routes from Mosul.

and irritating that I could not rest. It was torture. I pulled the dirty, smelly rags over my head to protect myself from their attack.

When morning came, everyone was getting ready to continue the trip. I was so tired I didn't have the ambition to move. Laughing, the cart driver asked, "They got you, didn't they?"

I was so weak and sick from the mosquito attacks, I did not know what to do. I could not continue my trip, yet I could not stay either, for I would starve or die of thirst. The man was kind enough to suggest that I ride with them on the oxcart. My head felt heavy, and I could hardly drag one leg after the other. I did not want to ride because I knew how much he valued his oxen. He depended on them to transport men back and forth for the railroad company near Mousul.

I thought that the evening's rest would do me some good, but the next morning I had a high temperature and was helplessly sick with malaria. I was thirsty all the time, but I had no water to quench my thirst. Then I had a fever and a chill. While everybody else was going to his assigned job, I could not even move. At noon, the leader came to me and said, "You had better go back to where you came from. You are sick! Sick! Do you understand? I will take you. I told you this was not your dish." To prove that he was right and he was satisfied, he promised to take me back without charge.

I don't know how many hours later I was told that we had arrived back in Nissibin. I had slept most of the trip and dreamed of the cool brook at home that had run day and night, singing soft music as it meandered from the hills above into our yard. The cart stopped, and I thanked the man who looked like a darkness angel. I saw a faint smile on his face as he disappeared with his cart, raising more dust clouds as he went on his way.

I had a hard time walking. I took it step-by-step until I reached the camp and Haroutoun, the only person in the whole world I could safely ask for a glass of water. When I arrived at his tent, he treated me like a long-lost brother and calmly whispered, "Do you know what's the matter with you? You are too independent. You didn't want to stay here. Now you are going to have to stay put. Besides, you have a fever, and I have to take care of you."

We both held deep and conflicting convictions. Haroutoun was conservative and deeply nationalistic. To him, members of the Protestant Church were not Armenians: "They live in a shell, wrapped up in dogmas." Nothing could be expected of them as Armenians. The only way to be a good Armenian was to have no ties binding you. Yet he cared for me because many years ago we had been students at the Armenian National Church School in Gurun. And later we worked and lived together in Aleppo. He often reminded me that I was different from the average Protestant because I could converse with him about Armenian literature.

Our views were far apart, but we were close to each other, as close as any friends can be—and he was hard to get close to. He was slow moving; each step he took was measured and calculated so that he would not make a mistake. He was slow to laugh, hard to persuade, but he was honest and sincere, as well as stubborn. We would argue about religion, and only on rare occasions would he blame the church for the suffering of the Armenian people. He would say that the church should not have told us to surrender our guns. We would have been much better off if we had fought with guns and ammunition; instead, we surrendered like lambs being led to the slaughter. On the other hand, Bishop Timaksian, who delivered a message from the Catholics, expressed his sentiments but gave the people a chance to decide for themselves.

George, who shared his tent, had nothing in common with Haroutoun. George was a Roman Catholic from Kharput. Rome offered salvation, and Rome could do no wrong. Sometimes it drove me mad to hear him carry on. I thought that the whole tent stank from the stale atmosphere, and I often found myself attacking him with Protestant ammunition. Pleading with me, he would say, "Brother Habib, I have nothing to say to you, but I'll pray for you."

Haroutoun tried hard to get some quinine for my malarial fever but all in vain. They did not sell it, and they did not have any. Often, I would turn from red hot to ice cold, from yellow to green. I could only drink tea without sugar. Haroutoun talked about me to Tossounian, a clerk in the office of the army commander. I knew him from Aleppo, and he brought me a few tablets of quinine he had managed to get somehow. Later he warned me of the dangers of being without papers. This army base had received daily orders to watch for those who did not have identification papers.

Haroutoun failed to get a job for me from his manager. Malaria had ruined my whole system. I was crippled between the fever and the chill. After a few days I dragged myself in and out of bed. I was wondering how different things would be if I had not taken that trip a couple of weeks before. Finally, one morning, I felt a little better; the fever had subsided somewhat. I could taste again. Haroutoun asked me how I felt. I had little strength in me, for the malaria had sapped nearly all of my energy.

Haroutoun knew a local contractor who had started some work around Nissibin for the railroad company. When I had regained my strength, he hired me. I had to walk back and forth, about five miles each way. Spring came and covered the hills with a fresh, young green. About two centuries before Christ, this city had been called Mutzpin (Mtsbin). It stood at the edge of the desert near the hills, a few miles southwest of the ancient city of Nineveh, and served as the capital of Greater Armenia for more than 150 years.* Now it was called Nissibin, and I was working on its railroad.

Walking and work helped my recovery, and I was content. Each morning I would cross a wheat field where the workers were. I would mark their daily work in my book and report it to the engineer's office. After a few weeks, Melik, the chief engineer's secretary, arranged a job for me. In the nearby mountains, about five hundred Indian prisoners were sent to build a small line from the hills to bring down wood for railway fuel. The engineer of the project had to travel out of the area, and I was assigned to supervise the job while he was away. I was to report the workers' progress, oversee the prisoners, and take care of the supplies and water under the protection of three army guards.[7]

At long last, my name was filed in the office of the commander of the camp, but he hesitated to sign it; I didn't know why. When I asked Tossounian what my chances were, he replied, "You can't push the commander. It is possible that he wants to see you in person. I saw your name in a file waiting for his signature."

Melik pressed the commander for his signature, and finally I was called in. I saluted the commander as a soldier should. A big mouth opened with a big shout demanding my name.

"Habib Georgi," I replied, and carefully answered each question with "Yes, sir." Something made me remove my hat all of a sudden. He shouted at me: it was against the regulations. I got so mixed up between the Eastern and Western ways of protocol that it didn't occur to me that he probably

---

*Mutzpin or Mtsbin was included in the kingdom of Tigran the Great for a time in the first century BCE but did not serve as the capital of Greater Armenia.

liked to yell, and that this was as good an excuse as any for doing so. For a moment I thought that I had lost grace; that it annoyed him to do something he didn't want to do. Later I found out that I should have brought him a gift acknowledging his generosity in putting his signature at the bottom of the paper.

"When are you going?" he hollered again.

"As soon as my papers are released from your office, sir," I said nobly, wondering whether my phrasing was wrong, too. He repeated, "What did you say your name was?"

Listening closely and watching each word I used in Turkish, I replied, "I beg your pardon, sir, you must excuse my poor Turkish." (It was not poor Turkish.) I emphasized the point that in Syria no one spoke Turkish well.

"We will send your papers tomorrow," he continued.

I thanked him and left the office, glad to leave such a silly interview and such a fuss. My papers did not arrive the next day, or the following day. Tossounian tried to push in his office to obtain the signature, reminding the commander that he expected me to get an important job after this project. "We may need him someday," implying that, although I could not pay for favors now, in the future I would be able to not only pay for them, but to do favors also.

When the papers (see figure 5.1[8]) were released, the engineer on the project took me with him several miles away from Nissibin. The train stopped, and on horseback we rode toward the mountains.

Mungesingh

The place in the mountains was isolated. Nobody ever would have expected to find men living there. The camp sat on the side of a hill, which led to the woods. The engineer made room in his tent for me and explained the plans of the work, to rush the wood supply to the main station. He told me that one of the guards was available in case of an emergency because we were totally cut off from any office by wire and train. He suggested that I keep a supply of fresh water and food and said that he would return in a few days.

The foreman of the Indian POW group was a tall, strong soldier in his thirties, dark and heavy. He proudly wore a khaki turban on his head. His long beard joined his long hair in a bun under his turban. Each morning,

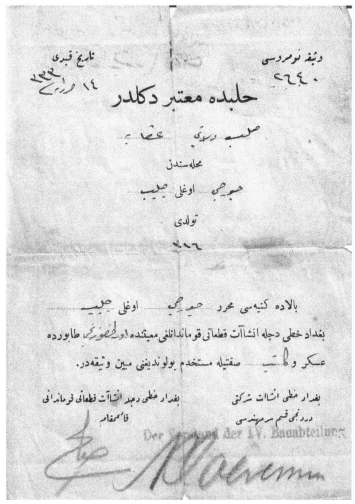

FIGURE 5.1
Minassian's Turkish/German Work Papers

we would talk about the day's assignment, keep a record of the sick, and make the rounds with the guards who took the prisoners of war to work. One of the guards would stay with me in the camp for protection.

When the engineer came back, he showed dissatisfaction with the pace of the wood supply. The operation was slowed down by the shaky lines and derailments, because the line had been made by untrained prisoners of war. The wagons derailed easily. I would hang around the camp and watch the people cooking and making bread, killing their goats, and getting together after dinner, lighting a cigarette and passing it around until they could not hold it anymore. They would not let anybody touch their water cups; instead, they would pour water into your palm from a cup. They used their rations sparingly, wisely, and without waste. In the morning, they would rearrange their hair, untouched by barber or scissor, wrap their long khaki turbans around their heads, and clean their pure white teeth with the charcoal left over from the night before, using their index fingers as a brush. If they were happy, they would sing in a soft voice, chanting, "O, Piyi, O Pache, Bombay, Baby, Both, Atcha," meaning, I learned, "O, Brother, O, Brother, Bombay girls are the prettiest."

One morning when the guard blew his whistle to get us ready for work, I came out of my tent to meet the group. I noticed that a few of them would not come out of their tents. I visited each of them. Some were only pretending to be sick, but others were suffering from fever. I saw a young man in his early twenties, pale and sick, sitting inside a tent. His head was held down between his legs; he was shaking from fever. I touched him and asked in English if he were ill. "Yes, Sahib," he said, "I have a fever."

I asked his foreman what the man's name was. He said Mungesingh. Knowing that if I excused him from work, everyone on the line would soon claim to be sick, I told his foreman to send the man to my tent to cook for me, and in a louder voice I said, "I need a cook," so that everyone could hear me. In my ration bag were only a few beans. The man raised his head and with pitiful, dark eyes, short of words in which to express himself, he bowed to me gracefully and went to my tent. I saw the guard watching while Mungesingh entered my tent. I whispered to the guard in Turkish that this boy was going to die very soon, and I suggested to him to take it easy with the boys because they were exhausted. The day was hot, and food and water were getting short. When I entered the tent, Mungesingh was curled up and could hardly breathe. I asked his foreman if he could wash the poor boy's face.

He said, "We hardly have enough water to drink." I went out and got some water from the guard and let the man wash his face and neck. Mungesingh remained pale and yellow, but he spent the night in my tent next to my cot on a piece of burlap.

Neighboring Arab tribes were giving us trouble, claiming that the railroad company was taking wood from their property. They even used guns to stop our workers. Arabs revolted against the Turkish government and sabotaged the railroad line.

One afternoon, two guards entered my tent and asked me if we could talk privately. I dismissed Mungesingh, but I told them that he did not understand Turkish anyway. One of the guards reminded me, "Those dirty pigs are not dependable." "This 'pig' is not dirty," I told him, "and they are very loyal if you are friendly with them."

I motioned that I was ready to listen. One guard took courage and told me that they were tired of their job, of working without pay. Food was scarce, and life was monotonous. Another added, "We know we can trust you." He stopped a moment, gathering his thoughts, and continued: "We are planning on joining the Arabs. They want us with our guns. If you join us, we will take you with us."

I pretended that I had not heard the last suggestion. I did not know how to take it anyway. So I played safe. This was a good opportunity, an adventure, I thought, but we were in a prisoner-of-war camp, and their safety was my duty. I thought a moment and finally told him, "You were sent here for a purpose. You have a duty to perform, and you are trusted with this job. Do you think that the Arabs love you? Do you know why they are asking you to join them? They want your guns, not you. Once you are there, they will be through with you. They will slit your throat, and that will be the end of you." Realizing the danger, I whispered, "Let's not whisper a word about this, and let's perform our duties." They left my tent and took with them a heavy burden. I was not prepared for their plan, and I did not want to be involved.

I had sent a messenger with a note to headquarters urging them to send us rations and drinking water. But the messenger had not returned, and the engineer who was supposed to be back had been absent for weeks. I was getting a lot of complaints about the food shortage and the guards' pressure on the prisoners. I tried to explain to their Indian leader that I, too, was waiting for the messenger to come back with rations. But I could not communicate very well with the prisoners' leader. He thought I was brushing him off. I noticed the resentment in his voice. He thought I was a more important man than I actually was. Every day I waited for the guard to come back with the rations, hoping it would dispel the tension. I noticed that the prisoners avoided me when I was around talking to workers or trying to calm them down. Most of the prisoners did not want to work, but their leader, to save face with me, convinced them to do so. But the work was slow, and the wood supply was getting short, regardless of my efforts.

On a Sunday morning, I heard a commotion. The head of the workers rushed to my tent, angry and almost shouting, "Did you order the gendarmes to beat my men?"

I came out of my tent and asked the guards why they were beating the prisoners. One of the guards said that they refused to work, so they were using their sticks to spur the prisoners on. I felt that it was to satisfy their ego, to show they were able to order prisoners. I called them to one side and, with a tone a soldier would understand, I reminded them of their purpose for being there and told them that they were complicating my work. It was getting harder and harder for me to make prisoners work, and added, "I am expecting the engineer very soon. We will receive food and water; in fact, if you want to be near the main station, I can arrange it for you." They were happy with the prospect of a transfer. They made the rounds of the camp, then left the workers alone. The leader of the Indian prisoners came to me and said, "Now it is your problem and your responsibility to make the men work. I cannot do anything with them anymore. They will not listen to me."

I asked Mungesingh to tell the guards that I wanted to see them. Then I asked him to leave us alone, but I noticed his shadow on the outside of the tent and knew that he wanted to know what I told the guards. He could not understand Turkish, so I was free. I made my Turkish as plain as I could, so that if Mungesingh could understand any, he would understand my reason for calling the guards. I told them repeatedly that soon the engineer would arrive, and we would have plenty of food, and I instructed them not to use the sticks anymore.

"Now I want you to go out without your sticks. Your guns will be enough for your duty." I called in the head of the prisoners of war and told him that it was better for them to start working as much as they could in order to prevent the guards from using extreme measures. He told me that it was against the law to beat a prisoner of war. Poor man, I could have told him that a lot of things were against the law, but we were cut off from the world. Instead, I told him that it was up to him, but that his cooperation would make it easier for me to make a good report.

Then the prisoners pretended that they were working, and the guards and I pretended that we were not watching. When evening came and darkness fell, Mungesingh had our lentil soup ready, each in a separate bowl. He bowed his head and in a very low voice told me how his countrymen felt about me, emphasizing the word "bad." In a plain, short sentence, he told me that when they talk like this, they are dangerous. I asked him what he was suggesting. He said, "You should leave the camp tonight."

When I told him that I did not know the road, he said that he knew the road to the station and would come with me. But it was not that simple. Prisoners of war, after midnight, had no business being outside of camp, and I did not have any business being out late with them, and what about the guards? Wouldn't they join the Arabs as they wanted to? And wouldn't the prisoners' lives be in danger? The more I thought about it, the more complicated it became, but I decided to take a chance. I told Mungesingh to slip away, to avoid the guards, and that I would follow. He went toward the telegraph poles in the east.

When I joined him, I noticed that the moonless night protected us. Step-by-step I followed him, always eastward along the telegraph poles. Finally, we passed the guards and took the direction that avoided the road. Soon we found ourselves walking on hollow ground, in the middle of the night, hearing our own footsteps. Dogs started barking in the nearby village. We took off our shoes and proceeded without even whispering to each other. We took a comfortable breath when we passed the dogs and walked silently, a short distance between us, full of anxiety and fear.

Many miles later, we noticed that our shoes were getting wet. One of my feet sank deep into the mud. Mungesingh reached for my hand and pulled me out. Soon we found ourselves in the middle of water. He asked me to jump first. I couldn't see the width of the space to make sure that I could jump over it. He repeated that I should jump. When I did, my left foot remained stuck in the mud. He jumped after me with his long legs and strong arms and once again pulled me out. I asked him if he knew where we were. He said, "No," adding, "I think we came the wrong way."

But not knowing which way to go, we followed the direction of the telegraph poles. All of a sudden, we heard gunfire. "Lie down," he ordered. He was an experienced soldier, so I did. A few more bullets whistled overhead as we lay there, breathless. Then he used his army training and crawled on his belly. I did the same—like a good soldier would do for a general. The only way that I could be saved was to obey and follow him.

I wanted to ask him why he had chosen this road, but I knew that he didn't want me to talk. This was not only his mistake but the mistake of both of us. We finally arrived back in Nissibin after midnight. I told him to take off his turban and to walk ahead of me until we passed the center of town. When he passed the center, I saw two MPs walking slowly. They passed me without suspicion because of my uniform. I joined Mungesingh near the bridge, which connected the city to the railroad station. The engineer's office was on the right of the workers' camp. A guard's voice stopped me, demanding, "Who goes there?" I nodded to Mungesingh to stop.

"A worker of the company," I replied. He noticed my cap in the dark and asked for my pass. I pulled out my identification card, but the poor fellow could not read. He called another guard, and hollered back asking my name.

"Habib, going to the center, Sulaiman's camp."

"Let him go," said the man. I motioned Mungesingh to follow me. The guard asked me who he was, and I said that he was my cook. When we entered the camp, we were stopped by another guard. I explained to him who I was. Nearby, Sulaiman asked me my name in the dark. When I said my name, he ordered the guards to let me go. When we approached Haroutoun's tent, I motioned Mungesingh to enter, and we raided the wooden box where Haroutoun kept his leftovers. Soon he awakened and asked what was going on. I asked him if he had any food for two hungry escapees.

In the morning I went to the head engineer's office to see Mr. Pfalz. I was angry but not afraid to tell about my experience. I put it to him point-blank: "How do you expect me to operate a camp, with five hundred Indians, without food or water? Besides that, you didn't even send my messenger back."

The officer calmly replied that he had sent plenty of water and bread to the camp on a horse wagon that morning. He said that it would arrive that afternoon. He added that they had not had any trains for three days.

Then I told him that I could not work in an isolated place like that without more security and rations and that I had no intention of going back. So, with this big man, who was as powerful as a general, I started to bargain. He promised to take me with him to the next railroad station with his official hand-pump rail car wagon. From there I would have a horse-drawn wagon to take me to the workers' camp. And in a few days, he would send a replacement and bring me back to his office for a new position. I agreed; I had no choice. I took Mungesingh with me. He was proud and happy to see me sit next to this high official.

Within a few days, the camp returned to peace and normalcy. The engineer in charge took my records and books and released me from my duties. I bid goodbye to my newfound friend Mungesingh, jumped on my horse, and followed the guardsman to the station. When I arrived, the guard met me and whispered, "You know, you gave us very good advice, Habib-effendi. We just received bad news from the other side of the hill."

Desert Flowers

When I returned to Haroutoun's tent, he informed me that I had a job waiting for me. I went to the engineer's office and met his secretary, Melik, who gave me a book with names: the daily report of workers' newly started contracts. My task was to check off each worker's name while he was on the job and report to the main office daily. The group's foreman was a Kurd, and his supervisor was a German engineer. He was loud, domineering, and would not tolerate mistakes, because he would not allow himself to make a mistake. He was a hardworking man, working for the Kaiser's victory. When I went to check the laborers, he was shouting orders to the foreman. A woman in rags and a man shook from the shouting.

I watched him shout out orders. I did not approach him, hoping his tirade would stop. When he calmed down, he came to me and said, "I guess you are the new timekeeper." I told him that I was. He said, "I will tell you what to do." I turned to him and said that it was not necessary—I had already gotten my instructions from the main office. He gave me a dirty look and said, "I wish you good luck. I hope you will be better than the last man." I came close to him to make sure he understood me. I told him that this was not my first job on the road, and to emphasize my point I threw in a few German words, which did not sound like very good German. But his Turkish did not sound very Turkish either. However, we understood each other. He kept repeating "Nicht"* to everything I said.

This station, newly opened, was the end of the line. The engineers had developed a new plan for making switches in a circle. When the train

---

*German for "not."

engine entered the circle, it could connect with either one of the lines, wherever the cars were. Therefore, it required more labor and time. They brought the prisoners of war—English, Russian, and Indian—and some Kurdish women and men and young girls, who were exhausted, dressed in dirty rags, and on the run from nearby cities. They poured into this section to escape the Arabs. There were some Armenian girls and women, runaways from harems in search of food and shelter. They would have liked to work, too, but no jobs were available to them. The company needed stronger bodies. The weak begged from the more fortunate for a piece of bread or shelter, but they were chased away. These undesirables were driven from one camp to another.

It was an open secret among friends and workers that the new timekeeper was an Armenian. One day the Turkish commander's secretary called me by my real name, "Hovhannes!" I turned back to see who was calling. When I saw him, I asked him if he was calling me.

"Yes," he said, and asked whether Hovhannes was my real name. "I heard Tossounian call you that, so I thought that I would also." But when he told this story to Tossounian in his office, he said that my real name was Habib, and the matter was closed.

One morning when I went to check the workers, the foreman informed me that four women were waiting for me regarding jobs. When I talked to them, they told me that they had run away from a nearby village and were desperately in need of food and shelter. They came to Nissibin with the hope of finding somebody to help them, and people had suggested that they come to see me.

At times, we let our heart dictate our logic, and that often brings trouble. Nevertheless, whatever the risk or the trouble, something compels us to do things simply for the satisfaction of doing them. I could not turn my back and just ignore these appeals for help. I was searching for a solution to the problem these four women faced when I noticed the sad and melancholy eyes of one of them, her tattered clothes hardly covering her body. Her kneecaps were dirty, her feet swollen and wrapped in rags. I opened my workers book, checking the list of names and nervously turning the pages. I saw one name had been absent for a week, a second one for a few days, a third and a fourth for two weeks. I asked the women if they could keep another name in mind besides their own, for I had found a solution. I said to the foreman that these women would work in place of the absentees.

Although he was a Kurd, even the foreman was happy with the arrangement, though I wondered why. I thought that he was trying to please me. I wondered whether he knew who I was. I wondered, too, if these four women knew who I was, or if, subconsciously, they knew that I was an Armenian. Satisfied and happy, I left the group and went back to the office to report to the head clerk how I had placed those four women. I told him how desperate they were. He smiled at me and said, "I hope it will work."

The following afternoon while I was on a routine checkup, I saw the angry German supervisor talking to the foreman in his strange Turkish. The man was bewildered, and the women were shaking. When I approached the German engineer, he asked me why these women wouldn't respond to their names when he called them? I asked him to stop shouting, and I called each according to the name in my book. Each responded. I told the engineer that we would settle our differences in the main office. I went there and handed in my resignation because I had been highly insulted. Mr. Pfalz promised to talk with the supervisor and tell him not to interfere—Melik had told Pfalz about my report the day before. To find out how these things had gotten so out of hand, I went to the foreman's tent after work.

A woman answered faintly from inside the tent. I waited outside and told her my name, and she opened the flap of the tent and invited me in. She knew me, but we had never met. It is not proper for a man to enter anybody's tent when the man of the house is absent. This is a law of the desert, but she insisted that I enter. I did so hesitantly, but adamantly refused to sit down.

She was blond, pure white, and polite. She made an effort to smile. I could see that she was an Armenian. It was not necessary to ask, although she seemed to be a strange flower cast upon the desert. But she took courage and identified herself.

During deportation, she had lost her mother and her sister from Darende. Her sister had been married in Gurun to a young man called Chokarian. Among the many successful merchants in Gurun was the well-known Chokarian and Company. This was her sister's husband. I told the girl how I knew the family. I did not want to waste any more time and wanted to leave, but she stopped me, begging me to do something for her. She said that she wanted to leave this place; that she belonged to her people and wanted to be with them. I told her that I would take her with me to freedom when better times came, and I promised to see her again as soon as I had a chance. I told her to tell her Kurdish husband that I had dropped in to see him.

When I returned to my tent, I saw that Haroutoun's face was full of disappointment. He had heard about my argument with the German officer and that I was being called a troublemaker. Haroutoun argued that without a job I was without protection as well. I told him that those poor women stood in front of me full of hope, believing I could do something for them. "You have not seen these women; anyone would have done the same."

He smiled and gave me a friendly hug and said, "I have news for you. My supervisor had trouble in the bakery shop, and he thinks that the man in charge is stealing. He always has a shortage. He begged me to convince you to take this job. The arrangement has already been approved by Mr. Pfalz."

Makroohy

So, the next day I went to the railroad station, which housed camps. In the center of the station stood two bakery shops, open day and night, which supplied all of the bread for workers, guards, and officials. The man I was to replace was already gone, and I was to take his vacated tent. At the entrance to the tent stood a pale, sick, quite unattractive girl of about sixteen. A woman was sweeping the ground of the tent. She told me that she used to work for the former boss of the bakery. She was strong and healthy looking, as peasant women are. "And what about that girl?" I asked.

She hesitated a moment, as if in search of words, then said, "Well, she used to stay with him," and she looked down in embarrassment. I was about to ask, "Why didn't he take her with him?" but looked at the young girl again and asked, "What is she going to do now?"

The older woman shrugged her shoulders, implying it was anybody's guess. I turned to the young girl and asked her name. "My name is Makroohy," she said, a choice Armenian name meaning purity. She blushed and hesitated, as if she did not want to communicate. But then she came near and revealed quietly the tragedy of her life. Like trees after a hurricane, we carry with us the mark of past disturbances.

I did not want to question her for fear of torturing her, so instead I said, "You will stay with this woman in her tent until I can get a job for you."

Turning to the older woman, I said that I would be very grateful if she would give her motherly attention and take care of her.

When I took over my job, I asked the workers to move my tent closer to the bakery. The older woman was to come and clean the place and sweep the floor. She asked if she could do laundry for me. We went to her tent; Makroohy was there, crying. She seemed like a broken leaf that had fallen in the springtime, prematurely to perish. Her previous master had refused to take her with him for he did not want to feed an extra mouth. I stood outside the tent and told her that the other woman would take care of her, that she was well protected now, and that I wanted her to be strong so that I could get her a job.

I returned to the shop to check the stock and get acquainted with the routine. The head man in the bakery told me that we did not need to have shortages because we had a guard between two shops. "But you know how it is," he said. "Our manager is loose in character and morals."

I asked, "Are you all Armenians here?"

He said that they were and introduced me to some workers, all with Turkish names. I told him that I must be called Habib. He nodded that he got the message.

Just as I was about to start my work, a tall English prisoner, Dick, stepped in and told me that he used to keep the manager's books. He was not only tall but quite handsome, healthy looking, and pleasant. We spoke English, and I insisted that we speak English all of the time. On my second round of the bakery, I noticed a guard with his gun on his shoulder. He saluted me. I stopped and talked to him, letting him know in no uncertain terms that nobody was to enter the bakery shop except those who worked there, and no one was to take anything from the shop without my permission, repeating, "No one."

He replied, "Yes, sir."

I was happy with my new assignment. I had a lot of responsibility, especially in catching up with the orders and taking care of the workers. And Dick was very helpful. As head baker, he wanted to be sure that I would not make any mistakes. He told me that in case of a shortage, we could reduce the size of the bread until it was level with the amount of flour we received from the storehouse. I learned that I was allowed to get more flour than I needed each day, so long as our books balanced. I took advantage of this privilege, for the extra bag of flour would come in handy if the train came in late or we had a shortage of supplies in the warehouse. These two bakeries supported the whole local railroad system and the prisoners' needs.

We raised our production from eight hundred loaves a day to twelve hundred loaves a day. No one was allowed extra bread, and no other shops were selling any. Consequently, within a short time, many strange people visited me looking for favors. I tried to ward them off, as I wanted, among other things, to justify the trust placed in me. A job like this, in times of scarcity and crisis, had many temptations, not the least of which were corruption and favoritism. Past experience had taught me a lesson I never forgot, and I decided to be strong and to resist temptation.

One day our camp commander sent his valet to the bakery with a note begging me for an extra loaf of bread. "If you please," the note read, and it was signed, "Noory Bay." This was my first temptation, and from high up the ladder it came. Shortly after, however, I was informed of a surplus of flour. So, the following day, the whole camp had a larger loaf of bread. The supply manager, Mihran, who had assigned me the job, asked me how it had happened that we had a surplus. I told him that I had counted all of the sacks for all of the prisoners of war, officers, and labor groups. "The sacks were always ready to go before the workers came for them, and I was in the shop from when I woke up until I went to bed at midnight." I told him that each worker left the bakery showing his loaf of bread to the guard; the guard would get an extra loaf of bread to show my appreciation for his aid.

Haroutoun visited my tent more often now and had dinner with me. He never asked for an extra loaf of bread and never received one. We understood that we both had to be careful and protect each other, but we had plenty to eat when he visited me.

The foreman one day asked the older woman who cleaned for me to leave word for me that he would be honored to have me in his tent to sip Turkish coffee with me. He gave me a warm welcome when I entered. His blond wife retreated to the hidden division in back of the tent. But her husband generously asked her to come and join us, calling me "friend." He told me that there was a labor shortage, and a contractor from Aleppo, Stepanian, had asked him if he could get some workers. He sent the four women to him.

Kikor

One afternoon, a child's cry awakened me from my nap. I jumped up from my cot and rushed out of my tent. A small boy was crying at the entrance to the bakery shop. I asked in a rather angry voice why he was making so much noise: "What is the matter with you?"

Wiping his tears with the back of his dirty hand, he replied, "They beat me," and continued sobbing. I asked him who had beaten him, and he said, "The guard." Carefully avoiding the guard, he came close to my tent. His disheveled, dirty hair, almost gray with dust, hid his little black eyes. He was no more than nine years old. His legs evidenced past struggles with the intense heat of the sun and dust—his kneecap was at the verge of cracking. His young feet were encrusted with mud and dust.

When I asked the guard why he had had to beat the boy, he replied that the boy was stealing bread from the bakery. But the boy answered, "I was just picking the crumbs off the floor." He looked like a Kurd, and to be sure I asked him his name. "Kikor." Not believing what I had heard, I asked again, "What did you [say] your name was?" "Kikor." I corrected him. You mean Krikor? "That's what my mother called me," Kikor said.

I asked him where his mother was. He shrugged his shoulder. "I don't know. To make sure that he was not lying, I asked him what his family name was. Again, with a shrug, he gave me the sign, "How should I know?"

My voice softened and I asked him the question that needed no answer, for I wanted to keep him talking. He answered, "Yes, I am Armenian."

I went into the bakery, picked up some fresh bread, crushed it and extended my hand to him. He took the bread gratefully with a sweet smile. He could not say thank you. He had never heard the word, never used it, probably never had occasion to use it. But he paid me in full with that sad, yet happy, smile. When a helpless child looks up to you with a smile, nobody in the world is greater than you, and you know it. I invited him into my tent, but he would not come in. He remained outside, near the entrance, selecting small pieces to munch on, using his robe as a tablecloth.

I asked him how he had happened to come to this camp. Putting his left hand on a piece of bread and ravenously savoring the crumbs, he told me that he had lived with an Arab family in some faraway hills and didn't know how he had gotten there. He didn't remember his father, or when or how he lost his mother. He remembered only the Arab's tent, tending the baby goats, and joining with the neighboring Arab boys to take the baby goats to the nearby hills. This was their daily routine. But one day, about sunset, when they were ready to go home, the baby goats were gone. They searched for a long time but couldn't find them. He knew that because he wasn't an Arab boy, he would be the one punished for this, perhaps even killed. The goats were more valuable than an Armenian child.

While the other boys went home, Kikor headed for the main road, where the German soldiers used to travel in big wagons without horses. He walked down the road and begged for a ride before the Arabs discovered him gone. He waited a long time, until dark. He started crying desperately. A truck pulled up where he was standing, and a German soldier, without asking why he was there, picked him up. When they arrived at the railroad station, they dumped him off. It was very dark, and he was cold and hungry. He slept in a nearby tent. He was afraid that somebody might discover him and return him to the Arabs.

In the morning, he begged for food and was chased and stoned like a stray dog. Suddenly, he caught the sweet smell of bread baking and followed the scent to the door of the bakery. He did not see anybody, but he did see the scattered crumbs on the floor. He bent down on his knees, crawling after each crumb until he found himself inside the bakery.

A strange thrill came over me. I had plans for Makroohy; someday she would be a pretty young lady, dressed up and attending school. And who knows? I might find a young man who would heal her past wounds. And now this homely little boy, hardly nine years old. If I could only keep him with me until new horizons opened, until things returned to normal. I would put him in a school. I would have a family of my own to start a new life.

What an opportunity I had, to be able to do something for these two lost souls and for the future of Armenia! I called the older woman to my tent and showed her my new "son" and asked, "Can you give him a bath if I provide the soap?"

"Yes." She nodded.

"You take care of him, and everything will be all right," I said, implying that I would not forget this favor.

Shortly thereafter a cheerful-looking little boy entered my tent, with dark eyes shining, ruddy cheeks, and a happy smile. His hair, faded from sun and dust, was now a rich dark brown. His doe-like eyes sparkled with happiness, but his kneecaps were still dark and grubby-looking from accumulated dust and sun. His gown simply hung on him; it did not protect him from the relentless sun and wind. I asked him to call the lady.

When she came in, I said, "I forgot to tell you to do something about his clothes," and I went to the bakery and got a flour sack. This would be enough for the desert, better at least than what he now wore. I asked her to fix it up; she said she would be happy to. I added that the boy must stay in her tent. "He will have whatever he needs," I said, "and I will get a larger tent for you, too." From that day on, Kikor and I were closely related. I did not even want to correct his name to Krikor.

It made me happy to have him around me. When I was not in my tent, he would fetch water, spread it over the ground and sweep the dusty floor, then bring fresh drinking water from the station pump. He now seemed taller, his head held high, because he belonged to that white tent.

As the days passed, Kikor and I grew closer and closer. He needed me and, I suppose, I needed him. My whole outlook changed. The purpose of living had dawned on me, becoming clear and distinct. Yes, I had a new reason for living, and the boy knew it. After work, when I was alone, he would come around to see if he could come in and give me a hug, or put his head on my knee, close his eyes, and listen to my future plans for him. I would say, "Someday we will be in a large city. I will teach, and you will walk to school with me. Someday you will dress like a city boy and have paper and pencils. And if you want, you can put your pencil behind your ear to show everybody that you can write. And I will buy you a new pair of shoes, something you have never had before. And I want you to keep them very shiny, always." But Kikor was not excited about his bright future; not concerned about learning. He wanted only to be assured that he would be with me always. He did not know how much I wanted that. It seemed as though he were a part of me.

My feelings for Makroohy, however, were different because she was a girl. I felt sorrow and pity, not joy and pride, as I did with Kikor. In fact, I worried about her; but I was happy that the strange hand of destiny had placed Kikor in my hands. How lucky and happy I was. Kikor, knowing this, always looked for privileges.

His flour-sack robe, of which he was so proud, made him look like a dark little boy in an angel's dress. He would eat and sleep in the older woman's tent, with more food than anyone else could have in this isolated land.

The desert had given us strange flowers, indeed: Kikor, Makroohy, and the blond lady in the Kurd's tent. Even Dick liked Kikor. Dick had wanted to learn a few words in Turkish so that he could talk to Kikor, but Kikor refused to learn the strange sound of English. He couldn't understand why Dick did not understand his Turkish.

One day Haroutoun informed me that Setrak Tossounian was sick and in the army hospital. I went to see him, my friend from Aleppo. While I was talking to him, a person wearing a loose nightgown walked toward me, like a ghost, without showing any emotion. It was a tragic sight. His cheeks were hollow, and he was a pale yellow; he could hardly walk. It was, indeed, a fearful sight. Finally, he reached me and, with a cold ghastly look, said "Habib?" I was even more upset and puzzled. I did not remember him. But I told him that that was my name, and he replied that his name was Angel.

"Don't you remember? Angel, from Darbasia? You know, we did not listen to you." Weak and short of breath he continued: "We went to Mardin,* to an Arab's tent, and he hid us during the day, and we were supposed to start our journey to the border that night. The police were informed, and we were arrested. They beat us badly, took away all our papers, and put us in jail, where they tortured us. Do you remember some of my friends?"

I asked him where they were now, and he said that they had all died.

Just a few months before Angel had been bright, healthy, and good looking, full of fun. He used to make the group laugh. And he knew how to get a few more loaves of bread from me when he came for the rations for each group. I never knew that a man could change so drastically in such a short period of time. I had a queasy feeling. I could barely understand what he said, I was so paralyzed from the shock of looking at him and from the stories he told. Finally, he felt dizzy and slowly walked back toward his bed. He covered himself, then stared at me from the corner of his eye, peeping from under his covers. Setrak and I were frozen.

Setrak was discharged from the hospital a few weeks later, and he told me that the unlucky Angel had died. His young body had been exhausted.

Grapevine 1918

It was now summer of 1918. We had no news about the war; yet, we had faith that the Allies would win sooner or later. In the meantime, thou-

---

*A town in southeastern Turkey, near the Tigris River and not far from Nussabin in Mesopotamia.

sands upon thousands would perish. The important thing for us was to get through each day, but each day the war would take more lives. If the world governments made their peace, thousands could be saved. We did not understand the diplomatic juggling of our young lives. We wondered what was holding up the victory, why the Allies were so slow.

We learned that Mr. Jackson, the American consul in Aleppo, had been called home.[9] We had only a faint idea why. So many things were puzzling, and our sorely tired hopes could not help but fade as time went on. The longer the war, the smaller our chances for survival. I had reached my twenty-third year, and I wondered how many more I had.

One afternoon, I saw Haroutoun walking slowly toward my tent; he appeared to be burdened with unbearable worries. When he greeted me, I asked if something was wrong. He said, "No."

"Then why this visit, and that worried look?"

"A friend of mine," he said, "who lives nearby, asked me to have tea with him and if I could bring you along."

I told him that I would not miss it, but I still could not understand Haroutoun's worried look. However, nobody had tea or coffee, and nobody ever had sugar, so I let Dick know that I maintain extra sacks of flour, so I stored many more sacks of flour.

A few days later, I got a note from Mr. Stepanian, the contractor from Aleppo, asking to see me. When I met Stepanian, he told me that his contract had ended. He did not say that it was finished, however, and he said that the workers would face starvation because he had no means of feeding them. I asked him if he would be gone for a while, and Haroutoun and I left for the lucky tent where tea and sugar were to be served

We entered, and Haroutoun introduced me to his friend. We sat down inside the tent and a few more men arrived. They arranged for a man to stand guard outside the tent.

The host started in a low voice. "We know that something is in the air, but we don't know exactly what it is. I am going to tell you a few things to put you on the alert for what changes may come. This meeting is not for the executives of the camps; it is not for everybody to know about, but only for a few trusted men. So, I will alert you." He paused to give weight to his next statement.

"We have noticed unusual activities on the line. For several days now, night trains have been leaving empty. This is something for us to think about. In fact, the train from the east does not stop here anymore, and nobody gets off it. All of the doors are locked, and the guards see to it that no one gets off or walks about the station when the trains arrive. Number two: some contracts have already been canceled."

A woman made tea for us and offered us some sugar. Haroutoun took one piece of the sugar and told the woman that I did not use sugar! She passed me by, and I looked up at the face of my Judas. He smiled, knowingly. The host noticed that I had not taken any sugar and asked me why. Haroutoun repeated his trick before I had a chance to open my mouth. Amazed, and trying to be polite, I told the man that Haroutoun was right and drank my bitter tea while everyone else enjoyed the sweet taste.

We had enough information to fill us with expectation. Each of us could draw our own conclusions. The evacuation of the army from Baghdad had begun.

I had received orders to provide two extra loaves of bread to each laborer who left the camp. The order also authorized me to maintain extra sacks of flour, so I stored many more sacks of flour.

A few days later, I got a note from Mr. Stepanian, the contractor from Aleppo, asking to see me. When I met Stepanian, he told me that his contract had ended. He did not say that it was finished, however, and he said that the workers would face starvation because he had no means of feeding them. I asked him why he couldn't let them go.

He grimaced. "How?"

"By train," I replied.

He said that they would not give him passage for his people. I asked him why he didn't talk to Mr. Pfalz about it. The train operation somehow came under the army's jurisdiction, and nobody could talk to or ask any favors of the commander of the station. I told him that I could not help him. Then he turned back to me and said, "How about those four women you sent me? They are still with me." I asked him what he wanted me to do.

He asked me if I realized that all of his workers were Armenian, men and women, all sixty of them, and that he had nothing to feed them. I told him that I would take back the four women, but he insisted that I must help him.

Through the office manager, Melik, Noory Bay arranged for the passage of the workers. We would provide their rations for two days: two loaves of bread each. My strange-looking four women, with their strange names, had passage, too. I do not know where they went, but the best we could do was to help them leave. I was glad that I had attended that meeting, even if I was cheated out of sugar with my tea.

Dick had a friend by the name of Grant, an Australian army pilot. He had helped the Germans repair their rickety one-engine airplanes. As a prisoner of war, Grant was charming, friendly, tall, and handsome. Despite the conditions for prisoners of war, he still had a good complexion. He visited Dick often and, to my satisfaction, he was friendly to Kikor. In fact, once in a while, he would get some chocolates from the German soldiers and bring them to Kikor, so he was a welcome friend in my tent. Often, he would tell me of his adventures as a pilot while fighting against the Turks near Baghdad. Thousands of soldiers were left without food and water. Under these conditions, they had to surrender—forty thousand of them, Indians and British. After that, they were sent to different parts of the country, but most were sent in work gangs to the railroad.

Noory Bay again sent his valet with a note asking me to do him a favor. He had an unexpected friend. "Would you please send me a couple of loaves of bread?"

The next morning, while I was roaming about the railroad station, Noory Bay pretended not to see me. I was fishing for news, wondering where his guest had come from. So, I walked up to him and greeted him as the commander of the station.

"Well, Habib-effendi. Salam to you," he said. "How are you, my friend?"

He was so warm and friendly that I became suspicious. He thanked me for the favor I had rendered him. I said that I would be glad to help any time; I didn't want him to be embarrassed with his guest. And, in a most friendly way, I reminded him that at his age he ought to be retired.

Smiling, he replied, "Because of the shortage of men, they made me a commander. That is why I am here." We both laughed. How true it was for many officers like him, and I wondered if he knew who Habib was. If he knew, would he be as friendly as this?

I received an order to keep the bakery shop working day and night and to produce as much bread as possible. Most of the work had stopped, and each worker was given an extra loaf of bread upon leaving. Our station was extremely busy, but for no apparent reason. So, I made a habit of walking to the station and back in order to find out what was up. Dick, my friend, wouldn't tell me why he was looking so happy lately, but I suspected, when I heard their whispers. Our grapevine was shaking again.

This time it was understood that all jobs would stop and all operations and activities soon would be transferred over to the Turkish army. It seemed that the army wanted all company employees transferred into the army, along with their records; we guessed what might happen to us. The German officials guessed, too, and their command refused to transfer over our records to the Turks. All of this happened suddenly. It meant that the war was ending.

Haroutoun had learned that passage was available, but for a high price, and that this was a secret. He was planning to obtain a ticket and leave this place. I had always thought we would stay together regardless. Yet he knew that I did not have enough money for the bribe. He said that we would be together, but he wished he had the money to buy my ticket, too. I shook my head. I did not want to go that way. I wondered if he could obtain those tickets, and if they were any good. Perhaps they would be good for a few stations, and then he might be stopped and dumped in the center of nowhere; no contacts, no friends, and short of money.

"I would not trust this man, whoever he is," I said. "I would wait, even if I did have the money to pay." But the next day, Haroutoun bought a ticket secretly and waited for his time to leave.

But when the time came, the train was not ready, and when there was room for him to leave, his pass was not accepted. The man who had sold him the ticket was gone. Haroutoun's pass was invalid.

Once again, we were warned to be on the alert. Things started happening fast. The prisoners of war were gathered for transferral to unknown places. The office force was getting ready to close their books and turn over operations to the army. We were told to maintain the railroad operations and were put under army control.

Haroutoun's assignment now was to listen at night for telephone messages in case a special message came for Mr. Pfalz, and for several nights he had not slept. He asked if I would relieve him one night. The job was top secret, but the main office gave its consent. Dick took over for me at the bakery, and I went down to the central office for the night shift listening in on the phone lines. For a long time, I listened and listened. I could not understand the words in code, but I knew no message had come for our office.

Then I heard a conversation in Turkish on one of the lines. One party ordered the other to get ready for a transfer: "Get ready to move soon. You will receive your orders. You will move on horseback, avoiding villages and the railroad line. We will start soon, and our group will meet you at ——." The voice faded away. I took a deep breath. I knew that this was a retreat for the Turkish army, but I didn't know where the conversation had originated, possibly from Mustafa Kemal Ataturk's army. This was important news, if we could only use it. The trouble was that I could tell this only to Haroutoun.

The next morning, when I walked from the office back to Haroutoun's tent, he asked me if I was sick. George was just getting up. I told Haroutoun that I was just sleepy and asked him to come and see me in the afternoon after I had my nap. He asked if I had heard anything important. Seeing George still lingering nearby, I told him to drop in at my place for tea. He knew that I did not have any tea and got my message.

When we sat down to talk later that afternoon, I made sure that no one was listening. I spoke in Armenian so that Kikor would not understand.

"We have to leave this place very soon," I said, and I gave him all of the details and information; this time we would be together. Haroutoun was now broke, as all of his money had gone for fake passes.

We decided it was best to leave soon, but we did not know how. We were employed by the company but subject to army regulations. We could not leave without permission from the army. So, our plan did not mean anything at all; worse yet, we could not run away. All railroad stops were checkpoints for civilians. I suggested that we take advantage of the knowledge we had as soon as an opportunity presented itself. In the meantime, we had to sit tight and pretend to be content.

Soon the prisoners were to be separated from the camp. We were worried about them and their transportation. We heard rumors of peace negotiations, but no peace was in sight for us. On the contrary, it was a most trying time, and we were worried that we would soon become army employees.

The management of the company ordered us to stop all activities. Shortly after, the German soldiers and railroad personnel, all but Mr. Pfalz, left the camp. My shop became the center of activity, producing bread for all who were leaving. Day and night, I kept the bakery open, often working until midnight, filling the unexpected orders that came in each day.

On one of these busy nights, I saw Kikor hanging around my tent. I told him that it was too late for a young boy to be up and I needed him to go to bed. He left but soon came back. I asked him what the trouble was. "Didn't I tell you to go to bed?"

"Yes, but . . ."

"But what?"

"They do not want me there."

"Who?"

"That English soldier."

"Dick?"

"No, the other one."

I rushed through the dark to Makroohy's tent. I called Grant in a raised voice. The flap of the tent was closed, and Grant did not answer. In an angry voice I again demanded that he come out like a man or else I would go in. The tent opened slowly, and Grant came out with a bottle in hand. I called him all of the bad names I could think of in English—barbarian, brute, taking advantage of a little girl!

My anger was justified. He knew that she was under my protection, and I considered him a friend. This was unforgivable. The bakery boys heard my screaming and hurried to the tent, while Grant told me to keep quiet; he was ready for a fistfight. The head of the bakery workers pushed him away, saying, "Oh no, you don't do that."

The other boys dragged me back to the bakery. I was shaking with anger and disappointment. Was there no decency at all in the whole world, even among Christians? The head baker offered me a glass of cold water and whispered in my ear, "You're a fool. I feel sorry for you. A girl like that does not deserve your protection. What are you trying to do? You are putting your life in danger, and it is not worth it. We have known for a long time what was going on, but we were waiting for you to wake up."

I went to my tent to sleep, but I could not sleep at all. My hopes and dreams were shattered. I was humiliated and disappointed in both Makroohy and men in general.

In the morning, Dick came by the tent and warned me coldly about acting again like I had the night before. He reminded me that Grant was popular. He was temperamental, and he kept a revolver. I told him that I was disgusted and did not want to see him at all. If he wanted to use his gun, I said, "Let him try it."

Dick was dissatisfied, for he knew that I regarded Grant as a degenerate English soldier, and he understood my disappointment. He knew how highly I used to think of them, and what a good friend I had been to them. He calmed down. Westerners seldom understand the moods, habits, and manners of the East, and he tried to excuse himself.

"Grant's action was uncalled for," he said. "After all, he is not British. He is from Australia. Grant is a mad man sometimes and unpredictable. I am worried only about you."

"A man should know a few basic things in life," I said, "and he should know how to act like a man. He is a brute, not a man, and we'll not talk about him anymore." I am sure that Dick sympathized with me, and he left my tent promising to talk to Grant.

That morning, I ordered the workers to take down the tent that I had provided for Makroohy and the older woman. I felt desperately disappointed and humiliated. The workers told them to leave the camp because I did not want to see them anymore; that was the last I saw of them.

Kikor now moved into my tent. Haroutoun paid a visit as soon as he heard about the night before and scolded me. His logic was the same as the man from the bakery: I had been foolish for doing missionary work for her.

"You know your obligation to your nation?" he asked. "First to get out of this whole mess alive. A barbarian like Grant can kill you, and nobody is responsible for you, nor does anyone care. Wake up! You are in the middle of nowhere. We have to get out of here, to organize and educate orphans. We must get out of here alive." A faint smile appeared on his face. "You sure picked a good one for future motherhood." I didn't have the nerve to argue with him, and he was surprised that I did not.

When Haroutoun's job was finished, they locked up the office and gave the keys to Commander Shoukry. Haroutoun moved in with me, waiting for passage out of Nissibin.

One day, I took a walk to the station to get news and say "Salam" to Noory Bay. I didn't learn much, but on my return Haroutoun told me that Mungesingh had been by to see me and was disappointed that he could not find me. Haroutoun handed me two silver majidias. "He said that you had loaned him these a very long time ago."

I wanted to see Mungesingh before he left, but I never had a chance to find him. He had wanted to repay a debt. This was, indeed, wonderful. I had never expected it. I wondered if Grant would ever do the same thing. Or Dick? No, it took a simple peasant boy from India, uneducated, but with high principles and ethics, and self-respecting Singh of India.

Haroutoun contacted his friend who had given us tea that evening before. This man could get information that nobody else could, and his sources were unknown to us. He told Haroutoun that we just missed being massacred. The German officials had objected to the removal of employees and insisted upon a guarantee of our safety. Then the official German staff left.

The English officers came from the front to take back their prisoners of war. The Turkish army retreated from the border of Baghdad, and Aleppo had now fallen into the hands of the British. It was the time for us to act fast, to leave this place, for the Turkish military was retreating toward Anatolia, in western Turkey.

When Noory Bay came to the bakery to take it over, I was there to greet him. He ordered me, as commanders do, to turn over all of my records to his army staff. The warehouse and the storerooms already were sealed, and he told me that the army was now taking over.

"Yes, sir," I told him. "And I suppose that you do not need my services anymore?"

"Yes, I do," he said.

"When you don't need me anymore, will it be possible for me to go home?"

He coldly answered, "I will let you know."

I understood that the night train had been transporting wounded soldiers from Baghdad to the interior of Anatolia. The next day I saw Noory Bay outdoors in pajamas and bathrobe like a civilian. He said that he was sick. We knew he was lying. He didn't want to wear his uniform.

Haroutoun and I secretly readied ourselves for departure. We emptied a wooden box of our belongings. I tucked my notes under my shirt once again and put a few coins in my coin belt under my shirt. We watched closely for a chance to get passage on the railroad. But Noory Bay had not released me. He would have done just about anything for me a few weeks ago, but the political climate changes fast, and so do politicians. In a few days, I finally secured my release. Noory Bay was very much pleased with the surplus of flour and grateful that he would not have to close the warehouse.

I made the rounds of the camp, anxious to see the blond lady with the Kurdish husband. They were gone. While Haroutoun and I waited for our train, I saw Noory Bay giving orders here and there. I made it a point to start a conversation with him, hoping that our past friendship still held, and asked him if it were possible to get a pass for a boy whom I was keeping. He cut me short, asking who this boy was. I said, "An orphan, sir," thinking that he would show pity.

"Don't worry about him. The government will take care of him."

The train arrived like an old man, hardly able to breathe or move. I told Haroutoun to move fast and hop on. I took Kikor to the tent.

"You are a strong boy, aren't you?" I asked. He looked at me, puzzled. "See this burlap sack? We are going to load it as high up as you are, and you are going to carry it alone to the station. When we are there you will jump up onto the train first and I will hand you the sack. You take the sack inside the train and put it down and stay behind it. You will stay until the train starts. I will be with you then." Although young, Kikor realized that this was a matter of life and death. He listened closely.

Now we had only to avoid Noory Bay and his staff. Kikor couldn't carry the sack either, it was bigger than he. He started dragging it. I lifted it a bit from the back to indicate that he was doing this for a copper coin. When we arrived at the station, I did not see Noory Bay, but I did see Melik. He greeted me and asked if I was leaving and if I had my wagon arranged. I said that I didn't. He asked me to wait a moment and left. Near the freight wagon, where the sign read ARMY OFFICIALS ONLY, he started a conversation with an officer and motioned me to follow him. He told the army officer that I was a very close friend of his and a worker, and introduced me as Mr. Habib. He added that all of the wagons were full and that I wouldn't be very comfortable with the immigrants. "I wonder," he said, "if there will be any room in your wagon for a friend?"

The officer, with great pleasure, said that he was sure that he could make some room and asked me to hop in. I thanked him and told him that I had to bring some of my belongings, and I called my errand boy. I whispered closely to Kikor not to jump in until I told him to. When the officer and his valet were gone and I was looking that we were not being watched, Kikor got his signal and jumped in. I gave the sack to him and he pulled it inside the wagon and stayed put.

I had a congenial conversation with the officials in my wagon. They wore uniforms indicating that they were high officials coming back from the front lines. They had their valets and a few suitcases. I went to my burlap sack in the corner and touched Kikor to reassure him. He touched me back happily. While the train rolled, I went to the next wagon to see Haroutoun. We did not know how this ride would end, how close we would be to our destination, Aleppo. We made arrangements to make contact at each stop, and I returned to my wagon.

Night fell, the officers finished their dinners, and their valets served them Turkish coffee prepared on an alcohol burner; then they slept. They slept while their future plans vanished.

Kikor and I slept with the hope of a new tomorrow. Before daybreak, I asked Kikor to crow like a rooster, as he had done in our tent at the camp to announce daybreak—cock-a-doodle-doo like a real rooster. I asked him to repeat it and then stop. While the officers ate breakfast, a valet asked his general if he had had a comfortable night's sleep. He said, "Thank you, Osman."

Then Osman said, "Sir, immigrants and workers are carrying their chickens with them. I heard a rooster from the next wagon."

I asked Kikor to repeat his trick. Then I brought him to meet the general. When he asked me his name, I said that the poor child had been lost and did not remember his name, but that I thought it was—I pronounced Kikor's name in such a way that it sounded Kurdish. The officer patted him on the head, and they welcomed this creature who crowed like a rooster and looked like a Kurd, accepting this as another strange event of the times.

When the train stopped at Ras ul-Ayn to refuel, an MP tried to come into the officers' headquarters. The general asked him what he wanted, ignoring his armband.

"Inspection, sir," the young soldier said.

The officer called him a jackass who could not read the sign ARMY OFFICIALS ONLY. The MP apologized for his mistake, saluted the officer, and left. Thus began our new day. Kikor had just had a new birthday. I'm sure that he would never forget that.

When the train stopped again, it was dark. I wanted to talk to Haroutoun. I told Kikor to stay put and that I would be back soon.

Haroutoun and I stretched our legs and discussed our plans. A man dressed in shabby clothes and patched pantaloons passed us. It seemed to me that I knew the face. I asked Haroutoun to turn and walk back again. "I think I just saw Sarkis." "Are you crazy?" he asked. But I was sure and wanted to return before he disappeared. I walked after the man, calling his name. He stopped, afraid—very much afraid. I came closer to him and said, "Sarkis? It's me." He froze, as if he had seen a ghost.

Haroutoun joined us. I hadn't seen Sarkis since the massacre on the hill before Aleppo. I tried to convince him that he should come with us to Aleppo, but he refused. He was responsible for his brother's widow and their children. Besides, he was working for a Kurdish *agha* and was at the station to sell raisins for his boss. He and his family were living in a nearby village.

The train gave its first whistle to start. I told him again to be sure to come to Aleppo and look me up, that I was sure I could get him a job, and we left him. Haroutoun was not as excited about seeing Sarkis as I was. Sarkis and I had been together in deportation, and we had lost each other. We had now met again.

Haroutoun and I decided to get off to change trains at the next stop, for our train was headed northwest for Anatolia and Constantinople. The other line would take us to Aleppo, which was now under British occupation. When we reached our stop, I thanked the officers and left. As the train pulled out, I talked with the workers waiting for passage to Aleppo, and they told me that the train line had been cut off between this stop and Aleppo. Haroutoun said, "Bad luck is always ahead of us, regardless of what we do." "How about walking?" I asked him. "Why, do you know the road?" he retorted sarcastically. "No, but . . ."

Haroutoun located a distant relative in the crowd who used to work with caravans, smuggling scarce goods in the black market. He had sold his mule near Antep in the hope of catching the train from here to Aleppo. He told us that he was trying to contact some Arabs who knew the road and a safe route to the city.

This road was dangerous because it ran through no-man's-land. The Turks had withdrawn, and the British army had not extended its protection that far, so thieves and army deserters survived here by robbing and killing travelers. There was no one to question or stop them. Fortunately, Haroutoun's cousin looked like a crook and a thief. He made contact with the natives and arranged for a tribesman to take us to Aleppo for a price.

We were short of water and food and had no protection. The desert wind chilled the group already cold with fear. We watched the hills where our help would be coming from. Our salvation depended upon a few crooked Arabs who might guide us to civilization.

At midnight a man came with a few camels and a donkey. We paid him the price our friend had agreed on, and he picked up our meager belongings and told us to follow. We followed one by one, "like ants moving their eggs to a new nest." We followed each other without breaking our chain, hardly seeing one another in the pitch-black night. Closer to the hill, we were motioned to stop. This looked like a second deportation for the group. But no, we could smell the clean air. Just a few more hours to salvation—that is, if we could make it.

Many things could go wrong. Our Arab guide could stop us on the road and rob us; deserters who roamed as organized desperadoes might rob and kill us. Here, there were neither rules nor government. But we took a deep breath of confidence when day broke, for we could see the green outskirts of Aleppo in the distance. A welcome sight! Our fears vanished with the bright day, and we smiled again and walked with new vigor.

Somebody pointed to a faraway flag. It was not the Turks' red flag with the crescent. It was the Union Jack, thank God. The caravan stopped, and we were told that our guide did not intend to go any farther. We did not know why. The elderly were worn out and could not continue. Kikor held my hand all night long and never complained, but when he saw the happiness on my face, he said, "Papa, is this the place?" I answered, "Yes!"

Haroutoun and I told the people to wait there until we returned from the British headquarters, where the flag flew triumphantly, spreading hope and confidence and security to those who saluted her. We were the only ones in the group who could speak English. Hesitantly, we approached the administration building. Nobody stopped us and nobody asked questions, and, thank God, nobody asked for identification!

I asked Kikor to take a nap, for the chase was over. He could sleep in peace now, next to his newfound Papa. The English flag provided a haven, gave all Armenians a new birth, and restored our belief in justice and decency.

6

The Return

The Joy of Being Alive

To OUR SURPRISE, the train into Aleppo was on time. It was the first time I had seen a British flag on the engine. This meant a thousand different things to a thousand different people who had survived the heavy hand of despotic rulers. It was the dawn of a new era.

We passed through the beautiful orchards on the outskirts of Aleppo. The engine whistled excitedly at our satisfaction, as if we were partners in victory. It seemed like a century had elapsed in the three years since 1915, so much had radically changed. We were delighted to see young English and Indian soldiers posted at the gate instead of the ragged Turkish guards. We took a carriage to the city's post office. Haroutoun and I were amazed by signs of Turkish soldiers, guards, or police. It must be heaven to live in a city like this. Kikor felt uneasy because he had never been in such a large city in all of his life, but he was excited and ready for the next adventure.

The driver stopped, and we took our belongings off the carriage. Kikor tried to help Haroutoun, the second member of his family. Haroutoun asked us to wait while he found a place for us to stay. I saw many new faces. Aleppo was a city alive with happy returning deportees.

A policeman, in the uniform of the newly created Syrian state, looked at me with the excitement of a cat seeing a mouse out of his hole and asked

me in Turkish where we were coming from. He was an old Turkish policeman with a new uniform.

"What difference does it make?" I replied in an icy voice. The policeman
left. He knew that I did not enjoy his inquiries; he knew, too, that he was
out of order.

While I watched all of this activity, I wondered how quickly the people
would come out of hiding. Haroutoun returned with his friend Onnig, who
had come back weeks ago from the desert to join his mother, sister, and
older brother. He asked us to stay with his family overnight and look for a
place the next day. Haroutoun asked me if I thought we should, dressed as
we were in old, filthy clothes and with a boy who looked like he had just
been captured in the wild. But Onnig insisted, and we agreed. He led us like
a city man, and we followed like immigrants, full of anxiety and wonder.

His mother gave us the Middle Eastern welcome for less fortunate
friends who need such hospitality, regardless of how much hardship it
might cause the hostess. We cleaned up, and I combed Kikor's hair, despite
his protests, and set forth for dinner. We hadn't had a hot meal for days,
and for months we had not had one like the one we had that night—stew
made of fresh vegetables, steamed chicken, and delicious bulgur pilaf.

To put Kikor at ease, we sat him by himself, for he had not yet learned
how to use a fork or knife and did not care much for a spoon either. His
were Arab table manners, using his hands and wiping them on the white
flour sack robe he wore. After dinner, we chatted and exchanged news. We
were especially interested in how the city looked after the British arrived.
Onnig told us that immigrants from all over were pouring into Aleppo
and organizing camps. "All of Aleppo looks like an Armenian immigrant
camp." Onnig's mother and sister talked with Kikor, asking him many
questions, which he could hardly answer.

When he referred to me as "My Papa, Habib," Onnig's sister asked him
who that was. Kikor was surprised that they had never heard my name.
Onnig told his sister that Hovhannes was Habib. His mother insisted that
we call the boy Krikor, that that was his real name. Kikor agreed without
question. The pilaf had worked on him; a full belly makes one agreeable.

The next morning Haroutoun and I went out in search of a room. Onnig
led us through the old streets of Aleppo to Bab al-Nasser, a two-story inn
with a coffee shop downstairs. We bargained with the innkeeper for an
unfurnished room; he promised to give us two cots. Kikor would sleep

on the floor, because there wasn't room for a third cot. We brought in our filthy-looking covers and our few belongings and went to a nearby Turkish bath, ready to start a new life in our newfound freedom—the three of us.[1]

I still looked like a railroad man, especially in my calfskin hat that Mousa had made for me. I remembered his smile when he told me that this would be a memento of our friendship. Where was he now? Did he survive and return home to his family in Constantinople?

But now it was time to dress for the city. I bought a *zouboun* oyro that the natives wear, a tweed jacket, and an English cap, which I proudly wore in place of a fez, the cursed headgear I had since childhood. Kikor looked like a patch on my new outfit. Haroutoun, always more practical than I, didn't want me to buy the boy anything because we were planning to put him in an orphanage. I convinced him that we should dress Kikor up and present him like the son of a father who cared about him, not like a deprived orphan. We planned to place Kikor in an orphanage because we could not do what needed to be done around the city with him along all the time.

I visited my best friend in the city, Mrs. Eskijian. She was alone with her two young sons and short of funds, but she kept busy with the incoming deportees. They remembered her and wanted her to help them make contacts. She was trying to carry on the great work of her late husband. She asked me what my plans were. Of course, I said that I wanted to continue my education as soon as I could, but right now I had to work.

"What will you do?" she asked. Before I could answer, she said, "You know, we are organizing a new orphanage with English funds, and we found out that none of our teachers speak Armenian; they are the only survivors of the state where Turkish was spoken. Fate and destiny provide a call for you."

She challenged me again, like she had after her husband's death. But I had decided not to become involved in anything that reminded me of the misery and suffering I had known. I insisted that my plans were to go to school and that frankly I was tired of seeing orphans. Then she said with a sad face, "Who will do the job?" I had no answer. Instead I talked about Kikor. She advised me to take him to the orphanage. "What would he be able to do in a hotel room?"

I told Kikor my plans. Disappointed and crying, he said that he would not be able to see me anymore and told me that he did not want to go to school. I tried my best to convince him that I would love him more if he could speak Armenian and read and carry a pencil on his ear.

The next morning, I took him to the orphanage, where I found a friend working as an assistant supervisor. He registered "Krikor" and asked me what his last name was. I told him I didn't know, and he suggested that I give him my last name so that the boy would have some means of identification. But I thought he should be named after his grandparents, assuming they were Krikorian, after the great Krikor the Illuminator.* The boy looked at me as if I had cheated him, denied him. But when I said goodbye, he came and hugged me as only a son could. It depressed me when he cried, but this was a decisive moment, and he had to do his share to cooperate. I don't know what Kikor thought that night or the next day when they sent him to class with the others, but I felt lonesome.

Before I left the orphanage, Professor Daghlian asked me to come to his office. He was the administrator, assigned to the job by the British occupying forces. He asked me to join the staff and help organize the school, reminding me, "We all need to do our best to prepare these children to be future citizens of the country. We are all soldiers and have a call to duty."

I decided to bargain. What grade was open for me? Reverend Norhadian had the upper-class children and was teaching reading. Professor Daghlian suggested, "How about teaching the next group Armenian?" That was what they needed, and that is what I agreed to do.

When, in a few days, I walked down to the orphanage, Kikor rushed up to me and hugged me again. "You did not come to see me," he said. I told him I would be here all the time because of my new job. He was as happy as he could be. I asked him if he liked his teachers. He answered me in Turkish, which sounded ugly to a man who is teaching Armenian. I told him that instead of saying "ha," he should learn to say "ayo" in Armenian.

"What's the difference?" he argued.

"So that they will not think you are a Turk."

He asked me how to say "ayo"† and repeated after me. I went to the office to see Mr. Gregorian. He introduced me to the other teachers and finally to Reverend Norhadian, the only other person teaching Armenian.

---

*Krikor or Grigor, anglicized as "Gregory," is the patron saint of the Armenian Apostolic Church, having converted Armenia to Christianity from paganism in the early fourth century. C. W. Dugmore, *The Journal of Ecclesiastical History* (Cambridge: Cambridge University Press, 1999), 268.

†Spelled "ayo," Armenian for "yes."

He told me that they had neither paper, nor books, nor pencils, just a blackboard, and that the hardest problem was to discipline them. These children had never had schooling and most were brought up and taken away from Turkish homes—some of them even thought that they had been separated from their Turkish parents. I found how true that was.

First, we had to establish discipline; then we could teach. The women teachers mothered the children and sometimes became their playmates during recess. They did so under the watchful eyes of the male teachers, who felt the misunderstanding among the children, the lack of communication, and the lack of interest in learning.

They were not seedlings but plants transferred under unfavorable conditions to strange grounds. We had a call to teach them discipline before we could teach them to read. The task seemed larger than we were. I realized that the shortage of men meant we had to do it ourselves until we could be replaced by those who were better for the job. On the other hand, the progress we made encouraged us, as did national events. Thousands upon thousands, learning that the British commanded Aleppo, came in from the desert and the unknown villages where they had been with hope for a new life.

An Armenian group was organized to make all newcomers feel at home in the city regardless of their meager funds. Camps were provided for those who needed a place to stay while searching for relatives, a lost member of the family, or a job. Each one had his unique story.

Young men were organized to revive Armenian culture, literature, and music. We had sorely missed this for the past four years, and we noticed that the returning deportees lacked Armenian manners and habits. They cared less about their nation than they did for themselves. One thing was certain: despite all of the misery, you could not find a single Armenian on the street begging for alms. If they were desperate, they would go to the church, stand in line, and somebody would drop a copper coin in their extended palm, but they would not do this outside the churchyard.

Aleppo was a beehive of activity for Armenians, and the natives were worried. The English had captured the city, but someday these poor devils, pouring in from all over and nowhere, would either take over the city or ruin it. They resented us.

Some Armenians believed that the Turks were agitating the natives (Arabs), but the British flag flew high over the city, reminding them of who ruled here.[2] My friend Sarkis had come in from the village where he had been hiding from the Turkish authorities and was now working as a servant. He still was afraid of communicating with anybody because, during the past four years, he had been running and hiding from people. He was conscious of his shabby clothes, which belonged to a mountaineer. I told Haroutoun that he must stay with us until he found a place to stay. I asked Sarkis if he would cook and shop for us and told him that he was welcome to stay with us and share whatever we had. We managed to dress him up in used clothes, which gave him more confidence and freedom to move about. We often talked of old school days, his outstanding achievements in classes and in games.

Haroutoun did not welcome this extra burden, but these extraordinary times demanded unusual sacrifices. Sarkis had next to nothing, but whatever he had, he gave to his brother's widow to take care of the children. Our meals were more expensive than eating out, but it comforted us to know that we were all together.

Kikor visited me more often than I liked. He showed no interest in school. His teachers tried to make him feel at home and gave him more privileges because of his sad past and his relationship to me. I tried to change his attitude and even scolded him. He would leave me, tears in his eyes, as if asking, "Why doesn't he understand me?"

The nationalist movement demanded much of our time. Besides our cultural group, we also belonged to an Armenian singing group. The nation was hungry for songs. There was a new, revived spirit in all that we sang. Meaningful and sentimental, they expressed our happiness at just being alive.

I noticed a strange phenomenon in the "returnees." People wanted to get married in spite of their meager means of livelihood. They lacked shelter, clothing, security, and occupation, but they came together with sweet dreams of a better tomorrow. They hoped to organize, plow, build new homes and schools for newborn children, and start the home fires burning once again. Religious and charitable organizations became active overnight, with more orphans from villages, huts, and unknown corners of the land. The people spoke many dialects, but they managed to communicate with one another and became attached to each other. An organization funded by Armenians from abroad began to trace and locate the scattered members of families, often with the help of the new government.[3]

Haroutoun and I worked to do our share. We wanted to bring the attention of the organization to some of the irregularities of operations, discrimination, and partiality. We asked Onnig and Haygaz to join us in publishing a weekly paper, *The Wasp (Bidza)*. We put our pennies together for mimeographing, and Haygaz drew a picture of a wasp with its wings spread for our logo. On the first page, we printed a warning: "Watch out for the Wasp—it might bite you!" We worked in a single room at an inn, and each of us contributed a column. Unfortunately, political unrest in the city forced us to close down after the third number. Yet we had brought about many improvements for the orphanage. The children calmed down, became more disciplined, and learned to play harmoniously.

The central committee of the Armenian organization responded that the Turks were planning demonstrations against the English and warned all Armenians to be cautious, alert, and to avoid any involvement. At this time, our Cultural Society was planning a recital—a rich program with Armenian music transcribed by Gomidas. I was to recite Daniel Varoujan's "The Spirit of the Nation,"* chosen to remind the nation of its glorious past. We were advised to cancel the evening, however. We were more surprised than fearful. The central committee told the English authorities that they suspected a Turkish revolt, and the English authorities just laughed at the Armenians. They assured us that nothing of the kind could happen under the British flag. But the Armenians were not convinced. The burned hand always remembers the fire.

Aleppo, a city in northern Syria, borders the Mesopotamian desert. For four thousand years it has been a commercial center. In the two hundred years before Christ, Aleppo was ruled by a succession of Assyrians, Babylonians, Egyptians, and Arabs. Each of these powers destroyed the city before abandoning it. The Persian, Greek, and Roman empires added to the destruction. In 1518, the Ottoman Turks occupied the city and ruined what little was left. But the city revived because of the fertile Mesopotamian land nearby. Now the city faced a new era. The immigrants and the British army brought a boom in business, and the center of these activities was the bazaar.

---

*He was a prominent Armenian poet, identified in Grigoris Balakian's firsthand account, *Armenian Golgotha: A Memoir of the Armenian Genocide 1915–1918*, Peter Balakian, ed. (New York: Vintage Books, 2010), 115.

It was a Friday morning, the Islamic Sabbath, and the bazaar was open each Friday as usual. I was ready to leave for the orphanage when I heard a shot. Sarkis jumped up. Haroutoun closed his mouth tightly, and we looked at each other. Our window was boarded up, as were all windows that faced Muslim homes. More shots. They sounded as though they were coming toward our inn. One shot came very close, then silence.

I did not want to be late for my class, so I left my room and went down to the entry gate on the street. The big gate was always locked, but the small door built into the gate was open. I opened it to leave, but somebody pulled me back by my jacket. It was the innkeeper.

"Didn't you hear the shots?" I asked him what it was. "I understand that there is some trouble in the bazaar. You had better go upstairs to your room and wait."

With that he bolted the small door. Sarkis and Haroutoun did not exchange a word. Each had his thoughts and fears. My return to the room frightened them even more. Haroutoun said, "It must be a mistake, the English are here . . ."

The shooting had stopped, but we heard the shouts of rampaging Arab mobs. We heard the door to the jewelry shop next door breaking. They broke open the shutters, stealing all they could. An Arab guard came to our room with his gun on his shoulder, his bayonet fixed. He was winding something he held in his palm. He kicked open our door and ordered us to come out. Sarkis was hiding under the bed, but with his legs exposed. I touched him and I told him to come out. I could not see Haroutoun either, but on the way out spotted him behind the drapes. Face-to-face with the guard, I did not know what to do. I knew I had to kill time before we went downstairs. I asked him if he had been told to ask us to go down, or did he want us to, and why? He said," Yes," and added, "You talk too much" and put his hand to his grenade.

At the door, I told the others to join me. Haroutoun was shaking as if he had a chill. Sarkis meekly followed us downstairs. We were ordered into the coffee shop, where people used to serve coffee and play backgammon. Another guard, in a Syrian uniform, forced everybody in and made them face the door. The women in the other rooms were terrified. They were all Armenians, new to the city and awaiting their families. A woman began crying and begging them not to harm her husband. I couldn't stand it anymore, so I came out of the crowd and directed my word to the woman, saying, "You shouldn't cry . . . you shouldn't worry. We have not done anything wrong. There must be some mistake."

A guard pointed his bayonet at me and said, "Shut up and get inside!" The bayonet, so close to me, convinced me to lose myself. In the meantime, a young man with an English army uniform burst in the gate and went upstairs to his room.

Another guard stopped him with a bayonet, and then he saw another guard leaving his room. He asked the Syrian officer angrily, almost shouting, "Are you responsible for what is going on here? What is that man doing in my room?" The guard raised the butt of his gun and tried to push him. The Armenian hollered again, "Oh, no, you can't do that to me. I have on an English uniform. You had better not."

There was some silence on both sides. A uniformed policeman came and told the guard to take the man out by the gate.

They pulled and grabbed him by his coat and threw him through the gate. We all waited for a shot. Instead, a civilian came, whispered to one of the policemen, and the policeman then whispered to the guard. In a short time, the place was cleared. The guards left us, and the police, in very smooth Turkish, told us that there had been a disturbance outside and that the guards had come to protect us!

"For your own safety, you had better not come out. We will let you know when it is safe for you to leave. We have a man outside the gates to guard you."

By the time Sarkis, Haroutoun, and I returned to our room, I had a chill also. This was too much for any one of us to bear after all we had been through. We sat silent. Finally, I asked, almost to myself, "I wonder what happened to that young man?" Then I turned and said, "You know, when they pushed us into that room and closed the door, I had a hunch that they were going to shoot us all, and if that young man hadn't come along and made a lot of noise . . . I think he saved our lives, risking his own."

Half an hour later, Indian soldiers on horseback were patrolling the city streets, calm, easygoing, as the English always are. Our guard was gone, and we thought we were safe. Soon the street resumed its normal pace, and Onnig came to make sure that we were safe.

The next morning, when I went to the orphanage, Esther came to me, surprised to see me alive, and cried, "You know what happened yesterday? The mob came and broke down the door. They wanted to come in. One of the teachers, Armenag, tried to stop them. They killed him while he was holding the door shut. He was only twenty-four years old and had survived the last four years of struggle to see freedom. The children were all panicky but calmed down when a British guard came."

If I had been on time for work, I would have been helping Armenag and probably killed.

After the riot, the British army took over the local civilian government, charging them with inefficiency.

By this time, Haroutoun was uneasy with Sarkis. I wanted to separate them to prevent an open break. I asked a friend of mine who was supervising a camp if he could give Sarkis a job. "My friend, let Sarkis come to the camp and give him some work to do." He agreed. A few weeks after, I visited them and found Sarkis with a pink scarf stuck in his front coat pocket and his coat sleeves down past his fingertips! He did not know how funny he looked, but he was very happy.

One day, when Kikor came to visit, we talked about the past, about his village and how he had escaped, the bakery shop, our train ride to Aleppo, and finally the orphanage. Suddenly, he asked, "What happened to that girl? The one I used to stay with?"

"You mean Makroohy?"

He said, "Yes."

"Perhaps she has gone to another city, or maybe . . ."

"Maybe?" he questioned.

I told him to go back to the orphanage, which he did. But that "maybe" haunted me. In the chill of the night, shaken by hunger and fever; in the dark, both physically and emotionally; lonesome and ill; had I been a friend or put the last stab in her back? Or, could it be that maybe from one tent to another, she had fallen lower and lower? Was she in the city streets, without hope or strength to pick herself up? And I wondered about all of the others who might have dragged her down. I asked myself: *Did my failure to understand her desperate need, my foolish pride, make me one of them? Had I refused her when what she needed above all was a friend, protection and love?*

The city was full of tragedy. Although the sea was now calm, the storm of war washed its debris on the shores of Aleppo. Tens of thousands of immigrants came here; poor and shabby; often crippled; with slashed necks, broken cheekbones, a missing hand, arm, or leg; or blinded during torture, marked by the heavy hand of misery. Hope enabled them to survive.

The Armenian population grew from ten thousand to thirty-five and finally to sixty-five thousand. All of them were waiting for leaders to direct them and create new ties for them. Groups were formed to meet their needs. The Americans were among the first to extend a helping hand, to shelter, feed, and provide jobs. Henry Morgenthau, seeing this vanishing nation, informed his nation from Constantinople. The people responded gallantly and graciously, organizing the Near East Relief.* With untiring effort, Morgenthau elevated his country to greatness, providing for thousands of orphans and many helpless widows, bringing hope to the hopeless and love to the forgotten people on earth. The nobility of man consists in the generosity of the heart and sensitivity to the needs of others.[4] Only the corrupt man can say, "I don't care."

Vartouhy

A new boy arrived in my class from a group that had escaped from a harem where his young sister had been captured. When they heard the news of the British occupation in Aleppo, they took courage and ran away. His mother found a job as a dressmaker, and the boy attended our school, but his sister's past experience made her cut herself off from everyone. She was only nineteen years old. The boy was handsome, neat and clean, and attentive. I was drawn by his good manners; he wasn't rough and careless like most of the newcomers, but he remained silent and melancholy. One day I started a conversation with him while the other boys were playing.

When I asked him how he and his family were getting along in this strange city, he smiled sadly and hesitantly confided that his sister had left them. His mother had tried to bring her back, but she had refused. When he told me that she was living in the red-light district, I tried to conceal my embarrassment, but I asked him his sister's name. "Vartouhy" (meaning rose), he replied, and he asked me if I would talk her into going home.

I told this story to Haroutoun that night, but he had already heard of the young girl from Gurun behind the red lights. He said, "Some friends

---

*Prior to the incorporation of the Near East Relief organization in 1919, American philanthropy was channeled through several organizations such as the American Committee for Armenian and Syrian Relief (ACASR) and the American Committee for Relief in the Near East (ACRNE).

are after her to bring her out of the place, but if they fail, they have a way to pluck her out. She is on their list now."

The next evening, I walked to the address to meet Vartouhy. A heavy-set woman with a thickly powdered face and mascara opened the door and asked me what I wanted. Her commercial smile seemed frozen on her face.

"Oh, you want to see Rosita?" she asked.

She led me to the courtyard and pointed to a door painted cherry red. After I knocked, a girl with an angelic smile opened the door and invited me in. She was congenial, warm, and happy. Her room was neat and peaceful, as if no visitors had even disturbed it. She offered me a chair, and I sat down automatically. She casually loosened her Damascus silk robe, exposing her body. But instead of admiring her beauty, I was looking for an escape, sorry that I had come. I took courage and said, "Well, I came here for a different purpose."

She gave me a strange look, and when I mentioned my name, her face saddened, and she quickly covered herself. I pleaded with her for the sake of her crying mother and her unhappy brother and told her the possibilities of the outside world. She told me that the outside world was hell and that she was running away from humiliating her mother. I suggested a boarding school; she may even marry in the future.

"I do not know why anyone, knowing my circumstances, would want to marry me," she replied. She reminded me of a Greek statue, a goddess with detailed perfection. "I know that I am a disgrace to my mother and my people, but it is too late." She began talking fast and nervously. Suddenly she asked me how I had found her place. When I told her, she became angry. I felt that I had failed and I wanted to leave, but I lingered; softly, without anger or resentment, once again I tried to offer the bright future of our people.

"You will be a queen in your family, surrounded with love and happiness." She looked at me in wonder. "Soon, very soon," I assured her, lamely.

With a heavy heart, her voice trembling, almost pleading with me, she said, "I want you to know that I am not a bad girl, but I am here. If the war had not lasted so long, I might have been saved. I was sold once. I am here at a better price."

"All that belongs to the past," I said. "We expect a better tomorrow, and nobody need know of your past. Let me help you, let me take you out of here," I begged. "You do not have to go home if you don't want to. We can arrange a boarding school for you, and when the time comes, you will be able to return to your mother and settle in another city."

"That happy tomorrow will never come for me," she said, and before she asked me to leave, I stood up to go. "Will you take care of my brother? I love him very much. Someday I am going to send him to the university."

She took my hand between her two palms. Then I left.

I had entered her cottage with the dignity of a judge and with the mission of a reformer, but I left feeling humbled, humiliated, and wiser. I often think of her, a spring butterfly caught in a net, a broken bud never to bloom, handled by many admirers, soiled and cruelly crushed, and thrown into the gutter. She had told me that she was not a bad girl; indeed, she was not. I couldn't help thinking that there would be no bad women without bad men.

The next morning, Vartouhy was still on my mind. Had I fallen in love with her? Of course not, I told myself. Nevertheless, the question of marriage popped into my mind. But, how could I? My honorable ancestors, wherever they lie buried, would rise from their graves and haunt me, saying, "How could you do this to us? What went wrong with you?" And my Puritan friends would say, "He went mad!"

Late that evening I found myself again at her cottage door, not knowing why. When I knocked, the same old woman came out and with a hoarse voice asked me once more what I wanted and then in a rude voice told me to get lost. When I insisted upon seeing Rosita, she told me to get away from there. "Rosita's gone!"

When I told Haroutoun that Vartouhy had gone away, he did not answer me immediately. Instead, he asked me how I knew. Then he said that the national organization had kidnapped her. She did not belong there; she was a disgrace to our national honor, which we could not allow.

The Year 1918–1919

It was November 1918, and the peace treaty had been signed.* The British and French governments were now administrators of much of the Middle East. The countries of Syria and Iraq were created out of remnants

---

*The reference is to the Mudros Armistice on October 30, 1918, between the Allied Powers and the Ottoman Empire, and the Armistice of November 11, 1918, between the Allied Powers and the German Empire.

of the old Ottoman Empire. Other cities nearby were now occupied by the French army under the peace treaty; therefore, people were free to return to their homes. The French authorities encouraged their movement and helped them as much as they could. But returnees found their old homes either destroyed or still occupied by Turks. They ignored the fact that they were not welcome in their hometown and managed to survive. After all, this was their homeland. For the Turks had overpowered them, taken their land, and thrown them out.

Yet, the Turks insisted on calling us "deportees," making us strangers in our homeland. Yes, the Turks resented us. The hatred harbored was deeply ingrained in their hearts. Yet many Armenians still roamed the large cities and Aleppo in search of a home and security.

I had a painful feeling that the promises inherent in the peace would not be realized. But the nation remained hopeful, for we, too, had contributed to the Allied victory. We had fought on the Caucasian front and in Palestine with General Allenby* and had volunteers in the French Legion Dorian (Légion d'Orient).

Woodrow Wilson introduced his Fourteen Points to be recognized by all nations in the League of Nations.[5] There was talk that the United States would accept the mandate of Armenia if Wilson's Fourteen Points were respected.

In order for our small nation to be heard by the great powers, we had to be unified, to put the nation's interest above all else. But selfish politicians seeking power caused disunity and disharmony. All of our wonderful plans perished in the internal struggles for power. And the hope and desire of a new homeland once again evaporated between two major political parties.

In vain, local organizations tried to do something for the returning mobs of dislocated people without the help of a central organization.

On New Year's Day 1919, Haroutoun and I spent the time reminiscing about the past four years. How fortunate we were to have survived so many struggles, so much hardship and danger. He suggested that we celebrate that night. We were walking along the main section of Babul Farrage. The big clock struck midnight. Haroutoun suggested that we enter a bar and clink glasses, toast our luck. But I heard the voices of my Puritan ances-

*General Edmund Henry Hynman Allenby led the Allied forces against the combined Ottoman and German forces in Palestine and Syria. See, for example, Matthew Hughes, *Allenby and British Strategy in the Middle East, 1917–1919* (London: Frank Cass, 1999).

tors telling me not to enter the "joint." How I have regretted this! To have refused a lifelong loyal friend, who, like a brother, had looked after me, guided me, warned me of danger, and who had shared so many experiences with me in misery and happiness. Now, when he wanted to celebrate the end of our misfortunes, I turned him down! He often teased me about this through the years. And each time my "virtues" made me blush with remorse and self-condemnation.

The editors of *The Wasp* had a meeting to discuss future plans. We wanted to know what each would do next. Haygaz would take his sister to Constantinople and join his father. Onnig would soon go to Bulgaria to join his brother. Haroutoun would go to his brother in Boston, taking his aged mother with him. I planned to go first to Constantinople in the hope of going to school there or finding a way to go to the United States. Such plans made life interesting and exciting.

That afternoon we were walking silently on the outskirts of Aleppo, where gardens bloom among shady apricot trees. Our thoughts were of how to rebuild the new nation; deep in our minds were thoughts of how we had failed in the past as a nation.

Haroutoun broke the silence. "We were robbed of human compassion for each other because our beliefs divided us, created walls that separated us from each other. Language, religion, and tradition were once the guardian angels of our nation; but this is not so anymore; they divide rather than unite us. It seems to me that the world would be a better place if there were no separation of dogmas or religions, which divide us from our real God."

I was staring at him, and he saw my surprise. "The only difference between a Roman Catholic and a Protestant," he said, "is that the Catholic learns how to bow to his priest and the Protestant to argue with his minister, and that is progress. Both—rather, neither—believe in this God that they pray to, nor do they believe in the Bible they may read. Their characters are brittle. As new social values replace the old, the new man will have the vision of a call in life, and he will meet his challenge. This new man will overcome his past prejudices, ignorance, hatred, and fear, and with this elevation, he will have a clearer vision to see the truth and be able to love his fellow men. This will be an awakening, a new birth for all men, a new world, a new religion in which the brotherhood of man will prevail. The time will come when people will be released from the dictates of a church.

Real freedom of thought will prevail. Man shall become self-sufficient and will attain sufficient understanding to know why it pays to be a man and behave like one."

The noble soul did not have the patience to endure the wrongs of the past, for he had suffered a lot at the hands of hatred. He boldly expressed his anger with the thought that some of us would not agree with him, but he would not deny his convictions in order to please us. Against his better judgment, Haroutoun carried within him the blood of his ancestors. He was a descendant of that great man Vartan of Gurun, who was crushed but never bowed. He would rather revolt—speak up—than consent in silence to wrong.

I submitted my plans to my friend Garabed, who was teaching me English. He objected to my leaving Aleppo and my duties at the orphanage, but I told him that I was sure I would return with broader knowledge and greater skill. I reminded him of how badly I needed the education to properly perform my duties. Of course, I could not escape my obligations to the nation, which needed every one of us and all that we could give.

In March 1919, Miss Rohner invited me to visit the grave of Reverend Eskijian, to commemorate the third anniversary of his death. "Only a few will come to remember the great man who died without fear," she said, "because he did all he could to serve his people."

I took Mrs. Eskijian and a few friends with me to the cemetery. They knelt and prayed. Some wept, as did his widow. My heart led once again as I stood silently by his grave and, without tears, remembered his smile and his oft-repeated, "Someday you will be able to pay back, my son." I heard his soft voice as I stood silently by his graveside, reading his tombstone. The orphans had dedicated these words—HIS SERVANTS SHALL SERVE HIM AND SHALL SEE HIS FACE. "We do miss him, indeed," said a voice, "but we are relieved from our agony of losing him, when He gave us a man like him." I raised my head and looked up. They were all looking at me. Since that time, I have been a proud member of "the family."

Professor Daghlian, the administrator of the orphanage, strongly objected to my leaving, and when I visited Doctor Altoonian for a physical, he amazed me with his expression of devotion to the future of Armenia. He tried in vain to sketch a bright picture of an organization for building a new Armenia. "We will be founders of this future nation. We are living in a proud and historic moment, contributing our share in the building and responding to the call and challenge. We have the opportunity of serving in our time."

But I knew that it was now or never. And I was convinced that we would never be safe among the unfriendly Turks, regardless of who the governing forces might be. I had been hurt too much in the past by the Turks ever to forget, and I had to listen to my own heart, despite all of those who pressed me to stay and accused me of desertion.

A family headed by a woman in her sixties also wanted to go to Constantinople. Her widowed daughter, two young granddaughters, and her widowed daughter-in-law had survived through the hiding, bribing, and tortures of war with funds her son had sent from Constantinople. When they heard that I was also going to Constantinople, they asked me to join them on their journey; they would provide my fare. At first, I hesitated, for I wished to be free of obligations, but a mutual friend convinced me that I would need friends when I arrived in the city. So I consented and met with their family. She was a gracious old lady, with a wry sense of humor and dignity and an air of authority. She smiled at me kindly and called me son. I told her that I was willing to go with them.

My sister Anoush was sad at the thought of our separation, but I assured her that I would send for her as soon as I could. But Kikor cried. I talked to him and told him how necessary this trip was. I promised to write to his teacher and said that someday we would be together again. He hugged me, and I felt the warmth of a child who, without a whisper or a word, hugs you close with trust and love.

I left him with renewed courage and visited a few more teachers and administrators to bid them adieu and leave them instructions for Kikor. I also visited The Reverend's wife and Miss Rohner, who took my hand in both of hers and wished me good luck. What an angel this woman was! I wondered whether we owed her personally or the church for the great service she had rendered humanity. My last visit was to Sarkis at the camp. I told him I planned to go first to the capital and then, one hoped, to the United States. He said, "I will be there, maybe even before you get to America."

When I came home, Haroutoun and I had a long talk. We promised to keep in touch. He would let me know when he was ready to travel to Constantinople.

I packed and began the trip with my newfound family. This time I carried six English gold sterlings in my safety belt, a few notebooks, and copies of the three issues of *The Wasp*. Haroutoun came to the station as he had done before when I was escaping to some desert. This time he bid me goodbye and wished me happiness. I helped the children with their bags and jumped in, taking the special seat next to the grandmother as the male head of the family. The children were happy and excited at the prospect of meeting their uncle. Their mother was talkative, as widows seemed to be. But the young widow was quiet, and I noticed by her conversation that she chose her words carefully.

The train seemed to drag the burden of the past along with it, moving slowly, hesitantly. A French company had operated this train originally with great efficiency, but then the Germans had taken it over. Now the French operated it again, with the same employees. It was more undependable than ever, and the unsettled political situation made it unsafe. We booked our passage with someone who had connections with the officials, because the railroad stations were crowded with people, mostly Turkish officials anxious to get transport to Constantinople for their own security. The women had prepared a lunch, and we ate on the train. I noticed that the daughter of the older woman wished to be treated with favor. I wasn't sure why, but I thought it might be because she had discovered that I favored her sister-in-law.

When we finished our lunch, the grandmother crossed her heart and thanked God for His blessings. When the train stopped, they asked me where we were. I told them that I would be back as soon as I found the answer and told them to stay put until I returned.

French uniformed soldiers were guarding the railroad gate and office. This was the station where we had stopped four years ago, before first reaching Aleppo with Mother. One of the women passengers approached the water faucet. A Turkish peasant pushed her to one side and reached for the faucet. A French soldier stopped the man with the butt of his gun, cursing him in Turkish for his uncivilized behavior. I noted that the soldier belonged to the Legion Dorian. The Turk was surprised and retreated—in fact, ran from the water faucet.

I thanked God for providing such a reversal. A few years before, when a shabbily clothed Armenian woman had approached the same water faucet, a Turkish guard had cruelly pushed her away. Happily, I went back to the train and told the ladies that I had seen some Armenian soldiers in French uniforms guarding the station. The old lady crossed herself piously and looked up to heaven, blessing the name of the Lord.

The fuel and water did not make the train go any faster. In the meantime, the engineer was advised to proceed cautiously because saboteurs were ready to blow up or derail the train. Most of them were Turkish army deserters who worked undercover to show their resentment of the new powers, especially the Turkish-speaking Armenian soldiers of the French Army.

We arrived in Adana, at the base of the Taurus Mountains, very late, but a coachman was waiting for us and took us to his house. Before we went to bed, he informed us that the railroad line had been cut between Adana and Constantinople. The next morning, we learned that we would not be able to continue our passage. The grandmother telegraphed her son in the capital explaining our situation and where we were located, and returned to the host and asked him to find us a house until we could move on. Then she turned to me and said, "You will be our guest during our stay in Adana."

We moved to a new house, against the wishes of our host, who had been a close friend of this family years earlier in Erzurum. Once we were settled, I decided to walk into Adana and enjoy the miracle of my freedom. I couldn't believe my eyes. The city hall was a beehive of activity. People were coming in and going out, with no questions asked. Happy and friendly shouts were heard in Armenian. Men in French army uniforms stood guard. This was a world of fantasy, unbelievable. I had to pinch myself, like the boy in the book of happiness, to assure myself that it was true.

I couldn't resist the temptation to speak to a guard in Armenian and ask where he was from. I approached one and actually asked him. He said that he was from America. When he learned that I was from Gurun, he said, "I have a friend, Afarian, who is from Gurun, and he will be here at three o'clock to take this post." I knew the man, but in the meanwhile decided to see the marketplace. I asked the guard for the shortest route there.

Before the war, Adana was a great center for commerce and transportation; it had produced cotton and fruit. There had been a factory for weaving cotton goods. But Adana was paralyzed now, stripped of all activity since the war. I saw a lot of activity between incoming immigrants and occupying soldiers. The Turkish officials shied away because they were unpopular with the new occupying forces. They were especially shy with French legionnaires who spoke Turkish.

It was now nearly three o'clock in the afternoon, and I was anxious to see my friend Afarian, who had joined the Legionnaires from America. He was at his post guarding the entrance of the administration building. He was surprised to see me, and I told him my story quickly, giving him names of the few people from Gurun who had survived. Not wanting to disturb him while he was on duty, I left soon and promised to see him again.

While still on city hall grounds, I saw a man rushing in. He was about forty-five years old and looked like somebody that I had known. He noticed me and stopped. "Is your name Hovhannes?" I said it was, and then I recognized him. He had been a close friend of The Reverend. After a long time in hiding, he had disappeared and now he was in Adana. He told me that he was organizing an orphanage and had secured a building to start classes, and that if I were interested in its progress and had the time, he would like to show it to me. I agreed, and on the way to the orphanage, he told me that there was a severe need of teachers and asked if I would work with him. I told him that I was on my way to Constantinople and that I was waiting for my passage.

"Do you know how long you will be here?" he asked.

"I don't know, but I expect to leave very soon."

"Just the same, I need you," he said. "We are organizing classes, and I want you to help us as much as you can."

I told him that I would let him know, but he insisted that he was sure I would do my share to help organize the classes. When we arrived, he introduced me to a few young men who already were engaged in forming classes. Vahan, who came from Caesarea, survived in hiding, finally reaching the city. He was about nineteen, polite, healthy looking, and obliging. He said, "How nice of you to consent to work and help us."

I told him that I would be glad to help, but that I was about to leave. When I went home, I told the grandmother what had happened. She agreed that I should work but asked me whether I was working under a Protestant minister or somebody of that undesirable denomination, although she knew that my parents were Protestant.

The next morning I was on the job, organizing the classes—thanks to the Armenian legionnaires. The classes filled with new arrivals who were pulled out of Turkish harems and brought to the orphanage. Many of these children hardly knew their names or their nationality.

The Legionnaires of the French Army

After the massacre of 1895, Armenians in Turkey tried very hard to send their young sons to the new world for their safety and education, and to protect them from political unrest. They might have thought of it as a temporary accommodation until the political horizons cleared and they would return home, but that opportunity never came.

But when the Turks allowed their subjects the freedom of travel, many young men left their homes, their families, and loved ones to enjoy the freedom of the United States and Europe. Many more joined them later.

The 1915 tragedy of massacres shocked the world and Armenians in Europe and in the United States. They heard strange stories about deportation, starvation, slavery, and slaughter. But they were cut off from the old world, their families, and had no way to contact them. Even American missionaries and counselors could not supply sufficient information. Their agony multiplied when the news reached them that many young girls had been kidnapped, children killed, and their churches burned. They were tortured by the knowledge that men, women, and children were scattered all over the desert. They could not reach them to protect them.[6]

In Paris, an Armenian Central Committee organized to help the French army.[7] Young men from France and the United States volunteered to join the Legion Dorian* to fight the occupation of Turkey. These young men had only one thought in their minds: to find their loved ones and rescue them from the grasp of the Turks at any cost, even loss of life. They abandoned their ties in the new world, their comforts, their jobs, and joined the French army to march on Turkey. Nobody could stop them. They took an oath to avenge the victims of the murderers. Revenge was the password of the time. Now they trained as regulars and fought under the French flag, glad of the privilege to be in a good cause.

They showed great courage and dedicated themselves to pay back the Turks for the cruelty they had inflicted upon their victims. As soon as the

---

*This has been transcribed incorrectly and actually refers to "La Légion d'Orient," which was a French foreign legion unit that later became the Armenian Legion (La Légion Arménienne) in 1919. Many Armenians volunteered to fight with the French in an effort to help defeat the Ottoman Empire. The Armenian volunteers (*gamavor*) played a key role in capturing the heights of Arara in Palestine and opening the way to Allenby's northward advance into Syria. See Susan Paul Pattie, *The Armenian Legionnaires: Sacrifice and Betrayal in World War I* (London: I. B. Tauris, 2018).

Turks heard about the Armenians fighting for both the French and General Allenby's English army, they quickly decided to surrender. They knew these boys meant business, and their time had come for sweet revenge.[8]

Cilicia

Cilicia, an area along the southern coast of Turkey, encompassing the Taurus Mountains and extending to present-day Syria, was the last stronghold of the Armenian kingdom. Armenians had struggled to protect their homeland for centuries from the Assyrians, Greeks, and Persians until they finally surrendered to the Roman Empire. It was the end of a kingdom, but the people still were tied to their ancient homeland.

Next came the barbarians from the Far East, the Turkomans from Central Asia who ruined the land, burned and killed. Then Seljuk Turks established a reign of terror. Still the Armenians rebuilt and plowed their land.

But in 1915, imperial Germany helped the Ottoman Turks to uproot this nation from its past. This was the cruelest blow of all. After World War I, few Armenians survived to return to cultivate their land and rebuild. Those who did were turned away, refused and resented as if they were strangers. The new mandated administrations of England and France were too busy with their own interests to pay attention to the tragedy of their new subjects. They quickly forgot the Armenian contribution to their victory in Palestine and in Cilicia.[9]

Brother Hampartzoum

We continued to wait it out in Adana for the government to repair the railway line into Constantinople. One afternoon I went to Adana's marketplace to roam around and enjoy seeing Armenian soldiers in uniform. Some stood guard, others were giving orders here and there. Many people were going in and out of one small shop in particular, and I wondered what it was all about. I saw a man sitting on the floor, fixing something with a hammer. I could not see what he worked on, but his face seemed familiar. Hesitantly, I entered the shop. He was busy sharpening a knife, and he asked his next customer what he wanted. He wanted to buy a kitchen knife, so the shopkeeper showed him one. Then the shopkeeper saw me but paid no attention. He continued his work. When his customer left he looked at me and asked if I wanted to buy something. His bass voice assured me that he was who I thought he was—Brother Hampartzoum from Sivas.

I asked him if he was Brother Hampartzoum, and he asked me how I knew him. I told him my name, adding that I was Bedross-agha's son. He jumped up and grabbed my hand in surprise and happiness. He had aged considerably since I saw him last. His smallpox scars seemed broader, and he looked as though he had suffered much. His speech and general movement reminded me of a caged fox. Finally, he asked about my father. I told him how and where he had been killed. A few tears rolled down his cheeks. He made no effort to wipe them away, perhaps fearing that I might notice. Then he asked about my mother. Seeing me look down at the floor, he wiped his tears from his face with the back of his hand, which was covered with grime.

I asked him about his family. While he had been serving in the Turkish army, his family had been deported; and since his release from the army, he had searched for his wife and children from the Russian border to Mesopotamia, and from there to Der el-Zor and Noory, then to Homs, Aleppo, and finally Adana. He asked everyone if they knew of his family, or had seen them, or heard about them. His words poured out. I did not know how to ease his suffering. Remembering his close connection with the church, I tried to comfort him, saying automatically, "Maybe this is God's will." I was well aware that no one could ever relieve the agony of lost loved ones.

He looked at me in amazement, as if to make sure he had heard me right, and replied in an agonized tone, almost scolding, "Don't say that; please don't. A God that wishes the torture, maiming, and the killing of a man like your father, your mother, my wife, and my young and innocent children is not a God anymore, but cruel, and should not even be mentioned. Please do not repeat that, you innocent, naive boy." He pulled out his handkerchief and wiped away his tears, not only of sorrow or suffering, but because of his separation from the God who had deserted him and his people in their hour of need.

This looked to me to be the death and burial of his faith, hope, and trust. It was bitter and very difficult for him to bury them. He insisted that I come and see him again. Luckily, a customer came and relieved me of my own torture and amazement.

Desperation gives a man two choices: He may become closer to his God, seeking protection from the evil he does not understand; or he may discard his beliefs and disassociate himself from his God, relying on his own wit to face the realities and misfortunes of life. Brother Hampartzoum was the only returnee I knew who did not want to return home to rebuild his birthplace, or to return to his people, or his God. He was a man without a God and without a country.

A few days later I met Afarian, my friend in the French army. I asked him how long he expected to be stationed in Adana. He looked at me thoughtfully and said, "We have a mission to perform, and we are going to stay until the mission is completed. The French army wants us to go home right now. It seems to me that there is a lot of double-crossing, but all of us are going to stay. We did not come here to fight and occupy territories and help attain their victory, but for justice." His justice had a double meaning, which I understood very well.

We could not get passage for our trip to Constantinople, for the railroad was not safe. So I continued my work at the orphanage. I enjoyed the friendship of my coworkers, especially Vahari. Finally, after six weeks of waiting, my new family obtained passage through a friend who had connections.

I would cherish the memory of these last six weeks in Adana all my life. Young, sunburned, happy Armenians educated to their mission enriched my heart. They showed a readiness to restore the lives of the youngsters, rescue them from abject slavery, even marrying the girls they took from the harems, the wishes to avenge the honor of their loved ones—parents, children, mothers, and sisters. This was the challenge of the time, and these young men met their challenge against all odds, proving that they were the sons of Haig and Vartan, great in victory and defeat. Volunteers reminded their sisters and brothers that they were not forgotten, even a thousand miles away from home, and brought hope to ravaged hearts. It was not unusual for these men to stay after their discharge. They were marrying young ladies with Arabic tattoos on their lips or foreheads that indicated they had once been owned by the master of a harem.

Finally, we were leaving the city. We took whatever belongings we could to the train. The service was better now, the trains livelier. We passed the greenery of the Adana countryside, almond and cherry trees in full bloom, with delicate, fragrant blossoms of white, pink, and red. It was a memorable, gay April day in 1919. The engineer was instructed to go cautiously and be on guard for saboteurs. I saw legionnaires on board, questioning passengers and checking their identification.

A Turkish family, a husband and wife with two young girls of about six and ten years of age, sat across the aisle from us. The man started a casual conversation with me, very polite, in fine Turkish. I responded. They were going to Konya, just over the mountains, and I told him that we were going to the capital. He noticed the fatherless children in my group, and the two women, hardly in their forties, without husbands. He did not ask me who they were. He didn't even ask me where my birthplace was, although he diplomatically called me a countryman. (Quite a switch from my previous train adventures.) It was understood that the children were orphaned and their mothers widowed, and that I had been left homeless, returning—no one knew where, nor to what.

He looked to me like an important man in the Turkish government, and it was obvious why he was anxious to leave Adana; criminals do not feel comfortable on the Day of Judgment, and that day was at hand.

I saw a volunteer of the French army questioning the passengers in Turkish about Turks who were fleeing the city, but they left Armenians alone. Just a few feet away one of them asked a man to show his papers. The high-pitched voice and angry tone shook up all of us. The man across the aisle smiled at me. He forcefully touched the shoulders of one of the girls, hugging her to show her that she was secure. I smiled back, without taking my eyes off of the little girl, hardly six years old. The soldier came close and asked if I knew the man across the aisle. I said that he was a friend, and the soldier left. The children's mother smiled softly, with gratitude, without speaking. When I turned to my group, the grandmother's face had turned to vinegar. She was disappointed in me and didn't talk to me for a long while.

When our train stopped at Konya, I was told that Mr. Partridge was passing through this station, possibly on the incoming train going to Adana. Wondering if the news were true, I waited on the platform. A train slowly stopped, and I noticed an American emblem on the wagon. The door opened, and I saw my friend, tall and blond. I hopped onto the train, my hand extended in joy.

He recognized me instantly and inquired about my father and family. He was shaken by the news, then asked me about the boys from Gurun. Hurriedly I told him all I knew. We spoke in Armenian. The whistle blew, his train started moving. While we were still talking, the second whistle blew to release the brakes. The train speeded up. I bid him goodbye without a word of thanks for the help he had given us during the deportation. I had to jump off. My last glimpse was of him waving his hand and saying over and over, "Take care of yourself." He was returning to Adana to reorganize a school for returning Armenian deportees.

After the evening meal, the grandchildren slept, and the grandmother went to bed. The two widows kept me talking about my future plans, about how badly I needed an education, and my desire to return to the newly formed Armenia. They smiled at me and did not discourage me when they learned that this home, rather a dream, had no concrete foundation. I had no money and knew no one in the city. They wondered how I was going to accomplish all of this. The grandmother's daughter drew closer and suggested that her brother in Constantinople, she was sure, would do something for me because he was a very wealthy merchant. But her sister-in-law reminded her that I didn't want help that way and turned to me and asked, "Isn't that true?"

Automatically I agreed with her, not knowing her motive or her meaning. Her sister-in-law left us. We whispered softly, occasionally letting a word go aloud to satisfy the listeners. I asked her what her plans were.

During the war, she said, she had managed to send her son to Constantinople. He was in school. "I would like to settle my husband's share of the business with my brother-in-law and get my part of the interest." But something was bothering her, and she was not going to let a stranger know what it was. One Sunday afternoon back in Adana, I had heard a family argument; their friend insisted to the grandmother and her daughter that they were wrong, and he said loudly, "She did not, she could not help it," and asked them to be tolerant toward her. But the sister-in-law told him that she did not deserve it. "My brother was gypped!"* So now they were going to cut her out of her share of the family wealth. I could have kissed this troubled woman, but I did not. Instead, I took her waiting hand and locked it in mine and said no more.

I heard the grandmother cough and thought it a very polite warning. She was sure that I was a friend but was not sure of her daughter-in-law. I

---

*This is a derogatory term for being swindled or cheated. It stems from the word "gypsy" and perpetuates a racist stereotype against the Roma and Sinti.

bid her good night and stretched out in my covers, near the grandmother, to show that her confidence had not been misused.

The next day the train stopped at Ismid station, just outside Constantinople. It was evening. The shadows of the trees draped the city and made the evening very desirable and restful. It was uplifting and romantic. I promised myself that I would come back and enjoy this beauty.

When we finally arrived at Haydar Pasha Station, we felt we had made quite an accomplishment. The grandmother's son was waiting for us. He took his mother into his arms, hugged her and kissed her on both of her cheeks, "How do you do?," and shook her hand. It hurt to see it, and I could not help wonder how much it must have hurt her.

7

Constantinople

The City of Paradise

FINALLY AT OUR DESTINATION in Constantinople, the grandmother graciously introduced me to her son. "I want you to meet our friend; he is going to stay with us." Her son shook hands with me and politely engaged me in conversation. A horse and carriage were waiting for us. He ordered the coachman to stop at *Nishan-Tash*. Although it was dark, I wanted to see as much of the city as I could. My host saw my excitement and explained each passing street. "This is Pera, the most lovely street in all of Constantinople." When the coachman turned to the right, he gave him the number of the apartment, and the carriage stopped at the door. We helped the ladies and children out of the coach.

I purposely ignored my new friend, leaving her alone to carry her own suitcase. A young lady appeared. She hugged her mother and kissed her sister and her sister-in-law. Then the grandmother recited her introduction to the hostess of the house, who graciously welcomed me. She said, "We will be happy to have you. We are indeed honored to have you with us."

A maid came and did her utmost to make us comfortable. We had a cool cherry sherbet made of tart cherry juice. It relaxed us. My friend went to her room and changed her dress. She returned all in black, her mourning dress after five years of widowhood. It was a noble gesture, naturally assumed by a widow, but she looked prettier in a dark dress; very gracious, more attractive even than the young miss. Her brother-in-law looked at her from the corner of his eye. No one said anything. I winked at her secretly when I thought it was safe to do so, for my heart was aching for her. Hadn't she suffered enough? Why was she receiving this humiliating treatment?

In the morning when we were served breakfast by the maid, I was conscious of my shabby clothes, but my host graciously started a conversation with me. He asked me what my plans were. I told him that I intended to go to school. He did not ask me if I had enough money, but suggested, in a very friendly way, "It takes a lot of money, especially if you want to go to Robert College."*

His mother interrupted. "He will stay here until he gets organized. Besides, he has no friends and does not know anyone in the city. We may do something for him," she said with a positive note. Her son left me alone to wonder how soon I should get out of this house with my shabby clothes. I felt like a patch of disgrace on his aristocratic dignity. I noticed that his young sister followed the conversation closely.

When he kissed his mother to leave for the office, his wife asked him to invite a few friends in for dinner. When the maid started cleaning the house, the young miss coyly asked me to take a walk around the block to see the city.

This was a choice residential neighborhood. The streets were beautiful. I went as far as Pera, the only Westernized street. People were dressed differently; they were well groomed, neat and clean. This part of the city was busy and gay. I took another walk on a side street and then returned.

The lady of the house opened the door with a friendly greeting, addressing me as Baron (Mr. in Armenian). When I stepped in, I glanced at the baron's clothes. It was very depressing.

"You know," she said, "you amaze me with your careful words and genteel manners. I never met a man from the interior like you." She asked me what my father's business had been at home.

---

*Robert College was founded in 1863 by American philanthropist Christopher Robert and Congregational missionary Cyrus Hamlin. With a campus overlooking the Bosphorus, it became a highly prestigious school with an international faculty and student body until the end of the Ottoman Empire. Robert College has gone through several transformations; in 1971, it was transferred to the Turkish Republic and has been renamed Boğaziçi University.

The grandmother entered the living room, sat by me, and told her daughter-in-law, "You people who are born and raised in a large city don't know anything about small-city life. They are educated, and I dare say that they are dependable and more real, down-to-earth people," implying that big-city people often were insincere and artificial, proper in manner and speech but not as trustworthy as they should be. And, she added, "He is a good boy. Unfortunately, his family was Protestant." In a friendly way, she suggested that I would soon learn. I thought that she was laying the groundwork for my adoption and that my religion was the only reason I did not qualify.

A short young man came to visit. He was in his early thirties, immaculately dressed. He reached out for the grandmother's hand and graciously kissed it, then the hostess, and finally the young lady, who held out her hand with a smile. He kissed it tenderly.

When the dinner guests arrived, I was seated next to the grandmother at the head of the table. This indicated to the guests my place in the family. The guests were charming society people. Then the lady next to me began a conversation. She asked me about the deportation and my family. She asked out of the sheer thrill and excitement of the adventure, not out of sympathy. The grandmother stopped her, reminding her not to stir unpleasant memories because a sore always bleeds a little each time the bandage is lifted.

But the young miss pleaded with her mother to let me repeat the story of Mutzpin, where I saw a stone pillar in the middle of the desert, about three feet wide and twenty feet high, with nothing on top of it but the nest of a lonely stork. The guests wanted to know where Mutzpin was. I told them that it was in an unknown section, called Nissibin, in the Mesopotamian desert not far from old Nineveh, or Mousul, but they did not know where Nineveh was and had never heard of Mutzpin. So I had to tell them that in the Armenian Apostolic Church in the Divine Liturgy of the Blessing of Saints, there is a reference to the bishop of Mutzpin.

My neighbor looked at me in wonder and asked, "Where did you study your history?"

"In Gurun."

"Where is that?" she asked.

"In some forgotten corner, far, far away in Asia Minor."

Grandmother interrupted and said, "Now, you know why he is my guest."

The next morning, I took down the address of Garabedian, the Armenian school next to the mother church of Galata. I had a long walk through the streets of Pera and asked a few people where I could find the Armenian Church. I was anxious to spot an Armenian, but in a city such as this, everyone looks alike. Finally, I arrived at a busy section of horse carriages and porters carrying big loads harnessed on their backs. A shoeshine boy approached me. I refused him, but asked him if he knew where the Armenian Church was. He looked at me, and with a big smile and told me to go to the second block and turn left, and I would see the church. He was still smiling as I left. I kept going and turned to the left. I saw a strange sight— an almost nude woman in a caged window. I was shocked and blushed. Although I didn't know a soul in the city, I was afraid someone would see me where I didn't want to be seen. Then I understood that strange smile on the shoeshine boy's face.

I rushed to the main street, where I found a neatly dressed middle-aged man. He looked Armenian. I asked him about the church. In Armenian, he asked me "Are you Armenian?" I said, "Yes," and he accompanied me to the church, then left me. When I went to the principal's office, he told me that the classes were already filled and that I was too late for registration. When I told him where I was staying, he was surprised. He asked me if my host knew that I wanted to go to school, suggesting that he could do a lot for me. Later, I found out that the grandmother had wanted to pay for my schooling but her son objected.

The following day I wanted to go to Koum Kapou. A friend of mine had given me a sealed letter and insisted that I deliver it to her mother, who would surely have a room for me. I walked on Pera again. This boulevard intrigued me from the beginning to the end of my stay in Constantinople. I walked steadily, admiring the shops and the window displays, like a farmer boy in a big city. I thought how wonderful it would have been to be born here, to be able to go to school in a great city like this. Finally, I crossed the drawbridge that connected the western part of the city to the eastern. What a great change! Everything became eastern! Men wore fezzes, and women covered their faces with veils. This was the real East, as "east" as could be. I turned down the street where the goldsmiths ply their trade and entered a closed market, like the eastern bazaar. Here you could buy anything you wanted, from Egypt, Damascus, Beirut, or Aleppo.

An Armenian goldsmith directed me to Koum Kapou: "You must go to Gedick Pasha, then go straight until you see the Armenian Church."

It was late in the afternoon when I met my friend's mother. I was happy to see her, for she was kind, and I felt like I had found a new friend. She made lunch, and we started talking about the past and how I knew her daughter, the time we had spent in the desert. She asked me about her grandchildren, whom she hadn't yet seen.

She opened the sealed envelope, read it and reread it, then asked me how her son-in-law was. Before I could answer, she said, "I understand that you are a very close friend of my daughter. Confidentially, how are they getting along?"

I told her that I did not know, that her daughter hadn't told me anything special. Then she asked me where I was staying. When I gave the name of the family and the address, she smiled weakly and said, "You do not belong there, my son. Let me take care of you. I will cook and look after you. My daughter asked me; I must."

I asked her how much she expected me to pay for my room and board. "I'm not going to charge you as a stranger. We will see." I was thrilled by this warm welcome from this woman toward a strange man. In the meantime, a young girl entered the living room. She was twelve years old. The woman said, "Meet my daughter; she is from my second husband."

She made me promise her that I would move in soon, and left her.

The following day, encouraged by my success, I took the address of the Bible House of the American missionaries. I met a young man as I entered the building. He noticed my uncertainty and greeted me warmly. His name was Aram. When I told him that I was from Sivas, he asked me if I knew Hurant Kulujian. I was surprised to hear that he was also here. We were close friends when we were children. Aram told me that my friend had some strange experiences in Sivas, that now he was married and living in Uskudar, across the Bosphorus from Constantinople, close to Aram's home.

"By the way," he asked me, "do you have any relations or a friend in New York City? I'm sure that I have seen your name on our bulletin board. Somebody was looking for you from New York, and our office was trying to locate you."

He directed me to the office to find out about it. He was congenial and warm and promised to tell Hurant about me. I asked Aram to direct me to the office of *Jagadamard*, one of the city's largest Armenian daily papers. Mousa, another friend of mine from the desert, had told me that he could be contacted there if I ever reached Constantinople. After a long walk in the afternoon, searching the strange streets and buildings, I finally saw a sign written in large Armenian letters: JAGADAMARD. I entered the office. The place was filled with strangers from out of town. They were all there to locate people or find a job. This office, the most active organization in the city, did all it could to help. I asked the man at the desk about Mousa, but I didn't know his last name. So, the man asked me how I knew him. When I explained, he said, "Oh, you want to see Baron Armenag." He took my name and asked me to come again. After I gave my name, I added, "Say Habib was here," to make sure Mousa would remember me.

The next day, when I met Armenag, he was full of charm and smiles. We greeted each other like long-lost brothers who had found each other. He ordered tea and some Turkish delight.

"Do you know who else is here?" he asked. "You won't believe it!"

"Who?"

"Sakally."

It was my happiest moment since I had left the desert. We talked about the past and our adventures and how we had managed to come to Constantinople at long last. Finally, he gave me the news of the newly formed Armenian government in Yerevan, the capital of Armenia. We made arrangements to meet again, and Sakally, too, of course.

Nature had created marvels in this part of the country: Constantinople, where a past civilization had reigned in Oriental splendor, the mecca of culture and commerce for centuries. Constantinople, circled by the sea, is one of the most beautiful cities in the world. Here, East does meet West, providing a strange mixture of nationalities. Persians in their native costumes; Hindus, more Westernized, wearing their characteristic turbans; Arabs in their agile desert robes; Egyptians and Greeks, Armenians and Jews, French and English, Bulgarians, Russians, Germans, and Turks. This is the Babylon of all nations and languages, a veritable paradise! Everywhere vestiges proclaimed its glorious past—the fascinating ancient buildings, churches, mosques, a comingling of architectures. The times change, but the remains of the Romans, Greeks, Byzantines, and others remind you who ruled here in the past. The Turks, through it all, held on to this gem and the country at large.

I made it a habit to leave my new home and enjoy the fresh beauty of it all. I was hungry for it. "What a shame it is," I mused, "that I had come here so late and under such unpleasant circumstances." But better late than never, and I was glad that I had finally arrived and intended to make the best of it.[1]

When I met Sakally and Armenag, they told me of the struggle for Armenia in the Caucasus. Sakally was learning Russian and planning to leave for the new fatherland. "They need us there; we do not belong here."

Armenag agreed with him, and they made me blush for my selfish, unpatriotic coolness toward the newly founded Armenia. I was determined to stay and find out what it was all about; and, if I failed to go to school, I would prepare for my long-planned trip to the United States. I intended to make my own decisions. On my return home, I told my host and hostess and the grandmother that I had found a new place to live. The grandmother was indignant and asked me if anyone had offended me. I lied graciously to make her feel comfortable. To the amazement of my host and the family, I moved to the humble house of a widow across the street from an Armenian Church of Koum Kapou.

Tragedy of Survival

Hurant Kulujian was working, and I could not see him because he lived in Uskudar. Aram told me that his mother was very much interested in meeting me and asked me to have dinner with them. We arranged a date and took a boat to cross to Uskudar. She received me with a gracious smile, as if I were related to her. There was so much more love and contentment in this humble home than in the last home I had stayed in. She had made *dolma*,* and the three of us ate the stuffed grape leaves until we could not take another bite. I enjoyed it very much, not because I was pampered and honored, but because I knew that I was a welcome guest in this house.

After dinner, Aram went to see if Hurant was at home and returned with him. I hadn't seen Hurant since 1914. I hadn't known whether or not he was alive. We embraced like brothers. We had so much to tell one another. When evening came, Aram's mother suggested that I spend the night with

---

*A popular Middle Eastern and Greek stuffed vegetable dish.

them, but Hurant convinced them that I should go with him; besides, he wanted me to meet his wife. I gratefully thanked Aram and his mother and bid them good night.

The floor in Hurant's house was bare, no chairs or furniture. A single kerosene lamp stood in the far corner. His shy young wife welcomed me with a genuine smile, but the obvious deprivations and need depressed me. When we settled down on the floor, I realized how difficult it had been to survive. Although they had not been deported, they had had their share of misery and then some.

As a child, Hurant was an outstanding violinist. He had given a concert in 1913. In 1915, he was drafted, but he was picked to go to the governor's mansion to entertain the governor and his guests. In the meantime, his parents and sister had been deported. The governor of Sivas had enjoyed his musical talent, but they did not want an Armenian in the palace's service. They asked him to accept the Islamic faith, or else. They changed his name and asked him to marry a Turkish girl to prove his faith in Islam. This was a very hard thing for an Armenian to do—against tradition and his vow to marry with love. An Armenian cook in the palace suggested that he marry an Armenian girl who had been adopted by a Turk and given a Turkish name. He could rescue her from the Turkish home and let the future take care of itself.

He did so, and when the Allied forces neared the town, he escaped with his wife to the big city, poor and desperate. Instead of enjoying life in their youth, they were suffering the tragedy of survival. In the morning after a light breakfast, they asked me to come again and have dinner with them. I promised them that I would as soon as I could, but the opportunity never came.

Through Aram of the Bible House, I found my brother's address in New York and wrote to ask if it were possible for him to send me a visa. Meanwhile, I met an Armenian minister and his wife in Gedick Pasha. They showed an interest in me and offered to help me in any way they could. At Aram's suggestion, I gave up the idea of going to school. Instead, I searched for work, but the town was full of immigrants. People came even from Russia, escaping the revolution. They were all desperate. They came to Constantinople to save their lives and found security under the Allied protection, but thousands were unemployed, desperately looking for shelter and food.

Haroutoun wrote to say he had to leave Aleppo and suggested that he bring my sister Anoush to Adana. It seemed that when the Allied forces came to an agreement with the Turks, plans for building new homes for Armenians were forgotten. Armenians had had clashes with the Turks in Marash and Antep and Hajin. Without the protection of the Allies, French and English, the deportees did not stand a chance. The Turks once more massacred Armenians, while the occupying forces looked the other way.

I was able to pay my room and board, but my savings were dwindling away. I had a few pennies to spend for fare, and I walked and walked the city in order to save money. Finally, I could no longer pay for my room. My sweet landlady started complaining about the price of food. She suggested that I take any job to make a living.

One Sunday at church in Gedick Pasha, a lady in a dark dress approached me and asked if I were Bedross-agha's son. When I said yes, she said that she was about to go to Sivas with missionaries and was glad to have seen me. Her name was Zabel. Her husband had taught in our school's carpentry shop. She had lost him, did not know where he was. That same day, a family invited me to their house for dinner; and when I told them that I expected some trouble from my landlady because I had no money or job, they asked me to move into their house. I told them that I couldn't do that as long as I owed money to my landlady. The lady of the house said she heard that the British army had an opening for an interpreter in the army warehouse.

I moved out with the hope that I would find a job very soon and pay my landlady. She agreed. She did not want to lose more money on me and gladly let me go. My new landlady was well educated. Her husband was a well-known merchant in a small town nearby. They had come to Constantinople for security. She managed to find work here and there, but her husband had not worked since their arrival in Constantinople. One morning she suggested that we should go with her to the British Labor Headquarters, where we might be able to apply for jobs. My hand shook because I did not know how to fill out an application.

They told us that they needed a checker. I asked what that was. The woman at the counter explained the job to me and added, "I am sure you can do it."

Happily, I signed my name at the bottom of the paper and left feeling hopeful. They assured me that I would hear from them soon.

My brother George sent no answer from New York. My shabby clothes were getting shabbier. My old khaki pants could not hold a press anymore. I was not sure if anybody would want me to work for them. I asked Aram to compose a letter to my friend Nilson in London. I had told him that he could write to me care of the Bible House. I signed it Habib to make sure that he would remember me from the Darbasia POW camp. I received an answer in a very short time:

Dear Habib,
It was a great surprise indeed to receive your letter. I am sure that you want to go to school now, but before I write about schooling, let me hear from you about your plans and please let me send you some clothes, which I am sure you need and if you are short of funds, let me know.

I thanked him for his letter and assured him that financially I was all right. I thanked him, too, for the offer of clothing, but told him that I did not need any. Still, I did not hear from my brother, or from the British Labor Headquarters. Soon I received another letter from my friend:

Hovhannes,
I have talked to my mother about the war since my return, especially of the life in Darbasia and the friendship that we enjoyed in those bitter days in the desert, and I told her, too, what you had done for our boys. She has asked me to write you and tell you that you are welcome in our house for as long as you wish to stay. My uncle, who is a judge in London, wants to provide you with all the needs for your schooling. I would love to hear from you. Let me do something for you. It is my turn.
                              Your friend,
                              Nilson

Six weeks had passed, and I had not received any answers from the British employment office, so I went to find out why I had not been called up yet. I saw a desk clerk who wore an Army uniform but who appeared to me to be Greek. I told him who I was and wrote down my name. He returned shortly and told me that no such name was in the file. I was annoyed, confused, and disappointed.

"I must have that job," I told him, almost shouting. I went on in despair, "Are you sure you looked in the right place? They promised to write me without fail."

An English officer passed and asked me what the trouble was. In sheer desperation, I poured forth all of the English words I could muster in an attempt to explain to him that I was promised a job six weeks ago and was waiting anxiously to hear from them. "Now this man," I said, pointing to the uniformed man, "tells me that he cannot find my application."

The officer asked me how I spelled my name. I wrote it on a piece of paper and thrust it into his hand, hope swelling within. After a few moments the officer came back with a smile, and said, "Indeed, it was there," and after a long pause, characteristic of the British, he said, "You must come here Monday and see me; I will take you to your job."

My heart beat faster. I visualized the end of my misery and deprivation. Now I could pay my landlady, maybe even buy a new suit of clothes, and bring my sister to Constantinople.

On Monday morning I went to the British Employment Headquarters and saw the officer, who took me to another office for my final review. They told me that I must have identification papers from a local establishment. All I had was a recommendation from the school administrator in Aleppo, but they wanted a local authority to verify who I was.

I went to Aram for advice. He suggested that I see Reverend Zenopea, the head of the Armenian Protestant Churches in Turkey, for he would recognize the name of the professor who had given me the recommendation. I rushed to Gedick Pasha, rapped at the knocker, asked the maid if I could see the Reverend. She asked my name and left me at the door. When she came back, she told me that the Reverend was very busy. I told her that it was most urgent that I see him. She went in again, and when she came out of the secluded privacy of her master's office, she told me the sad fact that I must come some other time.

So I returned that afternoon. I could not wait. Finally, a sober man, immaculately dressed, with a starched white shirt, band collar, came out. He looked as though he were ready for an official reception, cool and composed. I told him who I was and pulled out my recommendation papers, signed by the professor whom he knew well. He told me icily that he did not know me and could not help me. I reminded him that I did not know anybody in the city and that the Armenian Mother Church had recommended that I see him and that I was from a Protestant family. He repeated that he could not do anything, but that he would gladly give me some money from his small discretionary budget to help the needy. I told him that I was not begging for money; all I needed was his signature on a piece of paper to certify my name. He rudely turned back, told me that he was sorry, and closed the door.

I went home and told the story to my new landlady. She grew angry at the great head of the church who was not available to those who needed him most. She said that she could not understand this and wondered what was wrong. All evening long we discussed ways of getting a verification. The local minister of the church, who knew me, suggested that I go to the office of the untouchable— he would talk to me, the great man behind the locked door. When I arrived there, he put down a few words on a piece of paper to certify my identity and my name (see figure 7.1), then brushed me off, as

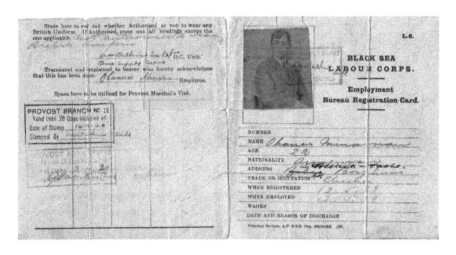

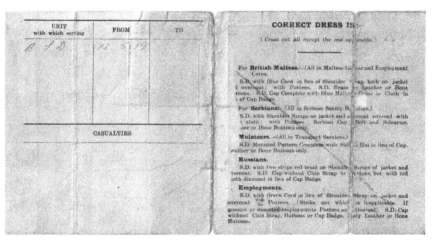

FIGURE 7.1
Minassian's Black Sea Labour Corps Employment Card, May 12, 1919

if to get rid of the poor, helpless, and undesirable. I promised myself that I would never forget this. But I thanked him and reminded him how important it was for me to get this job. I could see that he had met me—a nuisance, annoying him and disturbing his peace for such a triviality.

The next morning the man in the house, encouraged by my success, went to the headquarters with me. The officer asked us to jump into his small army car and took us to the main office for registration. We went to the desk, and the uniformed man saluted him. We showed our papers, and the same officer took us in his car to our assignments. We entered a door guarded by Serbian soldiers and were introduced to Corporal Sam, who was in charge of the army feed supply. We were under his command. Sam took us to the yard where hay and sacks of oats were piled. He gave us each a book in which to enter receipts and check the shipments. I couldn't understand a word of what Sam said. I asked my companion if he did. He said that he understood very little. How I wished that he would stay close to me so that I could tell the workers what Sam wanted me to do.

Kaba Tash was close to the palace and had been used by that sultan for wood storage. It overlooked the Bosphorus, and its large seafront was protected by heavy stone walls. Commercial boats docked here and unloaded; we reported the volume and weight of each load. I had to remind my corporal to talk slower so that I might catch what he was saying. He had a front tooth missing, and it was hard for me to know whether he was ordering, or shouting, or both.

A small Welsh fellow under Sam's jurisdiction was always asking me questions and wanting to know if I knew any women to whom I could introduce him. I told him that I was new in the city and had no connection with this huge ocean of people. He wanted a friend. This poor fellow seemed desperately lonesome. He was disappointed in me because I could not take him any place like other boys did, and so he left me alone. I noticed that his English was worse than Sam's. For example, when he called out an order, I didn't know if he was saying "fifteen sacks" of oats or "fifty sacks." I told him that it would be more practical if he wrote down the orders to prevent mistakes. I was always embarrassed to make such mistakes and constantly reminded myself that I must not lose my job.

My friend and I traveled back and forth to work from Gedick Pasha to Galata Bridge. We did not have to pay the toll for the bridge like the British Army personnel, and we were proud to show our passes and cross for free (see figure 7.2). My friend paid my carfare until I could pay my own. But the month flew by, leaving me flat broke. My landlady wanted to wash my

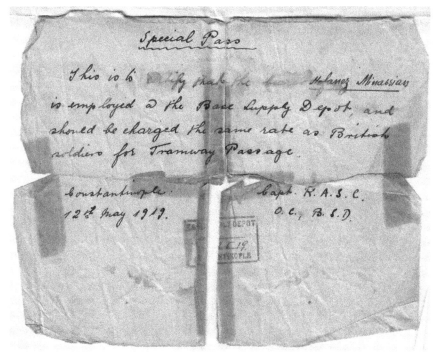

FIGURE 7.2
Minassian's Special Pass, May 12, 1919, British Supply Depot

shirts for me, but I had only the one I wore on my back. I would go to my room, take off my shirt, and leave it by the door for the landlady. The next day it would be washed and pressed so that I could go to work or church with the same trousers and shirt I had been wearing the previous day.

One day Sam told me that I could go to the army food-supply depot and receive rations. I took whatever the clerk gave me, including bacon, which I had never eaten before, a huge piece of yellow cheese, and a chunk of beef. I gave it to my landlady, to her delight. But the happiest day of my life was when the captain paid me my wages—two gold English pound sterlings for my first month's work. How grateful I was. And how lucky. And once more I remembered how unfortunate I would have been if the man behind the closed door, the disdainful head of the church, had not put his official stamp on a piece of paper, which enabled a desperate soul to survive. Yet, he had filled me with hate, not love.

My landlady insisted that I pay my previous landlady first and then her, but I divided my wages in two and paid them both, keeping a few pennies for myself.

I worked day and night, without earning extra for overtime, to show my appreciation. Whenever a boat was unloaded, the army would save the rental on the ship. The workers got used to me, and I got used to them. Most of them were Kurds from all over the country, and they were a hardy lot, strong and frugal. They worked under a contractor boss, who provided them shelter in a *khan*, where they would sleep and eat. They played backgammon or cards, smoked in the coffee shop until the wee hours, got a little tipsy, and in the morning, they would go to work all over again, at the shores of Kaba Tash.

These men, the most hardworking in the city, were also the most deprived. Most of them came from unknown villages and hamlets. They were sturdy, but the air in their rooms could kill a cow or a horse! Their food was the cheapest, even when they received wages. If they weren't getting paid, they got only a loaf of bread and a piece of cheese. The contractor who gave them jobs was also supposed to give them food and shelter and tip them a few pennies for booze to keep them happy. If they were young, this kind of life was unbearable, and they would never be able to return to their homes and marry or reach their families, who had waited for them for maybe five, six, or even ten years. Often, they died from diseases they picked up from living so close to the gutters of the big city. Or trouble might break out, and someone would die by the knife. But these men from the unknown hills never robbed. On the contrary, they always shared whatever they had and in case of sickness, they helped one another as though they were true brothers. They lived virtuously in the gutters of the big city.

They believed in working hard and earning a living. If they were not under contract, they stood idle under the Galata Bridge, leaning on their harnesses, waiting to be hired, even to earn a few honest pennies. The local people called them "professional hammals or porters," a title just above that of beggar, because they were paid "beggar's wages." They would carry anything that you could load upon them—house furniture, sacks of grain—from place to place, often climbing steep hills with sturdy steps, from market to the houses and from one warehouse to another, like beasts of burden. These Kurds were dependable, loyal, congenial, and trustworthy, in fact—trusted by all. Yet they were always in rags and filthy. Day by day, year in and year out dying, as they dreamed of going home once more to be the "light" of their huts, the fire of their families, which they called *ojak*.

I grew to know and respect these people who worked day by day, minding their own business, and happy to be able to work, just work. They would unload the boats and stack the sacks high up to the sky, building pyramids with the bales of hay. They would often joke and mimic the English soldiers, throwing in the few words of English they had picked up, saying, "Pardon," "Mister," "Yes," or "No."

Ahmad was a Kurd, and the strongest of them all. He was their leader, although they called him *kall*, because he did not have any hair on his head. He was a great show-off. They would load him with as many as six sacks of oats, each weighing about one hundred pounds. Without tiring or showing a sign of weakness, he would go around the boat and the storeroom. We also had some regular workers in our group who did daily tasks in the storeroom. Among them were two young brothers: the older one, Mustafa, became my favorite, and I always asked him to do a few errands for me. He was dependable, fine, and friendly. He had lost his father in the war and worked to support his mother. He lived in a shack where the rent was low, but he had to travel a long distance to the city. Jobs were rare and hard to come by.

Haroutoun wrote that he had arrived in Adana and had brought my sister with him. As soon as they heard from his brother in Boston, he would come to Constantinople to go the United States. He placed my sister with a family until I could ask her to join me. He reminded me that the political outlook was gloomy. The Turks were on the run again, determined to destroy the Armenians who had survived the previous massacres, right under the noses of the French and British occupying forces.*

My work became more demanding each day as contractors rushed shipments. I was forced to work nights in order to clear the decks. But Sam did not like my way of working. He tried to persuade me to forget the scale and instead just count each sack of grain, averaging the bags at one hundred pounds each. I noticed, however, that the bags were getting smaller, less than a hundred pounds each. Sometimes they weighed only eighty-five pounds. I showed this to Sam and reminded him that the army lost money by not weighing the bags and only assuming that each bag weighed in at one hundred pounds.

"Do what you are told to do," he said with disgust, "and the hell with the army!"

---

*Mark Levene, *The Crisis of Genocide*, vol. 1, *Devastation: The European Rimlands, 1912–1938* (Oxford: Oxford University Press, 2013).

When the captain of the supply depot visited us, Sam complained that I could not carry out orders or get along with the other army privates. The captain, a man in his late forties, asked me in a friendly manner whether I was all right and if everyone was treating me right. "Sir," I replied, "I am very glad to have my job, and I enjoy doing it."

"If anybody gives you trouble," he said, "just let me know." When he left, Sam wanted to know what we had talked about and reminded me that army regulations stipulated that I could only talk to the captain through him.

Meanwhile, our burlap sacks, which the workers patched daily in preparation for new shipments, began disappearing from the warehouse. When I told Sam about my discovery, he told me that I should mind my own business.

One day I came to work, and Sam was gone. The bookkeeper informed me that he would not be in that day; that he would never come back. A few weeks later, a sergeant came in to replace Sam. He introduced himself as Dick and said he wanted to know the operations in the yard. In the meantime, a Greek contractor came to visit him and complained that since I had had the job he was losing money because his loads were always reported short upon arrival. After he left, Dick wanted to know why we didn't count the sacks, which would be faster. I said, "No."

He gave me a strange look and left. The bookkeeper told me that Dick was not satisfied with my answer.

"You mean he did not like it?" Within a few weeks, a woman began visiting Dick in the afternoon. She was in her late fifties, her face was covered with layers of powder, and she was missing one eye. I found it hard to look at her, but Dick was very happy to see this not-so-attractive woman, a parasite in the big city, living off of easy prey, lonesome soldiers, and strangers in town.

The private working under Dick insisted that I stop using the scale in order to make the job go faster. Now I understood the meaning of the visit by the Greek merchant. I refused and gave my book to a Welsh soldier to do the counting, and I reported to the office that I would take the afternoon off.

When the captain visited us again, he approached me and asked how I was getting along with the new men. I hesitated, looking for the proper answer to the question.

"Whenever you have trouble," he said, "let me know. Meantime, do your work, my boy, as best you can."

A few days after the captain's visit, Dick showed me a notice from headquarters demanding that all shipments, whoever the checker was, should carry my signature; but the jugglers always get around regulations. Therefore, often I was told to go home earlier than I was supposed to. One morning, when I came to report for work and to check the orders for the day, Dick called me to say that the bookkeeper would not be in that day. The head of the Serbian guards had told me that the night before the foreman and the bookkeeper had been arrested for carrying sacks of sugar. Dick did not know that I had heard in detail what had happened the night before.

My work doubled as contractors poured in shipment after shipment. Often I had to sleep in the office in order to finish unloading the boats. I found a broken army cot to sleep on during the late nights I couldn't go home. When the rush was over, I asked Dick if I could have the cot for my use. He agreed because it was broken and the Turks had left it behind in the storage house. I asked Mustafa to carry it to my home in Beshig Tash, not far away from work. He hesitated and asked if he could take his brother with him.

I expected them back within half an hour, but they did not show up. An hour passed and they did not return. I knew that they would not take advantage of the order to waste time. Finally, his younger brother came back and told me that the Turkish guards had arrested Mustafa for carrying stolen goods! I asked my captain what to do. He sent a uniformed man with me to Beshig Tash headquarters to get him released.

They denied that anybody by that name had been arrested. So, we came back, told his brother to locate him and advise Mustafa that I was responsible for his having carried out the cot. He located his brother in the Beshig Tash jail. I went over there to see him but was denied admission.

I called the local police officer and gave him my officer's message and told him that this man must be found right away. Later he called, apologizing that he could not find any record of an arrest anywhere. The boy had disappeared, and I knew that they would make him suffer for stealing a Turkish cot.

Late in the afternoon a Turkish policeman asked for me at the gate. I told the guard to let him in. He informed me that he had come to verify what Mustafa had told him and asked me if I would go to the police station to verify his story. I agreed, but before I left, I told the office where I was going and that if I did not return in time, they should look for me.

The police commissioner was congenial and polite. He offered me a chair and asked me for the story of the stolen cot. I extended my cigarette case and he thanked me, complimenting me on my brand. I told him the real crime had been committed by the bedbugs that had tortured me for many nights. But I had grown used to that cot, and my office had given it to me for my comfort. That was the story, and I had asked Mustafa, my worker, to take it to my home. The officer wrote down each word, and when he had finished, he asked me to sign the report. So, I put my signature in Turkish underneath. He complimented me on my Turkish handwriting.

"Now, if you don't mind . . ." His voice and expression suddenly changed, and with what sounded like an order, he commanded: "Follow the policeman to the headquarters to state that in person."

In the meantime, a policeman brought Mustafa into the room. Without hesitation I told him, "You can go back to your work. That's why I came here." The police commissioner objected. "You both have to go," he said.

"I am not going anywhere," I said to the chief, "unless Mustafa is released. That's why I signed that paper," and I looked straight at him to let him know that he could not arrest two people for the same crime. He released the Turkish boy.

I followed the policeman, and we took the tram to Kaba Tash. As we passed the storeroom, I told him that I should stop and report in. The poor man knew what I had in mind—once I was inside the gate, no one would be able to arrest me. He begged me not to go in, saying that they would hold him responsible and he might lose his job. I gave in to him.

From the headquarters, they sent me to the international prison ward, which was in the center of town and looked like an old castle. A tall, husky English soldier registered me, asked my name, and started searching me. I objected and explained that I was employed by the English army.

"Shut up. You are a prisoner now." He demanded that I empty my pockets. They took me upstairs and put me behind bars with drunkards, thieves, and hardened criminals—the day's collection out of the city gutters.

The prisoners welcomed me and asked if I smoked. I pulled out my cigarette case and handed it to them. They all laughed; they thought that I might have been smoking hashish. The fellow next to me on the floor asked me what the charge was against me. When I told him the story of the cot, he said that I was good for a six-month stay. Another boy asked whether I smoked anything other than a cigarette. I replied, "No," without understanding what he meant. They brought in more drunks and thieves throughout the night, and none of us could sleep, because the newcomers raised hell.

I asked a man what most of these men were charged with and how long they had been here. Most had been there for three or four months and had never been interviewed. Sweat rolled down my back. I might be shipped to Malta and put behind the heavy walls there. When the soldier in charge came by with several visitors, he pointed at me and said I was charged with stealing an English army cot. I wondered when I would be interviewed. Tomorrow? Or ever? I was charged with being a thief without knowing how or why.

Noises from the nearby drunks and worry about future complications kept me awake all night. By morning I looked like a real criminal and felt sick from lack of sleep. At nine, the guard called my name. I walked down the corridor with him. There was a long line of prisoners, and the military police ordered us to keep in line. My friend Dadourian came in and saw me in line and started to talk to me. He assured me that I should not worry, that he would bail me out. The military police pushed him aside and told him that he could not talk to the prisoners. He gave the military police a dirty look and said, "Watch out. You can't do that to me. I'm an American citizen, and I have the right to talk to my friend."

The MP (military police) pushed him out of the hallway. He turned back and said, "I will see that you are out today."

After a few hours of waiting in line, I was called into the office. A tall, skinny English officer asked my name, the office where I worked, and why I stole the army officer's bed.

"Sir," I replied, "that is a false charge. I have not stolen anything at all," and I gave him the details. A Turkish civilian who commanded the Turkish police told the officer that that was what I had been charged with and that was why I had been reported. The English officer began conversing in French and, in an angry tone, reminded him that he shouldn't bring in any case without first having secured a clearance. He then called an MP and told him to take me to my headquarters to await investigation, and I was locked up until late afternoon. Finally, the officer in charge called me and told me to report to him by nine o'clock the next morning.

When I went to my office, Dick told me that the work had piled up, that he had made no progress with the new helpers. He asked me to work that night. I went home, cleaned up, ate my supper, and returned to work through the night.

In the morning, the captain told me that he had telephoned "many times" the day before asking for my release. He insisted that everything was all right and that I did not have to report back; I told him that I promised to and that I should hear the investigation. I was at headquarters before the officer in charge. He called the investigator and then called me in: "How lucky you were that it was not a British army cot. Did you know that?"

I said, "No, I did not," but that I knew it had been left over from the Turks, and we both agreed that the Turks had wanted to make a big issue of it.

"You were, indeed, a very lucky boy, and I am glad for you," and he released my belongings and billfold.

"Rush back to your office. Your officer is calling me and urging me to send you back at once. Go and take care of yourself."

I thanked him, dashed out, and hopped onto a passing tram. When I arrived at the depot gate, the head of the guard welcomed me with a big smile. Workers stopped to look at me, and I heard them whispering, "He's back." Then I heard their foreman say, "Let's get back to work."

The officer in charge greeted me as if I had been gone a long time. The Armenian who worked with me in the office made a remark to the uniformed man: "Wasn't it foolish to go to all that trouble for a lousy Turk?"

I said, "It was my duty to save him. I caused it." He gave me a funny look, meaning, how foolish can you get?

But as I was on my way to the warehouse with a handful of orders in my hand, Mustafa came toward me with a happy smile. Without a word, he bowed down, took my hand and kissed it, the greatest sign of respect in the Near East. I pulled my hand away quickly and shook hands with him. He said, "I never knew an Armenian would do this for a Turk!" He was so overwhelmed that he forgot to say thank-you, but his action had said plenty. This was rewarding, indeed. When I went back to the office, my Armenian friend told me how far behind they were in the work. I told him to call the labor contractor for more men.

"We will catch up tonight," I said. He asked me if I weren't tired, because I had worked all through the night before. I told him that I felt comfortable and relaxed. I said to him, "You know, that Turk will never kill an Armenian," and left the office to work.

Notes and Memories

The French army dissolved the Legion Dorian, and its Armenian members returned to France and the United States, their mission incomplete. The Turks chased returning immigrants from their homes. Once more they killed, burned, and looted. There was no protection by either the French or British occupation forces who had changed their plans. My friend Haroutoun wrote, "Once again we are double-crossed by our friends; our dream of a homeland is wiped out forever. Thousands more Armenians who managed to survive the deportations and previous massacres have been killed in cold blood." This was a crucial moment for the Armenian population, particularly in Cilicia. My friend now wanted to take his mother to the United States and asked me to direct him to the capital; I asked him to bring along my sister.[2]

In the meantime, Greek soldiers were stopped from marching to Anatolian cities, even though they had been promised territorial adjustments as a reward for their cooperation with the Allied Forces. They had captured one Turkish city after another, but the British headquarters in Constantinople ordered them to retreat. Thus, their dream of conquering their motherland was destroyed. Their great hero, Vanezaloss, no longer was in power on the Greek mainland.* While the soldiers fought heroically, the Allied forces pushed them back as if they were a defeated army. Their sailors and soldiers cursed the British, and the Armenians cursed the French. Destinies were lost in the political scramble. The Turks, a humble

---

*Eleftherios Venizelos (1864–1936) was a charismatic and controversial Greek politician during the early decades of the twentieth century. As prime minister, he led Greece into the First World War on the side of the Allied Powers and sought as a reward the creation of a Greater Greece that included Smyrna and the Ionian coast of Asia Minor. He was opposed by pro-German King Constantine, who was sent into exile but was restored to the throne by the Greek electorate in 1920, resulting in the fall of Venizelos and the collapse of the Greek military offensive against the Turkish Nationalist armies in Asia Minor, which culminated in the great inferno of Smyrna in 1922 and the expulsion of most of the Greek population of Turkey in 1923.

and now defeated nation, showed signs of resenting the occupying forces in the interior and grew bolder day by day.

They raised considerable trouble in Constantinople. One day they fought openly in the center of the Galata market. I was ordered by headquarters to stay at my job until told to go home. Two British soldiers with fixed bayonets came and accompanied me home, which caused quite a stir with my neighbors. My landlady was shocked when she answered the door and asked me what had happened. I said, "Hush," thanked the guards, and closed the door behind me. My Turkish neighbors, seeing this, asked my landlady what had happened to me. She told them that her tenant had been working for the British Army. She repeated her story to me and asked if I wanted to go out with the Turkish neighbor's daughter. "All you have to do is put a fez on your head," she said. I would not put a fez on my head for anybody, much less a Turk, and I was in no mood to make love to a Turkish lady. I had all I could do to keep my composure, for her suggestion had hurt me deeply.

Dildana

After peace came, those families that had lost a son, brother, or husband in the army waited expectantly. A great many soldiers who had been considered lost or dead eventually returned. This gave hope to others whose agony of waiting and uncertainty continued.

My Turkish neighbor had not received a letter from her son Shoukry for a long time. He had been sent to the Dardanelles,* but she never lost faith that her son would return. A friend of his had come home, and that strengthened her belief that Shoukry, too, might return. Her hopes dimmed with the chilling realization that she was wishing for the impossible, and then burned brightly, feverishly, against all odds. Shoukry's friend could not tell her that her son was dead.

I met the neighbor one afternoon while she was visiting my landlady. The two women asked me to join them in sipping Turkish coffee. She did not wear a veil, like other Turkish women, and she did not mind when I entered the same room, which was unusual. Instead, she welcomed me

---

*The narrow waterway between European and Asiatic Turkey connecting the Aegean Sea with the Sea of Marmara.

with a faint smile. She said that I was no longer a stranger; that she knew about me, although we had never met. My landlady had been bragging about me. I noticed that the years had not robbed her of her beauty. She had blue eyes and a very light complexion.

"You remind me very much of my son, Shoukry," she said. "Each time you come or leave, I can't help but watch you come and go. Your steps and your movements remind me so much of my son. That is why I know so much about you; and that is why my dear neighbor invited you to join us. I am grateful to her for this privilege."

Her Turkish had a certain charm and sweetness. She spoke sincerely, and her adjectives were chosen to emphasize a point. I liked her.

"But I am still hoping for my son's return," she added, hardly believing her own words.

Knowing about my experiences in the war, she wiped away her tears and said, "Son, we are all the innocent victims of vicious, evil spirits out to kill and conquer. True, I did encourage my son to join the army of our fatherland, for the glory and victory of our country; and also as a devotee of Islam and Osmanly, with a deep conviction of our duty to answer the call. The son, whom I raised with my own milk to boyhood, I should now be ready to sacrifice."

I tried to comfort her by suggesting that this was a duty, and, therefore, she had had to respond generously to her country.

"Indeed," she said, "an evil responsibility. What kind of country? A country that cannot even point to the place where my son was buried, so I might be able at least to visit his grave or place a memorial upon it. All this agony for a handful of dirt? What a country! Does a country have the right to demand the sacrifice of our sons for a worthless victory? What of a 'victory' without youth? A hollow, empty, distraught land—the land is empty. *Bosh*! The world is empty without my son! No," she went on in a whisper, as if she were exhausted or perhaps afraid that somebody would hear her. "No, no, no. All this isn't worth it! For days and days, I would go to his room, waiting for his return, dusting his bedroom, pulling his letters out to read over and over again. He would write, 'Mother, dear, dear little mother, it will be very soon now that I shall return home. You will be very proud of me when you see me.' And again, another letter would say, 'Dear mother, do not worry, I will be home very soon.' I can hear his voice still. How could he be dead? Oh, no; impossible!"

His clothes were still in the closet. She would take them out, lovingly brush them, then put them back and hang them up with care. On some nights, dreams of her son fighting untiringly under heavy artillery, like a brave Osmanly, tortured her. Her oil burned night after night. She lived in agony.

She had lost her husband in the same war—and now her son. Many nights, she would tire herself out with crying and fall asleep only to awaken to her son's voice. Even during the day, she would see him moving about the rooms as he had before he left. There was no end to this. She would talk to her son as if he were listening.

How merciless God seemed to her, and how barbaric the enemy. How vicious, unbelievably vicious, was her own country demanding the life of her own son at such a tender age to promote a silly and foolish war over a worthless borderline.

The afternoon sun had left the room. I noticed my landlady's silent tears. Dildana was nervously crushing her wet handkerchief in her palm. Her cheeks were hollow, as if she were melting away from the agony. My landlady had forgotten her neighbor's nationality and religion. Her misery had closed the gap. The room was cleared of prejudice and hatred. Only sympathy for this suffering mother remained.

My landlady informed me that I would have to move out because my friend Dadourian, who was also living there, was going to marry and needed larger quarters. She recommended that I look up a neighboring Greek lady who might have a room for me.

Many Armenians returned from America for the sole purpose of marrying orphans and widows to help heal and make them forget their tragic past, to give them a new home, and to create new hope—this was the least they thought they could do for those who had survived. Dadourian was one of these men. He was one of the lucky few who had managed to escape from Gurun early and immigrate to the United States before 1915. Now he ran a branch office for secondhand clothing and awaited the young lady's arrival as had been arranged.

One day he told me that someone from New York City had visited his office and had asked during the conversation if he knew me. Dadourian told him that we had been living in the same house for a long time. The man asked if he could see me to deliver a message from New York. I was excited and happy to meet Victor Lahanna, even though he questioned me as detectives do to be sure that they are talking to the right man. He asked me where my father was and what his name was and so on and on. When he finally was satisfied with my answers, he said, "Your brother George told me to give you fifty dollars." And he pulled out that amount in Turkish money. I thanked him, and we shook hands.

But brother George would not answer my letters concerning my visa; although we had never met, I wrote him a nice, carefully composed letter to express my thanks and my gratitude for his thoughtfulness, and I hinted again at my desire to go to the United States. I dropped the letter in the post office box.

I had not had a new suit since 1914, nor anything new or anything that fitted. I got by with only a jacket or pair of pants. I took the money and bought a blue serge suit from Schtine department store. Now I could go among the people and visit and keep proper company. I was proud of the suit and very grateful to my brother, but I wondered why he would not answer my letter or help me get a visa. I must go to the United States, I would tell myself; and I would, come what may, any way I could.

I wore my new blue serge suit proudly to church, to show off a bit, I must confess. Instead of sitting in the rear, I took a choice seat up front. At the end of the service, the minister greeted me cordially outside, and his wife spoke warmly as usual. She reminded me that I had promised to have dinner with them. Now that I had the proper clothes, I accepted the invitation and went with them. She introduced me to her brother, who became my trusted friend and banker. I do not know why I had so much confidence in this man. I would bring my savings to him, and he would place the money in trust for my future trip.

This same Sunday, I also met Hovsep, the son of our school janitor from Sivas. He told me that Mr. Partridge was in Constantinople at Robert College. I took off one day and went to Rummely Hissar to see him. When the door opened, he jumped up and greeted me. I noticed he had lost his old jovial smile. In fact, he was not responding to my conversation. He stared at the floor while I was talking, and he looked very sad. He reminded me that he was tired and needed rest. On his return to the interior, he had been tortured by the drama of a vanishing race and its manifold tragedies. He had struggled to help these unfortunate people but in vain. His heart could not take it anymore. He had lost his faith in humanity. I could not get a response to my inquiries and thought that I would do best by sparing him any cause for worry, so I did not revive the tragic memories of dire suffering. Instead, I held his hand between my own and bid him goodbye.

I learned later that he never recovered from that melancholy. The sadness had been too much for so sensitive a soul.

My aunt wrote and asked me about my family. She was the only relation to have survived. She lived in Samsun during the war and only recently had heard about me. She told me how happy she was that I was alive. She hadn't heard from her husband since he had left for the army. For many months, she had been hiding with her sons, thirteen and nine years old, and a six-year-old daughter. I wrote that I was planning to leave for America and asked her to join me.

In the meantime, Haroutoun arrived with my sister. It seemed to me that we were finally coming together, like remnants of a big storm. There was new hope and a ray of sunshine. I arranged for my sister to go to a school in Uskudar, and for Haroutoun to stay at my first landlady's house. In Koum Kapou, the Armenian district in Constantinople, he told me how miserable the deportees were in the interior and how the plan for a new homeland in the east had failed. Now the Turks were building up to prevent newcomers from entering their cities. As soon as his papers were ready, he would be leaving for the United States.

I gave up hope of hearing from my brother George. But I received a letter from Detroit, from my aunt's brother-in-law, telling me that my aunt would arrive in Constantinople soon and that they would send her a visa and ticket money. I wrote and asked if they could possibly get me a visa as well. Then I could bring my aunt and the children with me.

Cemetery of Shishly*

Shishly's Armenian Cemetery, with its beautifully carved marble mausoleums, was a famous museum. Here and there one could read dates, scriptures, and poetry on the gravestones of those who had shaped the nation. You would see the *catholigos*, or a member of Parliament, or an outstanding member of the sultan's advisers or the treasury or the state's architect. It was a city unto itself, whose members were chosen to reside

---

*Also spelled Şişli; a historic Armenian cemetery in Istanbul.

with fame. It was a thrill to wander among those familiar names of Armenian literature and history.

Years later, when I left Constantinople, the Turks had stolen the last remnants of Armenia and with it built something else for the new re-formed Turkey.

The Peteshan Garden

One evening, a few friends asked me to go with them to see a play by one of my favorite writers performed. It was Levon Shant's *The Ancient God*, and it played to a packed house. I didn't know so many Armenians were alive. They spoke the beautiful language that I had heard only in school. It is happiness to hear your mother tongue spoken that way. The actors performed the play perfectly. The story takes you back to when life was simple and love was believed to be at its best. And the surprise of it all was that the actors had survived.

After the play, we went to the park, where the soft moon shone through the treetops. There was very little light. Somebody touched me, saying, "Catch me!" I ran after her, but she disappeared in the dark. Then a boy touched me, and while he ran, a soft voice whispered, "You've got me." We were young and happy. It was spring, and we were in the park.

Rebirth of a Nation

It was late 1919. In the Caucasus to the east, Armenians struggled heroically to survive among the unfriendly Islamic nations that were trying desperately to choke this little nation. Thousands of Armenians perished trying to create a homeland, a country with its own flag, recognized by other nations—independent and free! This was the final call for survival of our fatherland.

The phoenix rose from the ashes, as our poets had promised. Alexander Hadissian had come to Constantinople from Erevan to speak about us about this miracle of resurrection.* This small nation, with its meager power, had shaped its own destiny and sprung from the dead with new vitality.

---

*Alexander Khatisian, prime minister of the Republic of Armenia in 1919–1920. The Armenian republic was formed in the Caucasus in May 1918 but was unable to survive the joint aggression of Soviet Russia and the nationalist forces of Mustafa Kemal Ataturk at the end of 1920. For a

The packed house of the Peteshan was ushered by the Boy Scouts, young and handsome, the future generation of Armenia. The place was filled with women and children, young and old, who came to witness the baptism of the union. The flag of new Armenia, unfurled in its glorious red, blue, and orange, electrified us. Automatically, everybody stood up, the band played the national anthem, and the Boy Scouts sang along. Some cried out loud, others silently, most cheered joyously; a few whispered thanks to God that they had lived to see this day, this miracle. It held a personal meaning for each witness. A son, a husband, a loved one, and the many, many who had died were with us. It had taken centuries to make this dream a reality. The nation was being reborn, and I was one of the very few fortunate enough to be alive on that day to witness it. As the ushers took their position to show the people the way out, I touched the arm of one of the boys to make sure I wasn't dreaming.

One day I was asked to visit the returnees' camps on the outskirts of Constantinople. There was music, and people were dancing tribal dances; a well-dressed girl exhibited her talent, for she was a new bride. People cheered her, clapped their hands, and sang. A boy of twenty joined his bride in the dancing. People threw coins as wedding presents. They were wise to marry and try to build a nest out of nothing. The nation was alive and happy once again, with the urge to live.

Notes

One Sunday I decided to go to Uskudar* and hear the new bishop from Ismerna (Smyrna/Izmir). Although the son of a Protestant minister, he became a bishop of the Armenian Apostolic Church, in the hope that he might be instrumental in reforming the mother church, which was long overdue for a change. The Armenians did not dare change anything that had been handed down through the centuries. It was too sacred to alter; but this man, the son of a Protestant, dared be the first to initiate reform. After the High Mass, he came to speak to us. His Armenian was excellent,

---

survey of this period, see Richard G. Hovannisian, *The Armenian People from Ancient to Modern Times*, vol. 2 (New York: St. Martin's Press, 1997), 275–346.

*Uskudar (Üsküdar), formerly known as Scutari, is a large and densely populated district and municipality of Istanbul on the Anatolian shore of the Bosphorus. https://en.wikipedia.org/wiki/%C3%9Csk%C3%BCdar.

Surviving the Forgotten Genocide

as good as Torkom Kuchakian of Sivas, or Timaksian of Gurun. He combined the excellent delivery of the high clergy with the vigor and boldness of a young man. He spoke about our vision—of the awakening of the new generation that was forging a new nation. He emphasized that in order to build the foundation, we must understand one another and show charity and tolerance. He was referring, of course, to the political parties. He had a way of saying it: "One for all, for the betterment of our nation."

But the mother church kept its doors closed to the light; its heavy walls had been built to withstand reformation. Years later, when the bishop proposed that they should marry, he was criticized, harassed, and finally forced to leave the church. He married, leaving the gate open behind him for others to follow. A few joined the Protestant Church; some who did not want to separate from the other church eventually were cut off, for they could not breathe the stagnant air of their church. Perhaps this is why the Armenian Church in later years became the social hall of political parties rather than the center for the worship of God. It lacked new spirit and leadership.

When my aunt arrived with her three children, I arranged with my landlady to have them move in with me. We formed a new family under my protection, and I was happy to do so because, besides my sister, she was the only relation I had left. We reminisced about my childhood, when she lived with us before she had gotten married. She would wipe away her tears silently and thank God for his grace in sparing my life. Finally, we talked of how soon we could have our papers ready to go to the United States. She told me how desperate they had been during the war. She could not hear from her husband, who served in the Turkish army. They did not have any food or shelter. They had to be hidden away in order not to be deported.

A Greek family took them in, but the city police discovered them and took them to police headquarters. The local Greek priest protested to the Turks, claiming that it was his ecclesiastic duty to protect them from deportation because her husband was fighting for the Turks in the Turkish army, serving the Turkish government. The local government set her free. They sold everything they owned to buy food, and she made clothes for the children from patches, going hungry many nights. When the peace was signed, the Near East Relief arrived from the United States. She got a job that enabled her to earn a few pennies. They contacted her relations in Detroit, and a lady who had seen me in Constantinople told her about me. That's how we made contact. We talked about old times again, especially about my father and his activities; then late in the evening, she gave thanks for this moment and prayed to God for my safety. We found still more reasons to be happy and then went to bed.

Father

Once again, your memory revived, and our forgotten wounds, not yet healed, are bleeding. You gave me a high standard and a purpose to follow to justify calling myself a man and my existence. You taught me to disregard worldly values and choose the moral path.

You taught me not to compromise, to choose the good and the right and to fight for it, never to lose faith in justice, and to walk straight and hold my head high, to face the world with dignity and pride. You told me that it is everybody's obligation to promote justice because that is the only way to preserve the good and protect the noble. Serving humanity is not only an obligation and a duty for each of us, but a privilege.

True, things have changed. But it was a great satisfaction to know that you are victorious when you do the right thing, even when you fail.

Had I not been through the blizzard of our times, it would have been a happy life, but it would have been a life without true value, without understanding. It seems to me that the bright side of life is not always the fullest or the richest.

Now they tell me that I act like you, speak so much like you, and I even read the "Tessavross" like an Armenian priest.

I wish that you could have stayed with us a little longer. I miss you very much.

Dream

It was a delightful spring. I was looking for my house, where I used to see blue sky and listen to the birds. I would enjoy the warm sunshine and listen to the passing brook on its way through the orchards, think about the future and wonder what tomorrow held in store.

But the houses were not there, nor were the trees. The birds were gone, too, and the brook had dried up.

I could find no one to talk to. Once this had been a close neighborhood—older women were called "aunts," and young girls were "sisters."

Fathers were the foundation, and mothers loved and catered to their families. Now there wasn't a trace of life.

Wherever I went I saw the aftermath of destruction, the ugly marks of a war-torn land. The city had turned into a ghost town. I crossed the wooden bridge that connected our street to the church, but even the church was gone. I found, instead, piles of stones. I kept walking toward the foothills, where once upon a time the well-to-do merchants lived, but I found only a few rundown shacks. Among the shacks, I found a shepherd boy in rags with a few scrawny goats. I tried to talk to him, but he would not respond. With hand motions, I asked him where everybody was and what had happened to the stone church.

He said only, "No, I never saw one."

I asked him what his name was, but he asked, "Are you one of us? You do not look like a Turk."

I told him that I used to live across from the church. "You remember the Armenian Church?"

"Oh!" he exclaimed, "You are an Armenian. Your people killed our people, burned the city, and ran away."

In a few short moments, I arrived in Sivas. The college, of which we were so proud, was burned. The American flag that had flown so happily over us was gone now. From the time of Mukitar to our own, this was the big city, the center of culture. Now it was isolated, desolate, without a trace of civilization. I walked toward Saint Nishan Monastery. Hundreds of green pines had died. The heavy gate had been left open. I wandered in—I could hear the echo of my footsteps. The place had been ransacked, its ancient treasures stolen. King Senekerim's chambers had been left bare; his golden chair was gone, golden crown and robe, all of the treasures of the church—gone.[3]

In the distance I could see Saint Ohanness's church, now a deserted mosque, with its extended crescent up against the misty horizon. The hills lay silent and the dead . . . Each step brought back the past tragedy; each stone was a monument of heroism. The struggle between the conqueror and the vanquished had ended, but the tragedy of war continued loud and bold.

Desperate and lonely, I hurried away from the scene and took the road to the city. The church and school yards were vacant. No trace remained of the old community. Only a few stray, emaciated dogs roamed what once were streets full of life.

I went to the marketplace and found a few shops open. People were entering the main mosque for their morning prayer. I approached a man and, with a friendly gesture and salutation, called him countryman. He ignored me and entered the mosque to pray. I found no trace of many of the shops I had known. So, I left the town and went toward Kizil-Irmak (Red River), following the old road to Douzi-Sar, but the prosperous village was gone. Just a few years ago, I had stopped here on my way home to Gurun as the guest of the village master. We had visited a school built with the aid of the young sons from America. All had been wiped out. The war had taken away all trace of human progress.

I saw an old peasant plowing the land with a tired, bony ox. I greeted him, asking where all the young men were and why he had to do the plowing all by himself. He replied, "Because my son did not return home from the war."

I asked again why the place was so dilapidated and why the field was not cultivated. "Where's everybody? What happened to the Armenians?"

He wiped the sweat from his brow with his saggy shirtsleeve and replied sadly, "Stranger, I do not know what you want to know, but I wish that it had not happened, what happened here. We all would have been better off."

Then I woke up. In the whole damned country I met only one wise man, and he existed only in a dream!

The New Hope

Mr. Dadourian helped process my application for a visa through the American consulate. My doctor suggested that my sister remain behind until her eyes were completely cured. I arranged for her to stay at a boardinghouse, in Mr. Dadourian's care. I wanted to leave as soon as we could get the boat. My Greek landlady told me that her niece wished to see me before I left.

She came the next evening, nicely dressed, as if we were going to a party. We walked along the sidewalks of Beshig Tash to where the big palace clock ticked away, by the shores of the Bosphorus. She had closely locked her arm into mine, and I could feel the comforting warmth of her body. She whispered, "Before you leave, I have a confession to make. You will not believe it, even when I tell you why I refused to go out with you. You were angry. Do you know why? Because I loved you very much!"

I loosened my arm, to be free to look at her face in the dark.

"Yes," she said, "very much—you were so young, so innocent." I gazed at her as she went on. "But now, I want you to know, and I want you to think of me, the girl who loved you so much that she did not want to go out with you!"

We entered one of the shops in Beshig Tash where they served chicken breast pudding sprinkled with cinnamon. Hand in hand, we finished our feast of love. I took her home. She asked me again, "Will you remember?" She hugged me graciously and said, "Au revoir," as if we were to meet again. For many, many years, I thought of this, for no love will ever match hers. Yes, this I do remember, with bittersweet nostalgia.

When I notified my office of my intentions, they tried to convince me that I had all of the security I needed with them. As long as the British Army remained in Constantinople, I was safe. By this time, the Allied armies were reducing their occupational forces, and I knew that sooner or later they would pull out. God forbid that they should leave before I did. Only I knew what would happen to me then. I made a fast decision that determined my future.

As soon as I heard that a Greek company had a boat leaving Constantinople for New York, I took my savings from Mardigian and bought tickets for myself and for my aunt and her three children. Dadourian asked me if I would take care of his nephew, a fifteen-year-old who was the only family member to survive the Turkish massacre. We all eagerly awaited the departure of the *Goul-jemal.*

We boarded the boat that had served as a troop carrier during the war and took our place below deck. It was dark and gloomy, but we were hardly aware of that. We knew only one thing: this ship would take us to the land of our dreams, America! Indeed, very few ever experienced the joy of breaking the shackles of slavery. We had freedom of movement, freedom from harassment, and freedom from being chased and hunted. We were on our way to becoming free citizens. This was a new birth.

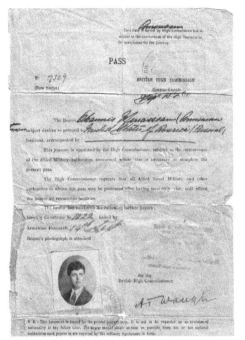

FIGURE 7.3
British High Commissioner, Constantinople, Permission to Journey to USA, with Minassian ID Photo, September 18, 1920

When the first whistle blew, I did not see a single person crying with regret. All were exhilarated by their separation from misery and tragic memories. When the second whistle blew, the boat began to move in earnest. At long last we were on our way. We were no longer interested in what went on about us or behind us. We drew a long, deep breath of relief as we sailed into the Dardanelles. The horizon was a clear blue, promising a peace we had not felt for many a year.

This was the spot where the Allied Powers had fought the Central Powers with their mighty warships, causing destruction greater than any before experienced in the history of mankind. Many, many young British, German, and other soldiers and sailors had died here. This was where Dildan's son had lost his life, as had the young sons of many, in the Battle of Chanak Kalla and Gallipoli at the Dardanelles—for the glory of their "fatherland."

When we passed the strait, we felt a new breeze, and our sense of freedom swelled. Our boat encountered and saluted a British warship standing guard, signifying power, dignity, and protection. We watched the new horizon, our hearts filling with hope for our future in the new world, the land of George Washington, Abraham Lincoln, and Woodrow Wilson; where the great Lady Liberty stood with her torch held high to welcome each new boatload of immigrants. The new horizon spread as wide as one could see. A new breeze swept the air clear and clean—it was the end of a nightmare and the beginning of a lifelong dream for a better tomorrow.

Salaam! Peace!

Appendix

WHEN I TOOK THE BOAT for the New World, I realized a dream of my childhood. I had a close association with Americans through my school and church, and I admired their ideals, their humanitarian efforts to serve, to help, and to uplift. This had made an indelible impression upon me, and I wanted to be one of them someday. Nothing could stop me from coming to see and live among these people.

I brought with me the few closely packed pages of notes that had faded during the desert chase. But like the wounds on the bark of a tree, memories of the past grow deeper year after year. At first, they paralyzed me, and I was unable to work on them. Within a few years, however, while I was working for the Ford Company in Detroit, I collected my notes and put them together under the title of "Forgotten People." In 1926, in New York, I also collected some notes under the headings "Vartan, the Reverend," "Makroohi," "Krikor," and "Please Look Up." I then decided not to inflict any sad memories on others.

These were stories of the past, and I wanted to forget them all, but the political situation remained the same—dark. In addition, there was the war in Vietnam. This, and the encouragement from friends, induced me to write. I did not want to preach a soft sermon but to shout loudly to the heavens and warn others of the big storm coming, for I had experienced such a storm before. If in doing so I have kindled the fire of compassion and enhanced the chances for brotherhood and peace, I shall be fully rewarded for my pains.

Yet this book is not complete, for there is no way to measure the depth of the sorrow, the misery, and suffering of the human heart. Words cannot adequately explain the pain, deprivation, and humiliation suffered by the thousands of victims of the cruel force of military might.[1]

Dear Aziz:

It has been a long time since we said good-bye. We were students at a college in the hills of Hoktar in the city of Sivas. American missionaries had come to Sivas to teach the gospel of love, democracy, and the better things in life.

You said you had come to learn English. Your father was liberal enough to send you to a school where you were the only Turkish boy among Armenians. You were brave. One day I passed you while you were sitting alone, watching bigger boys playing football. You smiled. I passed you, and I came back and I asked you if you were Aziz. You were encouraged and smiled again, happily. I was the first boy who greeted you. We talked in your native language. We did not say much, but we knew we were meeting on the same ground regardless.

Our friendship continued. We conversed about different things—our future destination, our hopes and our dreams. We had secrets and we talked about impossible things, like taking you to an Armenian church to hear the Mass on a holiday and you would take me to the Mosque to see Islamic praying some Friday. I also told you the story of the little boy Jesus. That was the year of 1913.

When school closed for summer vacation, we promised to see each other more, regardless of what happened. We would continue our friendship forever. You were sincere and noble. I was the only one in school who noticed your nobility, because I was the only one who was friendly to you. I always enjoyed your company. You were charming, an aristocrat. Later you wanted to learn Armenian so you would be able to say "paryloos" and converse with me in my language. It was fun. Each day we added more Armenian words. You were happy, too.

This did not last long. Summer came, and I went home to spend the summer with my parents in Gurun, a small city south of Sivas. On foot we traveled for three days, passing many Armenian villages with wheat fields. Peasants were getting ready for the new crop. My parents were very happy to see me. They were proud of me with the expectation that soon I would graduate from school and would be a useful citizen and a man.

When I went back to Sivas the following autumn to continue my education, I was informed by our principal, Mr. Partridge, that the school would be closed that year because of war. Then I returned home. Winter passed in isolation. But spring came, and spring in the Valley of Gurun is paradise. We all were busy doing our daily gardening chores. Later in April we were told to be ready for deportation. After many days of traveling on foot, I found myself separated from my family, friends, relatives, and neighbors. I was lonesome and in search of shelter. In Aleppo a good man gave me shelter and food, but he died soon, and I was orphaned again. Later, when I was in the Mesopotamian desert, I worked for the Baghdad railroad as a clerk.

Late in 1918, I arrived in Aleppo with an orphaned eight-year-old boy. In Aleppo I placed him in a British orphanage for Armenian orphans and left for Constantinople. The city was jammed with many returning deportees and many Russian runaways from the revolution. They were all desperately in search of work, all wanting to start a new life.

Many months after I found a job in the British Army as a clerk; my Turkish helped me. Many working there were Turks. I often thought of you, but there was no chance to see you. I wondered if you joined the army in the Dardanelles. I hoped not. I wondered if you were killed in action. Nobody would kill you if they knew you. But it was war, and nobody thinks during war.

I also thought I wouldn't be in the Mesopotamian desert in search of shelter if there were more like you in high places. That's why the memory of you never left me. You made me learn to love someone who is not supposed to be loved. Your sweet smile, your noble self, your greeting of "inchbess es."

In Constantinople I met a young boy, Mustafa, who was desperately trying to support his mother, who was a war widow. He was jailed while he was working for me. I got him out of jail. When he returned to work, he bowed and tried to kiss my hand. He wondered why an Armenian would do this for a Turk. He did not know my secret: I knew you.

I tried very hard to enter a school in Constantinople. I was turned down so finally I left the country of my birth, country of my boyhood happiness and misery. I came to the country of my dreams. It was not a strange country. People were kind to me, and they were friendly. New York City was the only city where I was not afraid of the police. I desperately tried to enter a school but I was unable to concentrate on studies due to the tragedies of the past.

Finally, I got a job at a Ford factory, laboring hard for a living. This was all I could do. I was deprived of the opportunity of a normal boy's education. Sleepless nights, dust and smoke from the foundry, and the smell made me sick. Now I am gray and live with my wife in Santa Barbara, a city near the ocean, with stately mountains behind it.

Our grandchildren wanted to know about my past, reviving old memories. That is why I am writing this letter. I am sure you will be glad to know that I am comfortable. I hope this letter will reach you somehow. When you read it, *do not cry for me*. I am well-adjusted [*sic*] in a country that stands for peace, freedom, and happiness, but I miss you, dear Aziz.

One last thought. On the Fourth of July our flag flies proudly in our yard, telling everybody that we are one of them.

John Minassian,
October 8, 1984

Notes

Introduction

1. Among the most concise and illuminating summaries of the latest interpretations and main events of the genocide is Adam Jones's "The Ottoman Destruction of Christian Minorities," 200–250, in *Genocide: A Comprehensive Introduction*, 3rd ed. (New York: Routledge, 2017).

2. Great Britain, Parliament, *Treatment of Armenians in the Ottoman Empire: Documents Presented to Viscount Grey of Fallodon, Secretary of State for Foreign Affairs*, preface by Viscount Bryce (London, 1916).

3. The first major oral history project, which the Armenian Assembly started in 1979, was funded by the National Endowment for the Humanities. Professor Richard Hovannisian at UCLA has been the leading academic adviser and initiator of similar projects by audiotaping seven hundred survivors. In total, there are close to three thousand interviews of survivors, about nine hundred of them on videotape. Donald E. Miller and Lorna Touryan Miller, *Survivors: An Oral History of the Armenian Genocide* (Berkeley: University of California Press, 1993), 27 and 212–13.

4. Donald Bloxham, *The Great Game of Genocide: Imperialism, Nationalism, and the Destruction of the Ottoman Armenians* (Oxford: Oxford University Press, 2005), 55.

5. Taner Akçam, *A Shameful Act: The Armenian Genocide and the Question of Turkish Responsibility* (New York: Henry Holt, 2006), 156.

6. Akçam, *A Shameful Act*, 211.

7. Ronald Suny, *"They Can Live in the Desert but Nowhere Else": A History of the Armenian Genocide* (Princeton, NJ: Princeton University Press, 2015), xx.

8. Suny, *"They Can Live in the Desert but Nowhere Else,"* 133.

9. *Deutschland und Armenien, 1914–1918: Sammlung Diplomatischer Akten-stuecke,* edited by Johannes Lepsius (Potsdam: Der Tempel Verlag, 1919).

Preface

1. Jackson informed Ambassador Morgenthau in April 1915 about the collusion of Germans and Turks in the incitement of mass theft and violence against Armenian "infidels"; by August 1915 he concluded that the campaign was systematic and total. In addition to his reporting, Jackson also assisted in relief efforts on behalf of Armenian survivors and has been recognized for saving thousands of lives. See Peter Balakian, *The Burning Tigris: The Armenian Genocide and America's Response* (New York: HarperCollins, 2003), 251–63, 289–90.

2. President Woodrow Wilson had appointed Morgenthau, from a family of well-to-do German Jewish immigrants, to the Sublime Porte (Ottoman government) to represent United States interests. However, the flood of reports that landed on Morgenthau's desk about the massacres of Armenians in 1915 consumed his attention and led him into an intense communications campaign; more than one hundred news articles appeared in the *New York Times*. Frustrated by the relentless Ottoman policy and the inaction of American authorities, he resigned his post in 1916. He wrote his memoirs and account of the genocide in *Ambassador Morgenthau's Story* (Garden City, NY: Doubleday, Page, 1918), also available at https://archive.org/details/ambassadormorge00morggoog.

He depicted Turkey as "a place of horror" and expressed his own exasperation: "I had reached the end of my resources. I found intolerable my further daily association with men, however gracious and accommodating, [who] were still reeking with the blood of nearly a million human beings." Morgenthau became a renowned human rights activist and philanthropist, helping to organize the major fund-raising effort of the Near East Relief Fund on behalf of the Armenians and other persecuted Christian minorities such as the Assyrians and Greeks.

Chapter 1: Sivas

1. For relevant materials on the province of Sivas and its Armenian population, see Richard G. Hovannisian, ed., *Armenian Sebastia/Sivas and Lesser Armenia* (Costa Mesa, CA: Mazda Publishers, 2004).

2. In the years preceding the First World War, Ottoman rulers subjected Armenians to waves of persecution, including mass violence in the Hamidian Massacres of 1894–1896, when some one hundred thousand Armenians perished and thousands more were forcibly converted to Islam or had to flee to other lands. During the First World War, Armenian men were recruited into the Ottoman army, but contemporary observers and postwar scholars have shown that the intention of the perpetrators was to expend able-bodied Armenians in battle or in unarmed labor battalions and to murder those who had not died at the front or from hard labor. See Grigoris Balakian, *Armenian Golgotha, A Memoir of the Armenian Genocide 1915–1918* (New York: Vintage Books, 2009), xxxiii. For a recent survey of interpretations, see Uğur Ümit Üngör, "Fresh Understandings of the Armenian Genocide: Mapping New Terrain with Old Questions," 198–213, in Adam Jones, ed., *New Directions in Genocide Research* (London: Routledge, 2011); Bedross Der Matossian, "The 'Definitiveness' of Genocide and a Question of Genocide: A Review Essay," *Journal of the Society for Armenian Studies* 20 (2011): 173–87; Ronald Grigor Suny, Fatma Müge Göçek, and Norman M. Naimark, eds., *A Question of Genocide: Armenians and Turks at the End of the Ottoman Empire* (Oxford: Oxford University Press, 2011).

3. Christianity was adopted in Armenia as the state religion in the early fourth century AD. In later centuries, Armenia was subjected to waves of foreign incursions by Arab, Byzantine, and Turkic armies and finally lost its autonomy in the late fourteenth century with the conquest of the Cilician Armenian kingdom by the Muslim Mamluks of Egypt, who were then succeeded by the Ottoman Turks in the sixteenth century. See George Bournoutian, *A History of the Armenian People*, vol. 1 (Costa Mesa, CA: Mazda Publishers, 1996). Religion is often cited as an underlying source of conflict between the Armenian population and their Muslim overlords.

4. Ronald G. Suny, *"They Can Live in the Desert but Nowhere Else": A History of the Armenian Genocide* (Princeton, NJ: Princeton University Press, 2015), 5–6. The Ottoman conquest of the Armenian highland began under Sultan Selim I (1512–1520) and was consolidated under Sultan Suleyman (1520–1566). See Dickran Kouymjian, "Armenia from the Fall of the Cilician Kingdom (1375) to the Forced Emigration under Shah Abbas (1604)," in Richard G. Hovannisian, ed., *The Armenian People from Ancient to Modern Times*, vol. 2 (New York: St. Martin's Press, 1997), 1–19.

5. On Armenian political parties and the movement for a "free Armenia" espoused by *Dashnaktsutiun*, see Gerard J. Libaridian, "What Was Revolutionary about Armenian Revolutionary Parties in the Ottoman Empire," 82–112, in Suny, Gocek, and Naimark, *A Question of Genocide*. The Armenian Revolutionary Federation is a nationalist-socialist party that was founded in 1890. The party

still operates in the post-Soviet Armenian republic and throughout the Armenian diaspora communities. See http://www.arfd.info.

6. Both the Turkish and Russian rulers made some gestures regarding reforms to address Armenian grievances in their imperial jockeying over territory and peoples. For the nineteenth and early twentieth centuries, see Richard G. Hovannisian, "The Armenian Question in the Ottoman Empire," 203–38, in Hovannisian, *The Armenian People from Ancient to Modern Times*, vol. 2. For the period during World War I, see Peter Holquist, "The Politics and Practice of the Russian Occupation of Armenia, 1915–February 1917," 151–74, in Suny, Gocek, and Naimark, *A Question of Genocide*.

7. The Armenian (Hamidian) Massacres in 1894–1896 were the first well-documented, massive Turkish campaigns against the Armenian population of the Ottoman Empire. Aside from the killings, tens of thousands fled the country, and many were forcibly converted to Islam. The associated plunder of homes and businesses economically ruined families, and the destitute numbered in the hundreds of thousands. It was highly publicized, and, like the nineteenth-century "Bulgarian Horrors," fueled a Western essentialist view of Turkish "barbarism" as an imminent threat to Christianity. For an extensive bibliography on the subject, see George Shirinian, *The Armenian Massacres of 1894–1897: A Bibliography*, at https://zoryaninstitute.org/publications/#resources.

8. During the Armenian genocide, Miss Graffam refused to abandon the girls under her care and marched with them all the way to Malatia, where she was forced to turn back to Sivas. See Susan Billington Harper, "Mary Louise Graffam: Witness to Genocide," 214–39, in Jay Winter, ed., *America and the Armenian Genocide of 1915* (Cambridge: Cambridge University Press, 2003).

9. On the growth of Armenian intelligentsia and national identity, see Razmik Panossian, *The Armenians: From Kings and Priests to Merchants and Commissars* (New York: Columbia University Press, 2006).

10. On the American and Armenian connections made through the diaspora and missionary movements, see Peter Balakian, *The Burning Tigris: The Armenian Genocide and America's Response* (New York: HarperCollins, 2003); and for an account by the Armenian Protestant Church, see Leon Arpee, *A Century of Armenian Protestantism, 1846–1946* (New York: Armenian Missionary Association of America, 1946).

11. Abdul Hamid was forced to become a constitutional monarch with limited authority in 1908 and was then exiled to Salonika (Thessaloniki) in 1909 after an abortive countercoup that resulted in the death of thousands of Armenians in the city of Adana and throughout the region of Cilicia.

12. On the Young Turk revolution and its aftermath, see Bedross Der Matossian, *Shattered Dreams of Revolution: From Liberty to Violence in the Late Ottoman Empire* (Palo Alto, CA: Stanford University Press, 2014).

13. Mkhitar Sebastatsi (Mekhitar of Sebastia, 1676–1749), noted theologian and scholar, founder of the eminent Armenian Catholic Mekhitarist order on San Lazzaro Island in Venice. The Mekhitarists had a profound influence on the Armenian intellectual revival of the eighteenth and nineteenth centuries. See Minas Nurikhan, *The Life and Times of the Servant of God, Abbot Mechitar, Founder of the Mechitarist Fathers* (Venice: San Lazzaro, 1915).

14. The Sanasarian Academy, located in the city of Erzurum, was an Armenian language institute of higher learning founded in 1881 through the munificence of Mkrdich Sanasarian. It drew students from throughout the Ottoman Empire and the Caucasus. Agop J. Hacikyan, ed., *The Heritage of Armenian Literature*, vol. 3, *From the Eighteenth Century to Modern Times* (Detroit: Wayne State University Press, 2005), 337.

15. Spelled Astghig or Astghik. According to Armenian mythology, Astghik was born from the waves of the sea and habitually took a bath in a certain stream every night; she is considered the goddess of love and beauty. http://www.arme niapedia.org/wiki/Armenian_pagan_culture.

16. Today Aleppo is the largest city in Syria. During the Ottoman Empire, it was a major center of trade and commerce. Gàbor Ágoston and Bruce Masters, *Encyclopedia of the Ottoman Empire* (New York: Facts on File, 2009).

17. The last King of Vaspurakan, from the Artsruni dynasty, who ruled in the tenth century. See Simon Payaslian, *The History of Armenia* (New York: Palgrave Macmillan, 2007), 70–74.

18. On the Hamidian massacres, see above, notes 7 and 17. The issue of a direct order from the sultan is a disputed one. Robert Melson argues that the sultan "initiated or tolerated the massacres." No single order has turned up, but scholars infer that a campaign of such targeted force could only have been done with the sultan's approval. See Robert Melson, *Revolution and Genocide: On the Roots of the Armenian Genocide and the Holocaust* (Chicago: University of Chicago Press, 1992). Donald Bloxham argues that the subsequent genocide beginning in 1915 was the culmination of a combination of internal and external forces, mainly driven by the Ottoman search for solutions to stave off decline under increasing pressure from the Western powers. See his *The Great Game of Genocide: Imperialism, Nationalism, and the Destruction of the Ottoman Armenians* (Oxford: Oxford University Press, 2005). On the centennial of the genocide, historian Ronald G. Suny countered the essentialist view of Turks as

inherently genocidaires with a nuanced explanation of the historical context of the war. It was the Young Turk leaders' "affective disposition" toward a perceived Armenian threat that led them to make specific (inhumane) choices. See his *"They Can Live in the Desert but Nowhere Else."*

Chapter 2: Gurun

1. A national hero, Vartan Mamigonian (Vardan Mamikonian) was the commander of the Armenian forces at the Battle of Avarayr against the powerful Persian Sasanian armies in 451 CE. Ronald G. Suny, *Looking toward Ararat: Armenia in Modern History* (Bloomington and Indianapolis: Indiana University Press, 1993), 4.

2. Sahag (Sahak), an Armenian patriarch, was central to the story of the Battle of Avarayr. He died in Persian captivity and subsequently was sainted. The battles led by the Mamigonian clan preserved the right of the Armenians to practice their Christian faith. See Elishe, *History of Vardan and the Armenian War*, translated and commentary by Robert W. Thomson (Cambridge, MA: Harvard University Press, 1982); Vahe Haig, *The Fifteen Hundredth Anniversary of Saint Vardan the Brave, 451–1951* (Fresno, CA: Diocese of the Armenian Church, 1951).

3. In 1914, the Young Turks joined the Central Powers—Germany and Austro-Hungary—against the Entente—Great Britain, France, and Russia—in a desperate attempt to strengthen and restore their empire after having suffered territorial losses in the Balkan Wars (1912–1913) and forced to accept a European-imposed reform in the Armenian provinces. See Ronald G. Suny, *"They Can Live in the Desert but Nowhere Else": A History of the Armenian Genocide* (Princeton, NJ: Princeton University Press, 2015), xviii; Mustafa Aksakal, *The Ottoman Road to War in 1914: The Ottoman Empire and the First World War* (Cambridge: Cambridge University Press, 2008).

4. Viscount Bryce, *Treatment of Armenians in the Ottoman Empire, 1915–16, Document Presented to the Secretary of State for Foreign Affairs* (London: 1916), cites this independent American Armenian journal several times.

5. As Raphael Lemkin observed, the destruction of cultural heritage and its bearers (intellectuals, craftsmen, merchants) was a definitive element of genocide that largely has been subsumed by focus on the mass murder. Peter Balakian's research on the ruins at Ani shifts attention to the cultural "vandalism" of architectural monuments. See Balakian's "Raphael Lemkin, Cultural Destruction, and the Armenian Genocide," in *Holocaust and Genocide Studies* 27 (Spring 2013): 57–89.

6. The Tashnagtsutiun (Tashnag) or Dashnaktsutiun party was founded in 1890, having as its goals the political emancipation and administrative autonomy of the Armenian provinces of the Ottoman Empire, as well as social-structural and economic reforms. The party, like the Hnchakian party formed in 1887, advocated the use of violence if necessary and trained freedom fighters (fedayis) to help Armenian peasants defend themselves in the late nineteenth and early twentieth centuries. Anny P. Balakian, *Armenian-Americans: From Being to Feeling Armenian* (New Brunswick, NJ: Transaction Publishers, 1993), 94. See also Gerard J. Libaridian, "What Was Revolutionary about Armenian Revolutionary Parties in the Ottoman Empire," 82–112, in Ronald Grigor Suny, Fatma Müge Göçek, and Norman M. Naimark, eds., *A Question of Genocide: Armenians and Turks at the End of the Ottoman Empire* (Oxford: Oxford University Press, 2011).

7. The author presumably is referring to Emmanuele Tesauro's *La filosofia morale* (1670), written in Italian and translated to Armenian by Mekhitarist Father Vrtanes Asgerian as *Emmanuel Tesavros, Imastasirutiun Baroyakan* (Venice: Bortoli, 1793).

8. This was the American Board of Commissioners for Foreign Missions (ABCFM), the first American foreign missionary society, established in 1810 by New England Congregationalists. Missionaries established an extensive network of schools, orphanages, hospitals, and colleges across Anatolia and Armenia. Many missionaries remained in the region during the First World War and were first-person foreign eyewitnesses to the destruction. See the Armenian National Institute website, http://www.armenian-genocide.org/missionaries.html.

9. For a survey of modern Armenian romantic and patriotic prose and poetry, with translated excerpts, see Agop J. Hacikyan, ed., *The Heritage of Armenian Literature*, vol. 3, *From the Eighteenth Century to Modern Times* (Detroit: Wayne State University Press, 2005).

10. A *khan* was typically a "way station" or "inn," often used by travelers but also used as an enclosure or a marketplace. The deportees from Sivas and Zara were thrown into the *khan* in Sivas, where they were devoured by lice and ravaged by disease. During the Armenian genocide, this type of concentration camp became a deathtrap, with corpses piled on top of one another or left as food for the dogs. See, for example, Raymond Kevorkian, *The Armenian Genocide, A Complete History* (London: I. B. Tauris, 2011), 647.

11. Komitas or Gomidas (born Soghomon Soghomonian in the town of Kutahia in 1869) was an Armenian priest, composer, singer, choirmaster, and musicologist. Founder of the Armenian national school of music and a pioneer of ethnomusicology, he was arrested and exiled by the Turkish government in April 1915. Through the efforts of American Ambassador Henry Morgenthau and

others, Komitas soon was released, but the stress of the deportation permanently affected his mental health. In 1919 he was taken to Paris and spent the rest of his life in a psychiatric clinic. He died there in 1936. See Rita Soulahian Kuyumjian, *Archeology of Madness: Komitas, Portrait of an Armenian Icon* (Reading, England: Taderon Press, 2001); Alan Whitehorn, ed., *The Armenian Genocide: The Essential Reference Guide* (Santa Barbara, CA: ABC-CLIO, 2015), 159.

Chapter 3: Many Hills Yet to Climb

1. Armenian king and for a short time emperor, circa 96/95–55 BCE. See Nina Garsoïan, "The Emergence of Armenia," 52–60, in Richard G. Hovannisian, *The Armenian People from Ancient to Modern Times*, vol. 1 (New York: St. Martin's Press, 2004).

2. On the Armenian kingdom of Cilicia, see Richard G. Hovannisian and Simon Payaslian, eds., *Armenian Cilicia* (Costa Mesa, CA: Mazda Publishing, 2008); and Jacob G. Ghazarian, *The Armenian Kingdom in Cilicia during the Crusades (1080–1393)* (Richmond, Surrey: Curzon, 2000).

3. Also known as Osmanli. The Armenian kingdom of Cilicia was conquered by the Mamluks of Egypt in the fourteenth century before the Ottoman conquest in the sixteenth century. See also Heather Ferguson, *The Proper Order of Things: Language, Power, and Law in Ottoman Administrative Discourse* (Palo Alto, CA: Stanford University Press, 2018); and Raphaela Lewis, *Everyday Life in Ottoman Turkey* (New York: Dorset Press, 1988).

4. The role of the German military leadership and of economic developers (mostly with railways) is still being researched and disputed. Latest research concludes that the Germans were more focused on military strategy, security, and conserving resources to win the war than in colluding with Turks in a campaign of total destruction of the Armenians. The German missionary Johannes Lepsius, who condemned the genocide and was described by Franz Werfel in his novel *Forty Days of Musa Dagh* as a "guardian angel of the Armenians," has long been honored as an outstanding humanitarian and eyewitness source, but he was not representative of an official German role in perpetration of or a policy to halt the mass murder. See Wolfgang Gust, ed., *The Armenian Genocide: Evidence from the German Foreign Office Archives, 1915–16* (New York: Berghahn, 2014); Eric P. Weitz, "Germany and the Young Turks: Revolutionaries into Statesmen," 175–98, and Margaret Lavinia Anderson, "Who Still Talked about the Extermination of the Armenians? German Talk and Silences," 199–220, in Ronald Grigor Suny, Fatma Müge Göçek, and Norman M. Naimark, eds., *A Question of Genocide: Armenians and Turks at the End of the Ottoman Empire* (Oxford: Oxford University Press, 2011).

Chapter 4: The Reverend of Aleppo

1. Hilmar Kaiser, with Luther and Nancy Eskijian, *At the Crossroads of Der Zor: Death, Survival, and Humanitarian Resistance in Aleppo, 1915–1917* (Reading, UK: Taderon Press, 2002), 45. See also the Ararat-Eskijian Museum website at http://ararat-eskijian-museum.com/hovhannes-eskijian.

2. Peter Balakian, *The Burning Tigris: The Armenian Genocide and America's Response* (New York: HarperCollins, 2003). See also historical archives of the *New York Times*, in which several articles from 1915 refer to these events. http://www .nytimes.com/ref/timestopics/topics_armeniangenocide.html.

3. Kaiser, *At the Crossroads of Der Zor*, 48–60.

4. Carol Rittner and John K. Roth, eds., *Rape: Weapon of War and Genocide* (St. Paul: Paragon House, 2012).

Chapter 5: Escape

1. Kurds collaborated in acts of genocide against the Armenian population in the Ottoman Empire and were themselves subjected to repression and assimilation. See Taner Akçam, *The Young Turks' Crime against Humanity: The Armenian Genocide and Ethnic Cleansing in the Ottoman Empire* (Princeton, NJ: Princeton University Press, 2012); Uğur Ümit Üngör, *The Making of Modern Turkey: Nation and State in Eastern Anatolia, 1913–1950* (Oxford: Oxford University Press, 2011), and his "Geographies of Nationalism and Violence: Rethinking Young Turk 'Social Engineering,'" *European Journal of Turkish Studies* 7, no. 7 (2008), http:// ejts.revues.org/2583.

2. The number of British military taken prisoner at Kut al-Amara was about fourteen thousand, although the Mesopotamian campaign already had cost more than twenty thousand British casualties. The enlisted men were treated harshly by their Turkish captors, with the mortality rate on the death march northward and during some thirty months as prisoners reaching as high as 70 percent. For accounts of British former prisoners of war, see, for example, E. W. C. Sangers, *In Kut and Captivity, with the Sixth Indian Division* (London: John Murray, 1919); H. C. W. Bishop, *A Kut Prisoner* (London: John Lane, 1920); F. A. Harvey, *The Sufferings of the Kut Garrison during Their March into Turkey as Prisoners of War, 1916–1917* (Ludgershall, Wiltshire: Adjutant's Press, 1922).

3. By mid-August 1916, some two hundred thousand Armenians were reported dead in the Deir el-Zor district, another fifteen thousand deportees in Aleppo were driven into the desert, and thousands of Armenian prisoners held in Sivas have been killed. The Turkish Interior Ministry was enforcing the dissolution of

the Armenian Patriarchate and the coerced assimilation of Armenian orphans. In the military campaigns, the Turkish army battled the Russians in historic lands of Armenia in Mush and Bitlis, and some sixty thousand Turkish casualties were reported in battles in the Caucasus. Complaints by German officials, including by the ambassador about the Turkish handling of Armenians and Turkey's interference in waging the war, resulted in a German-Turkish diplomatic crisis and change of the German ambassador. http://www.armenian-genocide.org/1916-2.html.

4. This interpretation of the German dominance in conceiving of and promoting the policy of genocide may be colored by the timing of this memoir being written after the Holocaust. However, recent research has shown that German weapons companies (Mauser, Krupp) supplied Turkish forces, which used these guns to kill Armenians. Thus, besides logistical support and training that the German High Command lent to the Turkish military, German arms manufacturers provided materiel. One German officer stationed in Urfa wrote to his wife in October 1915 that German infantrymen shot Armenian civilians in the local churchyard. In 2015, German president Joachim Gauck admitted to Germany's "co-responsibility" for the Armenian genocide. See Count Eberhard Wolffskeel von Reichenberg, *Zeitoun, Mousa Dagh, Ourfa: Letters on the Armenian Genocide*, edited by Hilmar Kaiser (Princeton, NJ: Gomidas Institute, 2001); Jürgen Gottschlich, *Beihilfe zum Völkermord. Deutschlands Rolle bei der Vernichtung der Armenier* (Berlin: Ch. Links Verlag, 2015).

5. Thomas Edward Lawrence volunteered for military service on the outbreak of the war, was sent to Egypt, and became a liaison between the British and the Arabs in mounting the Arab revolt. See T. E. Lawrence, *Seven Pillars of Wisdom* (New York: Penguin Classics, 2000); Gertrude Bell with Georgiana Howell, ed., *A Woman in Arabia: The Writings of the Queen of the Desert* (New York: Penguin Classics, 2015).

6. Raymond Kevorkian, *The Armenian Genocide, A Complete History* (London: I. B. Tauris, 2011), 969.

7. Budheswar Pati, *India and the First World War: 1914–1918* (New Delhi: Atlantic Publishers, 1996).

8. This document granted Minassian a certificate of employment necessary for him to use as proper identification within Eastern Anatolia. However, by using a different non-Armenian name in the body of the text and explicitly denying its use within the district of Aleppo, it also reveals the strategies used to mask Armenian identity and the limitations on movement members of this community faced in the early decades of the twentieth century. Thank you to Dr. Heather Ferguson for preparing this caption and the translation below.

Date of register:
14 Haziran 1333/June 14 1917
Document number 2640

Not valid in Aleppo
From the neighborhood of Aqaab[?] in Aleppo
Jurji son of Jalib/Habib
Born in 1316 (1900) (Rumi date system)

This document shows that Jurji son of Jalib/Habib, whose registration entry is written above, is in the service of the Tigris construction sectors command (*kumandanlığı*) of the Baghdad railway. He is a soldier and clerk (*katib*) in the nineteenth battalion (*tabur*).

(*on the left*)
Baghdad railway Tigris construction sectors command
Governor (*kaymakam*)
Salih

(*on the right*)
[Stamp in German] Chief of Fourth Building Department
Baghdad railway construction company

Verso (other side of document with Ottoman seal)
Recorded on 5 Ağustos 1334/August 5, 1918
Tigris construction sector
Baghdad railway nineteenth battalion construction division

9. The United States entered the world war in April 1917 on the side of the Allies against the German Empire. Although diplomatic relations were severed between the United States and the Ottoman Empire, war was never declared. On American participation in World War I, see, for example, Edward M. Coffman, *The War to End all Wars: The American Military Experience in World War I* (Lexington: University Press of Kentucky, 1998); Robert H. Zieger, *America's Great War: World War I and the American Experience* (Lanham, MD: Rowman & Littlefield, 2001).

Chapter 6: The Return

1. Salma K. Jayyusi, Renata Holod, Attilio Petruccioli, and André Raymond, eds., *The City in the Islamic World*, vol. 1 (Leiden and Boston: Brill, 2008).

2. Youssef Choueiri, *Arab Nationalism: A History and Nation State in the Arab World* (Hoboken, NJ: Wiley-Blackwell, 2000). Holocaust research has spawned a field of aftermath studies focused on trends in genocide survivor experiences, with analyses on survivor testimony, trauma, return to life, and generational transmission. See James Waller, "The Social Sciences" and subsection on "Current Trends in Social Science and Holocaust Studies," 673, in the *Oxford Handbook of Holocaust Studies*, edited by Peter Hayes and John Roth (New York: Oxford University Press, 2010). For an example of comparison of survivors, see Maud Mandel, *In the Aftermath of Genocide: Armenians and Jews in Twentieth-Century France* (Durham, NC: Duke University Press, 2006); and an informative summary of aftermath themes by Adam Jones, *Genocide: A Comprehensive Introduction*, 3rd ed. (London: Routledge, 2017).

3. Peter Balakian, *The Burning Tigris: The Armenian Genocide and America's Response* (New York: HarperCollins, 2003), 280.

4. The League of Nations was created after the First World War as an international organization to provide a forum for resolving international disputes. It was a part of President Wilson's program for peace and at the end of the Second World War evolved into the United Nations Organization. See https://history.state.gov/milestones/1914-1920/league. And for Wilson's Fourteen Points, see https://en.wikipedia.org/wiki/Fourteen_Points.

5. "Tales of Armenian Horrors Confirmed," *New York Times,* September 27, 1915, 5; "Tell of Horrors Done in Armenia," *New York Times,* October 4, 1915, 1.

6. Thousands of Armenians in exile in Paris and in the Diaspora in the United States fought in the First World War on all fronts. Philippe Landau, "Brothers of Weapons and Fate. Jewish and Armenian Volunteers in the French Foreign Legion (1914–1918)," *Archives Juives* 48 (2015): 28–50. See Herbert Adams Gibbons, *Armenia in the World War* (1926), http://www.armenews.com/IMG/Armeniaintheworldwar Gibbons1926.pdf.

7. Marilyn Shevin-Coetzee and Frans Coetzee, eds., *Empires, Soldiers and Citizens: A World War I Sourcebook* (Hoboken, NJ: Wiley Blackwell, 2013), 73–77.

8. David Fromkin, *The Peace to End All Peace: The Fall of the Ottoman Empire and the Creation of the Middle East* (New York: Henry Holt, 2009); Eugene Rogan, *The Fall of the Ottomans: The Great War in the Middle East* (New York: Basic Books, 2015).

9. Jennifer Balint, "'Doing Government Business': The Ottoman State Special Military Tribunal for the Genocide of the Armenians," in Kevin Heller and Gerry Simpson, eds., *The Hidden Histories of War Crimes Trials* (Oxford: Oxford University Press, 2013); Vahakn Dadrian and Taner Akçam, *Judgment at Istanbul: The Armenian Genocide Trials* (New York: Berghahn Books, 2011); Samantha Power, *A Problem from Hell: America and the Age of Genocide* (New York: Harper, 2007).

Chapter 7: Constantinople

1. See Ebru Boyar and Kate Fleet, *A Social History of Ottoman Istanbul* (New York: Cambridge University Press, 2010).

2. See David Gaunt, Naures Atto, and Soner O. Barthoma, eds., *Let Them Not Return: Sayfo—The Genocide against the Assyrian, Syriac, and Chaldean Christians in the Ottoman Empire* (New York: Berghahn, 2017).

3. See the new interdisciplinary work on Armenian culture in the aftermath of genocide, for example, the research of Anoush Tamar Suni, *Invisible Stones, Buried Histories: The Ruins of the Armenian Community of Van*, https://www.youtube.com/watch?v=LrY7xbLmUC4. Of particular importance are the publications and conferences of the Hrant Dink Foundation in Istanbul, created after the assassination of this prominent Turkish Armenian journalist and editor in 2007.

Appendix

1. The humiliation continues with the persistence of Turkish denial of the genocide. Richard G. Hovannisian, "Denial of the Armenian Genocide in Comparison with Holocaust Denial," 201–36, in R. Hovannisian, ed., *Remembrance and Denial: The Case of the Armenian Genocide* (Detroit: Wayne State University Press, 1998); see Taner Akçam, *A Shameful Act: The Armenian Genocide and the Question of Turkish Responsibility* (New York: Macmillan, 2006); Jennifer M. Dixon, "Defending the Nation? Maintaining Turkey's Narrative of the Armenian Genocide," *South European Society and Politics* 15 (2010): 467–85. Also see work on cultural erasure and archival heritage, Heghnar Watenpaugh, *Missing Pages: The Modern Life of a Medieval Manuscript from Genocide to Justice* (Palo Alto, CA: Stanford University Press, 2019).

Index

Note: Page references in *italics* refer to illustrations.

7–8; retreat toward Anatolia, 164;
Soviet Union and northeastern
borderlands, xviii–xix. *See also*
Hamidian massacres; Turks and
Turkey; Young Turks

Partridge, Ernest C., 8, 17–18, 71,
85–86, 193–94, 222–23
Partridge, Winona, 12–13
Peteshan Garden, 224, 225
Pfalz, Mr., 133, 149, 150
Phillip (village barber, doctor and
dentist), 59–60
Protestantism: Armenian refugees
and, 81, 87; Congregationalists,
4–5; Haroutoun's thought on, 183–
84; identity as Armenian and, 4, 32;
Puritan teachings of missionaries,
103–4

Rajah, 114, 116, 117–19
Rakupian, Rupen, 11
Ras ul-Ayn, 166–67
refugees in Aleppo, 75, 76, 78–79;
aid from Armenians, 80–81;
conditions during winter of 1915,
97–98, 99; food for, 112, 113;
girls, 97; John Minassian's contact
with hidden, 99; Morgenthau
and, 89; Nazaret-efendi, 82;
number of, during winter of
1915, 98; orphanages, 84, 86, 89,
96, 97, 101–2, 104–5, 111, 112;
as Protestants, 81, 87; rescue of
Anoush and Vahan Minassian,
83, 84, 86; Sevajian and, 80, 82;
travel to, 72–73; typhoid epidemic,
89–90, 99. *See also* Eskijian, The
Reverend

religion: Bedros and, 18–19;
desperation and, 192; Haroutoun's
thought on, 183–84; horrible events
and, 191; identity as Armenian
and, 4; Islamicization, xvi–xvii,
xix; as underlying cause of conflict
between Armenians and Muslim
rulers, 239n3. *See also* Christianity;
Protestantism
Republic of Armenia, xviii, 224–25
rescuers, xxv–xxvii
The Reverend. *See* Eskijian, The
Reverend
Riggs, Elias, 104
Robert College, 198, 222–23
Rohner, Beatrice: background, 96;
John Minassian leaving Aleppo
and, 115, 185; orphanage run
by, 111; postwar remembrance
ceremony for The Reverend, 184;
protection offered by, 112, 113
Russia, promises to help Armenians,
240n6

Sahag, Sourp, 32, 242n2
Sakally (Armen): aid to refugees,
122, 123–24; appearance of, 121;
background, 122; characteristics of,
121, 126, 128; in Constantinople,
202, 203; John Minassian leaving
and, 131
Sam (Corporal in British army), 209,
212–13
Sanasarian, Mkrdich, 241n14
Sanasarian University, 13, 214n14
Sardarabad, Battle of, xviii
Sarkis (friend): Arab raids and, 176–
77; deportation of, 55; Haroutoun
and, 174, 178; hidden by John

Vahan (teacher in Adana), 188
Vahari (friend), 192
Varjabed, Garbo, 7–8, 33–34, 47
Varoujan, Daniel, 175
Vartan (shopkeeper), 37, 38, 42–43,
    97
Vartouhy, 179–81
Varudjian, Daneal, 41
Venizelos, Eleftherios, 218
violence, rejection of, x–xi

The Wasp (newspaper), 175, 183
Werfel, Franz, 244n4
Wilson, Woodrow, xviii, 182;

Morgenthau and, 238n2
World War I. *See* Great War

Yanikian, Gourgen, x
Young Turks: Great War and, xviii,
    131, 242n3; motto, 10; overthrow
    of sultan by, 10; Tashnag party and,
    38; Three Pashas and, xvi, xvii

Zabel, 205
Zara, deportations from, 243n10
Zenger, Marie, 8, 14, 18
Zenopea, Reverend, 207–8
Zohrob, Krikor, 39